Carl Schmitt's International Thought

An unrepentant Nazi, Carl Schmitt remains one of the most divisive figures in twentieth-century political thought. In recent years, his ideas have attracted a new and growing audience. This book seeks to cut through the controversy surrounding Schmitt to analyse his ideas on world order. In so doing, it takes on board his critique of the condition of order in late modernity, and considers his continued relevance. Consideration is given to the two devices Schmitt deploys, the *Großraum* and the partisan, and argues that neither concept lives up to its claim to transcend or reform Schmitt's pessimistic history of the state. The author concludes that Schmitt's continuing value lies in his provocative historical critique, rather than his conceptual innovation.

WILLIAM HOOKER currently works as a lawyer at Clifford Chance in London. He previously researched and taught international political theory at the London School of Economics.

Carl Schmitt's International Thought

Order and Orientation

William Hooker

CAMBRIDGE UNIVERSITY PRESS
Cambridge, New York, Melbourne, Madrid, Cape Town, Singapore,
São Paulo, Delhi

Cambridge University Press
The Edinburgh Building, Cambridge CB2 8RU, UK

Published in the United States of America by Cambridge University Press,
New York

www.cambridge.org
Information on this title: www.cambridge.org/9780521115421

First published 2009

Printed in the United Kingdom at the University Press, Cambridge

A catalogue record for this publication is available from the British Library

ISBN 978-0-521-11542-1 hardback

For Arthur, my grandfather

Contents

Preface   *page* ix
Chronology of Schmitt's life   xiii

1   Introduction   1

2   Schmitt's 'international thought'   11

3   Unravelling sovereignty   34

4   Histories of space   69

5   Acceleration and restraint   102

6   *Großraum*   126

7   Partisan   156

8   Conclusion   195

Appendix. Carl Schmitt in international relations:
    a bibliographic essay   203
Bibliography   218
Index   227

Preface

My first exposure to Carl Schmitt was in 2001–2 when I had the good fortune to study the history of political thought from 1890 to the present under the supervision of Martin Rühl, then of Queens' College, Cambridge. In this setting, my first reading of Schmitt was in the context of thinkers such as Nietzsche, Weber, Sorel, Franz Neumann, Adorno and Horkheimer, all of whom were grappling in their varying ways with the political problems of late modernity. Schmitt stood out from this field both for his polemical force, and for his profound neglect among English-speaking scholars. At this time, none of Schmitt's post-war works were available in English translation, and except for the occasional efforts of Gary Ulmen as editor of *Telos*, there was virtually no English language scholarship on *The Nomos of the Earth*. The 'gap in the market' for serious study of Schmitt as an international thinker seemed self-evident.

In 2003 I produced a master's thesis entitled *Justus hostis: Carl Schmitt on Public Enmity*, returning a year later to embark on a Ph.D. studying themes of theological truth and order in Schmitt's view of world politics. Throughout this period the LSE provided a stimulating and supportive environment for the pursuit of what was often a necessarily solitary research agenda. In particular, I was enormously lucky to have Chris Brown as my supervisor. Chris's support comes not only in the form of constructive remarks and sage tactical advice, but most agreeably in the form of food, drink and great fun. I am sure he would accept of himself the description 'interested in Schmitt, but certainly not Schmittian', making him an informed and sympathetic reader of my work. I hope that he has now overcome early misgivings that he was somehow complicit in siring an underground 'Schmitt School' at the heart of the LSE.

Kim Hutchings and Nick Renngger acted as my Ph.D. examiners. They happily agreed to pass the Ph.D., but also gave detailed and very constructive attention to areas in which I could strengthen my research and sharpen my critical approach. They have both gone beyond the call of duty in their support and their proactive encouragement for me to take my work forward. I am also extremely grateful to Gabriella Slomp and an anonymous reviewier, both of whom read a first draft of this book, and provided numerous suggestions, criticisms and conceptual challenges. That I have not followed all of the advice so generously given in no way lessens my appreciation.

Many others at the LSE and elsewhere have also helped to shape my research and, ultimately, this book, through their generous suggestions and criticism. Margot Light and Mick Cox have been constant in their enthusiasm, and an excellent source of advice and guidance. I am also grateful to Doug Bulloch, Barry Buzan, Simon Curtis, Joe Devanny, Spyros Economides, Philippe Fournier, Rune Henriksen, Stefanie Ortmann, Serena Sharma, Ewan Stein, Louisa Sunderman and Peter Wilson for their various remarks and suggestions.

Tom Burn, David Matthews and John Matthews have frequently asked the sort of probing non-specialist questions that force one to re-evaluate some fundamental tenets of the thesis. I am grateful to them for the interest they have shown. Greg Callus deserves particular thanks for being a great well of knowledge and insight across the broad spectrum of political thought. I am also indebted to him for his help with the dreary task of indexing.

In exploring the religious and theological aspects of the thesis, I have been fortunate to develop links with the ECPR Standing Group on Religion. I am grateful to Giorgio Shani for chairing a panel at the ECPR Conference in Budapest in September 2005 where I had the opportunity to present an earlier version of Chapter 3 of this book. I also developed certain themes from Chapters 3 and 4 at the IPSA Conference in Fukuoka, Japan, in July 2006, in a panel chaired by Jeff Haynes. I am grateful to Giorgio and Jeff for including me in these events, and for their stimulating discussions of my work. I am also grateful to other participants for their criticisms and encouragement, and in particular to Vendulka Kubalkova, Mustapha Pasha and Richard Ryscavage.

None of this would have been possible without the relentless support and assistance of my family. Firstly, I thank my grandfather and my brother James, for their interest and encouragement. My parents have remained enthusiastic about my research, and have given me more material and emotional support than one could wish for. I am especially grateful to them for providing me with a peaceful and focussed environment in Tewkesbury in which to work, often denying themselves the utility of their country retreat in the process. Without the many productive hours I spent there, it is doubtful whether this thesis would ever have come to fruition.

Last, but in no way least, my thanks go to Sarah. In the course of completing this thesis she obtained the dubious honour of becoming

'Mrs Hooker'. She has helped me to avoid the worst pathologies of mind that total immersion in the work of Carl Schmitt can sometimes threaten. She has borne my frustrations with grace, and her simple confidence in me has headed off my pessimism at the pass. I am very fortunate.

Note on sources, translation and citation

Efforts at translating Schmitt's work into English have been somewhat patchy and piecemeal. Wherever a recent and reliable English translation of a work exists, that translation will have been used in this thesis. This includes George Schwab's translations of *The Concept of the Political*, *Political Theology* and *The Leviathan in the State Theory of Thomas Hobbes*, as well as the MIT Press series of translations including *Political Romanticism* and *The Crisis of Parliamentary Democracy*. Gary Ulmen's 2004 translation of *The Nomos of the Earth* is of great value in opening up Schmitt's more emphatically international work to an English-speaking audience. Ulmen has also recently completed a translation of *Theory of the Partisan*.

For the most part, Schmitt showed a preference for writing extended essays of between 3,000 and 10,000 words. Several of these have been published in English in the journal *Telos*, although there is no comprehensive English-language collection of Schmitt's essays. Many of the most important of these have been collected and published in three German-language volumes. *Positionen und Begriffe im Kampf mit Weimar–Genf–Versailles 1923–1939* (Hamburg, 1940) brought together thirty-six of Schmitt's essays written before the Second World War. Its focus, as the title implies, is on works that tend to concentrate on the post-1919 international order, international law and the political conditions of Europe. *Staat, Großraum, Nomos: Arbeiten aus den Jahren 1916–1969* (Berlin, 1995) brings together a further thirty-nine essays written over a longer time period. Edited by Günther Maschke, it is the most wide-ranging and comprehensive collection of Schmitt's works. It contains sketches of many of the ideas that Schmitt would subsequently work up into book-length pieces. Maschke also prepared a heavily edited collection of Schmitt's works entitled *Frieden oder Pazifismus? Arbeiten zum Völkerrecht und zur internationalen Politik 1924–1978* (Berlin: Duncker and Humblot, 2005). There is a certain amount of overlap between the works contained in this latter work and the other two volumes.

Some of these essay pieces are extremely important in their own right, and provide points of interconnection between Schmitt's more substantial works. Still others represent work in progress and, as would be expected, are worked up in more detail into monographs. In such contexts, I have tried in so far as is possible to emphasise the more major monographs, utilising Schmitt's essay pieces only to clarify ambiguity, or to trace particular lines in the development in his thought. Since this is intended as an account of Schmitt's specific understanding of the historical fate of the international system and not as an intellectual biography or a comprehensive survey of Schmitt's oeuvre, selectivity has been a necessary part of the exercise.

Where no English-language translation is available, or where available translations are provisional, unreliable or arcane, all translations are my own. For the most part, Schmitt is an extremely direct and stylish author, and the common difficulties of rendering 'academic German' are blissfully avoided. Nevertheless, where there may be some ambiguity of meaning, I have adopted the practice of reproducing the original German either in parenthesis or, with longer passages, as a footnote. Following Ulmen, I have taken the step of rendering the phrase *Hegung des Krieges* as 'the *bracketing* of war'. The verb 'to bracket' appears, in this context, to have become a common standard in English language, and to use a different phrase would threaten confusion. Nevertheless, as the later discussion of Schmitt's concept illustrates (see below, p. 21 n. 27, and p. 80), this is by no means an unproblematic translation.

Consideration is also given to a comparatively small amount of unpublished material from the collection of Schmitt's papers at the State Archive in Düsseldorf. The *Schmitt Nachlaß* contains almost 500 archive cartons, and includes correspondence to and from Schmitt, handwritten notes, sketches and early drafts, as well as Schmitt's collected library of books and essays, complete with marginalia. For details of the contents of the archive, see D. van Laak and I. Villinger, *Nachlaß Carl Schmitt: Verzeichnis des Bestandes im Nordrhein-Westfälischen Hauptstaatsarchiv*, Siegburg: Republica-Verlag (1993). I am grateful to Herr Professor Jürgen Becker for permission to access the archive in July 2005, and to all the staff who provided assistance in finding materials. I have adopted their suggested form in citing material from the archive. HStaD designates the Haupstaatsarchiv Düsseldorf. RW265 is the unique identifier for the Schmitt collection. There then follows an individual folder number. Since many folders contain several items collected thematically, I have endeavoured to identify the specific material under consideration.

Chronology of Schmitt's life

1888   Born in Plettenberg in Westfalen
1914   Publishes habilitation thesis *Der Wert des Staates und die Bedeutung des Einzelnen* (*The Value of the State and the Significance of the Individual*)
1915   Graduates in law from Strassburg University
1916   Marries first wife, Pawla Dorotić (divorced in 1925)
1921   Professorship at the University of Greifswald
       Publishes *Die Diktatur* (*On Dictatorship*)
1922   Publishes *Politische Theologie* (*Political Theology*)
1925   Marries second wife, Duška Todorović
1926   Professor at the Hochschule für Politik in Berlin
1932   Professor of law at Cologne University
       Publishes second edition of *Der Begriff des Politischen* (*The Concept of the Political*)
1933   Professor of law at the University of Berlin
       Joins the Nazi party
1936   Organises anti-Semitic conference of jurists calling for the elimination of Jewish influences in German law
1937   Publishes *Der Leviathan in der Staatslehre des Thomas Hobbes* (*The Leviathan in the State Theory of Thomas Hobbes*)
1942   Publishes *Land und Meer* (Land and Sea)
1945   Arrested by Soviet forces in Berlin
       Rearrested by the Americans and interned awaiting possible trial at Nuremberg
1946   Released without having been indicted
       Returns to enforced retirement in Plettenberg
1950   Publishes *Der Nomos der Erde* (*The Nomos of the Earth*)
1963   Publishes *Theorie des Partisanen* (*Theory of the Partisan*)
1985   Dies in Plettenberg aged 97

1   Introduction

It is not uncommon for the end of wars to herald the sentiment that 'nothing will ever be the same again'. To be sure, wars leave scars both emotional and physical. They leave tales of loss and instincts of vengeance. But in the political theory of Carl Schmitt, war is above all a political act. 'War is the existential negation of the enemy.'[1] It leaves concrete changes in the configuration of politics. It draws new lines on maps, and creates new lines of authority of men over other men. No matter how infrequent or limited, warfare is a necessary corollary of Schmitt's understanding of political life. And as such, the observation that war inflicts permanent changes on social life is, for Schmitt, nothing more than an observation that the history of the state rolls on.

Yet, amidst the destruction of Berlin in 1945, Schmitt was preoccupied with a quite distinct and more fearsome sense that 'nothing will ever be the same again'. Arrested by the Russians in April of 1945, arrested and re-arrested by the Americans, interred and questioned by the Nuremberg prosecutor, Schmitt suddenly became an actor in what was, for him, a more startling moment of change. Nuremberg seemed to cement a process that had preoccupied Schmitt for the past twenty-five years. War was no longer simply an affair of states, to be settled in the moment of defeat or victory. It was also a matter of right and wrong and an issue that implicated individual morality. Long after the real substance of battle had been determined, the quest to ascribe guilt continued. And even if Nuremberg could find no evidence to bring an action against him personally, Schmitt nevertheless became emblematic of that guilt. Schmitt became a character in the story of the end of the Westphalian state.[2]

---

[1] C. Schmitt, *The Concept of the Political* (trans. G. Schwab), Chicago: University of Chicago Press (1996) p. 33.

[2] For the story of Schmitt's interrogation by the Nuremberg prosecutor Robert Kempner, see J. W. Bendersky, 'Carl Schmitt at Nuremberg', *Telos* 72 (Summer 1987), 91–6. The same issue of *Telos* reproduces a transcript of some of Schmitt's interrogation: J. W. Bendersky (transcr.), 'Interrogation of Carl Schmitt by Robert Kempner', *Telos* 72 (Summer 1987), 97–107. See also J. W. Bendersky, 'Carl Schmitt's Path to Nuremberg: A

The year 1945 marks the rough mid-point of Schmitt's intellectual career. Doubtless the year is significant in the study of Schmitt for reasons we shall explore. But, perhaps above all, it is significant for its place in staging the personal drama of Carl Schmitt – for turning Schmitt into part of the story that his own work was attempting to analyse. From his internal exile at Plettenberg, Schmitt became the unacceptable face of Germany's intellectual past – a dangerous, shocking dinosaur who doggedly refused to adapt to the changed circumstances of the Federal Republic. Even today, more than twenty years since his death, engagement with Schmitt's theories of the state and the international system elicits deep discomfort. Indeed, it is hard to think of another intellectual figure who provokes quite such polarised views. And as a consequence, the analysis of Schmitt's work has increasingly become a process of advocacy. Those who are interested in Schmitt become engaged in a process of exhumation, whilst Schmitt's opponents try to keep him buried. The frequent response of those hostile to renewed interest in Schmitt is that he was an arcane and reductive Nazi who has little to offer current debates. Yet it is a sentiment often accompanied by its apparent antipode – that the invocation of Schmitt is dangerous, seductive and destructive. Since both instincts cannot be correct, it is clear that work remains to be done to cut through the drama, and to situate Schmitt's project more impartially.

The story at stake here is Schmitt's study of the slow decline of the sovereign state, and with it the international system based on the formal equality of states. The detailed timing of this story is unclear. To be sure, 1945 (or, more precisely, Schmitt's realisation of Germany's imminent defeat some time earlier) is an important moment in shaping Schmitt's own conclusions. Likewise, 1919 and the determination of the aftermath of war through legal measures form a prominent place in Schmitt's critique. Heinrich Meier suggests that by '1931–32, Schmitt sees himself facing a changed political situation', and that 'in 1932, Schmitt believes himself already able to look back at the "liberal age" in which "political viewpoints were robbed, with special pathos, of all validity and subordinated to the normative prescriptions and 'orders' of morals, law, and economics"'.[3] Perhaps from a German perspective, 1933 is the key date. As much in celebration as trepidation, Schmitt himself concluded of the day Hitler took power that 'one can say that on that day "Hegel

---

Sixty Year Reassessment', *Telos* 139 (Summer 2007), 6–34, and a further transcript of Schmitt's interrogation: J. W. Bendersky (transcr.), 'The "Fourth" (Second) Interrogation of Carl Schmitt at Nuremberg', *Telos* 139 (Summer 2007), 35–43.
[3] H. Meier, *Carl Schmitt and Leo Strauss: The Hidden Dialogue* (trans. J. H. Lomax), Chicago: University of Chicago Press (1995) pp. 21–2.

died'".[4] The twin questions that preoccupied Schmitt were why this dissolution had come to pass, and what the future of world politics would look like without the 'Schmittian' state.

Carl Schmitt was one of the most profound and most prolific theorists of international order in the twentieth century. He also enjoyed extraordinary intellectual longevity, allowing him to forecast and trace the political changes to international order under conditions of late modernity. Schmitt's immense range across legal, political, historical and theological canvasses provides an enormous, synthetic, arch-conservative world view. For all of the moral, personal and professional failure that attached to Schmitt's life, he has left a legacy of political categories and critical positions that continue to enjoy wide appeal in contemporary study of international order. He is also a figure who sought to transcend the terms of debate in any one field of intellectual activity, thereby creating challenging and innovative ways of viewing global politics. His arrival as a serious object of debate in international political theory is overdue.

Schmitt is of manifest value to a variety of scholars, whether based in international relations (IR) theory, public international law or political philosophy, whose central concern is the deep theoretical framework of world politics and global order. We should welcome the gradual reduction of knee-jerk hostility to the use of Schmittian categories in debate. Schmitt's famously parsimonious definition of the political as the distinction of the enemy is a provocative addition to debates on *pouvoir constituent* and should be of interest both to those who continue to assert the validity of the state as the basic political unit, and those who look elsewhere for the contemporary political dynamic. In addition, Schmitt offers a rich and rewarding historical analysis of the theme of power and restraint in the concept of the state that might prove a useful resource to those who assert the value of the state as the 'least bad option' for world politics. *The Nomos of the Earth*, written towards the end of the Second World War, is a vastly ambitious history of world politics that also provides a passionate defence of the triumph of the European state system. The great breadth and erudition of what is, in a self-evident sense, Schmitt's *magnum opus* appears destined to guarantee a place for *Nomos of the Earth* in the canon of essential IR reading.

However, for all its analytical depth and vast ambition, Schmitt's international thought represents a failure. Probably even by his own admission (and at least as early as 1946) Schmitt had run out of convincing ways to

---

[4] Schmitt, *Staat, Bewegung, Volk: Dreigliederung der politischen Einheit*. Hamburg: HAVA (1933). Herbert Marcuse remarks that this is the point at which he cannot bear to read any more of Schmitt (see *Negations*, Boston, MA: Beacon (1968), p. 275 n.79).

theorise the new foundations of global political order.[5] It is the intention of this work to illustrate the way in which Schmitt's understanding of the 'history' of the state form prevented him, *ipso facto*, from envisioning change to the foundations of international order. As such, it is a rejoinder to those who see hope in Schmitt's post-1945 work for a reordering of global politics along lines that, whilst transcending the Westphalian state in one way or another, nevertheless retain the vital public enmity that makes Schmittian politics tick. By contrast, we contend that Schmitt's eschatological-historical position results in a sterile conundrum in which Schmitt was torn between an ultra-reactionary defence of the flawed state form, and a breathless anticipation of an apocalyptic world unity.

A part of this project will be to examine the degree to which such talk of apocalypse is metaphor. Metaphor or not, however, it becomes clear that Schmitt regards the global ascendance of liberal universalism as a catastrophe. And in the face of such a pacified globe, the only position consistent with Schmitt's historical interpretation of this crisis is to await the inevitable but unknowable implosion of a formless order. The language Schmitt uses to consider this scenario is unfamiliar and uncomfortable for those interested in international political theory. We are hardly well equipped for discussion of the restraint of the coming Antichrist, portended as it is by the political unity of the world, and prefiguring the apocalypse! Nevertheless, it is hoped that by examining the intellectual roots of this position, the way in which Schmitt related it to the contemporary history of the state, and, in turn, the impact of this view on Schmitt's political decisions, it will be possible to draw illuminating parallels with more familiar accounts of the uncertain political underpinning of the contemporary international order.

This work will consider the way in which the two devices Schmitt creates to theorise post-1945 world order fail to convince, each in their own way. On the one hand, Schmitt developed a concept of *Großraumordnung* that might, in simple terms, be contemplated as a pluriverse of continental empires.[6] One might regard the *Großraum* concept as broadening out of the state concept into a more viable territorial space. At the same time, a *Großraum* is imagined as something qualitatively different from the state in that its binding cultural content is less organic, and the mechanics of political control are more self-evident. On the one hand, it changes the

---

[5] See C. Schmitt, *Ex captivitate salus*, Cologne: Greven Verlag (1950).

[6] The *Großraum* concept has been especially popular with 'Schmittians' of the Left, who regard the concept as holding some hope of encouraging a European political space that resists the universalising tendencies of global economics and American hegemony. Fuller consideration is given to this appropriation in the following chapter.

territorial basis of politics to contain the pressures of technology and communication. On the other hand, it is a decisionist entity laid bare.[7]

The other key concept in Schmitt's post-1945 work is that of the partisan.[8] This is a more reactive and reflective category that Schmitt seems to see as the last political corrective to abject universalism. Indeed, Schmitt's historical account of the rise of the partisan in Spanish and German resistance to Napoleon makes clear that the category is intended, by definition, as a somewhat desperate response to imminent global unity. Yet the partisan, whilst convincing as the locus of political reaction, and perhaps recognisable even today in localised, particularist movements such as the Zapatistas, cannot provide the basis for a new view of international order. As I shall argue later, the very concept and self-awareness of the partisan is itself parasitic on the disorder and sense of imminent collapse that Schmitt commits himself to redress.

The partisan is an echo of politics, and lacks the inter-subjectivity necessary for the kind of politics described in *The Concept of the Political*. As Gabriella Slomp has convincingly argued, the form of politics that the partisan represents is qualitatively different from inter-state politics and, crucially, offers no basis for stability.[9] In short, the partisan has the same twilight quality that haunts much of Schmitt's post-1945 work, and provides a challenge to those who seek to reconcile Schmitt's theory of the political to the contemporary world. If the partisan is all we have left, we have already abandoned the idea of a meaningful political order. Following Schmitt, we would be forced to choose between disorder and the absence of politics – hardly a choice at all.

Given his belief in the immutability of politics, this failure of imagination is at once shocking and disconcerting. After all, one of Schmitt's most famous contributions to political thought is his definition of the political as a realm that prefigures and survives the concept of the state. The opening line of *The Concept of the Political* (1932) makes it clear that the state is only a temporary manifestation of politics: '[t]he concept of the state presupposes the concept of the political'.[10] If even Carl Schmitt failed to imagine a convincing political order without the Westphalian state at its core, one is left to wonder how the terms of political debate that Schmitt left to us

---

[7] See Chapter 6 below.

[8] Schmitt wrote *Theorie des Partisanen* during 1962, stimulated in large part by an attempt to find a political analysis or, even, justification, for General Salans in Algeria (*Theorie des Partisanen: Zwischenbemerkung zum Begriff des Politischen*, Berlin: Duncker and Humblot (1963)). See Chapter 7 below.

[9] G. Slomp, 'The Theory of the Partisan: Carl Schmitt's Neglected Legacy', *History of Political Thought* 26:3 (2005), 502–19.

[10] Schmitt, *The Concept of the Political*, p. 13.

can be reconciled to the contemporary world. Furthermore, if the position is one of despair, how far should we share what his most sympathetic biographer, Joseph Bendersky, described as Schmitt's 'almost chronic fear of disorder'?[11]

The Concept of the Political, Schmitt's most famous work, is chock-full of dire predictions of what will ensue if the opportunity is not taken to protect and entrench the division of states as 'the most intense and extreme antagonism'.[12] If the march of liberalism continues, and 'state and society [are allowed to] penetrate one another', Schmitt can envision only a facile world of entertainment.[13]

A politically united people becomes, on the one hand, a culturally interested public, and on the other, partially an industrial concern and its employers, partially a mass of consumers ...

These dissolutions aim with great precision at subjugating law and politics, partially into an individualistic domain of private law and morality, partially into economic notions. In doing so they deprive state and politics of their specific meaning.[14]

Schmitt predicts that the march of liberal individualism will result in a situation in which the concept of the state becomes impossible. 'Every encroachment', he predicts, 'every threat to individual freedom and private property and free competition is called repression and is *eo ipso* something evil'.[15] Schmitt's implacable hostility to the triumph of liberalism within the state, and cosmopolitanism among states, provides his work with its constant polemical slant. Leo Strauss characterised the mission Schmitt sets for himself as motivated by a desire 'to replace the "astonishingly consistent systematics of liberal *thought*", which is manifest within the inconsistency of liberal *politics*, by "another system", namely a system that does not negate the political but brings it into recognition'.[16] It is precisely this challenge that motivates many of those most interested in Schmitt today.

Liberalism, then, is the immediate and evident target of Schmitt's thought.[17] Much has been made in recent times of the potential theoretical

---

[11] J. W. Bendersky, *Carl Schmitt: Theorist for the Reich*, Princeton: Princeton University Press (1983), p. 97

[12] Schmitt, *The Concept of the Political*, p. 29.   [13] *Ibid.*, p. 22.

[14] *Ibid.*, p. 72.   [15] *Ibid.*, p. 71.

[16] L. Strauss, 'Notes on Carl Schmitt: The Concept of the Political', in H. Meier (ed.), *Carl Schmitt and Leo Strauss: The Hidden Dialogue* (trans. J. H. Lomax), Chicago: University of Chicago Press (1995), p. 85.

[17] It must be noted that Schmitt was also concerned to attack Marxism–Leninism as perhaps an even more profound threat to the existing order. In many respect, Schmitt treated Marxism as a more extreme and more explicit outgrowth of liberalism, with its self-conscious and avowed commitment to dissolving division and reducing man to his economic status. See Chapter 7 below.

value of Schmitt's insights in the context of post-Cold War politics, when the triumphant ascendancy of liberal internationalism has seemed so likely. Yet the optimism and political activism of many contemporary 'Schmittians' seems strangely at odds with the contours of Schmitt's own hopes and fears. Behind Schmitt's vociferous critique of liberalism, there lies a deeper and far more important concern for the nature of the political world, and the seriousness of human life. It is only by examining the theoretical and, at times, personal and psychological basis of Schmitt's concerns that a fuller picture can emerge of precisely what motivated and aggravated the old man from Plettenburg.

This work will argue that Schmitt's pessimism about the prospects for international order springs from a particular and peculiar concept of history. According to this position, Schmitt's view of time is distinctly determinist, yet coloured also with a normative attachment to the ordered universe of the *jus publicum Europaeum*. Rather than turning to history for the tools to theorise this sense of unravelling over time, Schmitt tended instead towards theological interpretations of time. Whilst Burckhardt and Meinecke continued to be of interest to Schmitt, the focus of his interest tended to be on the political manifestations of their work in context, rather on the theory of history per se.[18] Schmitt's only consistent and mainstream position on the philosophy of history was his profound hostility to teleology, remarking as he did on the 'deep antithesis between the scholastic ahistorical approach and a historical mode of thinking, in particular the 19th century humanitarian philosophy of history [which] exhibits the self-conscious arrogance of an idealist philosophy of history'.[19]

In short, Schmitt regards conventional historiography as tending to bifurcate into either feeble Hegelianism of the progressive state, or else a history of *personae morales* infused with 'the psychological phenomenon of Renaissance individualism'.[20] Schmitt's own historical approach, exemplified in the breathtaking history of the idea of the state in *Nomos of the Earth*, thus, in a sense, eschews its status as history. It has only a loose concept of time and change, and is concerned instead with the possibility of concrete order. It is a history of orders punctuated by moments of radical change. Stability, rather than change, is the yardstick for Schmitt. Yet the modern history of the state directly affronts this emphasis on the stability of concepts. To Schmitt, the very possibility of

---

[18] See C. Schmitt, 'Zu Friedrich Meineckes Idee der Staatsräson', in *Positionen und Begriffe im Kampf mit Weimar–Genf–Versailles, 1923–1939*, Berlin: Duncker and Humblot (1994).
[19] From a discussion of Vitoria's scholastic objectivity in Carl Schmitt, *The Nomos of the Earth in the International Law of the* Jus Publicum Europaeum (trans. G. Ulmen), New York: Telos Press (2004), pp. 107–8.
[20] Schmitt, *Nomos*, p. 144.

nomic order appears threatened. The decline of the state reflects a wholly unprecedented increase in the *pace* of history. Rather than a moment of reformation, Schmitt fears that the current process of dissolution is terminal.

Thomas Hobbes is the key figure in fleshing out this essentially eschatological vision of modern history.[21] A difficult and contested figure throughout Schmitt's work, Hobbes comes to represent the intellectual origins of the modern state in the maxim *protego et obligo*. As such, Hobbes is seen as the intellectual bridge from the *complexio oppositorum* of medieval, ecclesiastical politics, and the quasi-religious sovereignty of the modern state. Hobbes is at once hero and villain in Schmitt's account. His remarkable conflation of God and politics in the modern state allowed for true unity of the Commonwealth; the existence and persistence of concrete orders of men organised as potential fighting units; and the survival of political authority that was, in the final analysis, absolute. At the same time, however, in failing properly to subordinate the 'covenant' of the people to the power of the sovereign, Hobbes opened up a conceptual gap that has been widened ever since by the liberal assertion of the primacy of individual *veritas* over the *auctoritas* of the state.

This, it is argued, gives the most valuable insight into Schmitt's account of the decline of the modern state. The seeds of the erosion of the state were sown in its very creation. In leaving open a space for private morality, the Hobbesian state allowed for the creation of a moralising individualism that came to oppose the very logic of the state, and challenge the 'validity' of the authority placed above them. Schmitt's 'story' of the state is a rueful tale of a brilliant political concept that has inadvertently ushered in an unstoppable tide of depoliticisation. This 'story', with its identified origins and predicted, dire ending, dominates the way in which Schmitt thinks about modern politics.

Besides this story of the unravelling of the state concept from within, Schmitt presents an ancillary narrative of an aggressive external attack on the state concept from the sphere of international relations. Not only do the 'people' gradually assert their 'rights' against the state; the very spatial and territorial basis of the system of states as a whole is challenged conceptually, accelerating the decline of the *Nomos*. First England, and then the United States, succumb to a radical concept of oceanic space that is logically inconsistent with the territorial basis of the European state.

---

[21] Only Donoso Cortes compares to Hobbes in terms of the degree of intellectual debt Schmitt openly acknowledged. Our study of Hobbes will focus on Schmitt's pamphlet of 1938, *The Leviathan in the Political Theory of Thomas Hobbes* (trans. G. Schwab), Westport, CT: Greenwood Press (1996).

This confrontation of Land and Sea, between the 'telluric' European state and the Atlanticist latitudinarianism of the Anglo-Saxons, creates a second historical dynamic that interacts with the failures of the Hobbesian concept. The combined effect is nothing short of disastrous for Schmitt.

In exploring this diagnosis of decline and a search for new principles, it has been necessary at times to avoid dealing with Schmitt's works strictly chronologically. The premise is that Schmitt was engaged in two related but distinct intellectual processes. On the one hand, an analysis of decline and, on the other, a search for new principles to remedy that decline. It is hardly surprising that Schmitt continued to sharpen his critique at the same time as exploring positive responses. Indeed, the latter included all manner of both intellectual and, perhaps more significantly, *political* moves throughout Schmitt's life, including his advocacy of Presidential rule under the Weimar constitution, and his eventual decision in favour of Nazism. In the context of his search for new principles of world order, therefore, Schmitt published his theoretical proposal of a politics of large spaces four years before he published, in *Land and Sea*, a fully formed critique of the conditions that might necessitate a shift to large-space politics. For the sake of clarity and the thorough exploration of Schmitt's ideas, the approach taken here is to break down Schmitt's ideas logically into retrospective and anticipatory categories. Where appropriate, every effort has been made to clarify chronological inconsistencies, and to explain the links between Schmitt's critical reflection and his search for new principles (links that often exist within the same work).

Instead of a strictly chronological approach, the work is instead organised broadly into two halves. After an initial review of Schmitt's oeuvre and emerging secondary literature on Schmitt as an international thinker, Chapters 3, 4 and 5 focus on his understanding of the history of the international system. Chapter 3 essentially concerns sovereignty as an historical phenomenon, and the creation of a radically 'internal' political space in the European state. By contrast, Chapter 4 addresses what might be termed the 'external' facets of Schmitt's account of international history. Here we address Schmitt's ideas on territoriality, geopolitical determinism and the spatial conditions of international order. In both chapters, the emphasis is on extracting the deeper assumptions and theoretical insights that characterise Schmitt's nascent theory of history. Chapter 5 seeks to draw several of these themes together in the idea of historical acceleration. It emphasises the important link that Schmitt draws between political order and the social experience of time, and the feedback relationship that he argues to have existed between the system of international states and the theoretical possibility of order.

As such, Chapter 5 links the first, historically orientated half of the book with the second, forward-looking section. Chapter 5 draws together the historical themes that constitute Schmitt's sense that we face a present 'crisis'. Chapters 6 and 7 go on to examine his attempts to respond to that crisis productively, and to produce an agenda for future order. The chapters focus in turn on the two key conceptual innovations through which Schmitt attempted to think beyond the state and towards some new principle of world political order and stability. Both chapters seek to illustrate the difficulties Schmitt had trying to reconcile his pessimistic theory of history with these bold attempts to define a new basis for world politics. His image of the future never escaped his complicated and theoretically entangled fascination with the past. Despite the imperatives he set for himself as a harbinger of change, Carl Schmitt the historian wins out against Carl Schmitt the politician.

Jacob Taubes described Schmitt as the 'apocalyptician of counter-revolution'.[22] It is a phrase that sums up the tension between the depth of Schmitt's antipathy to the emergent triumph of universalism, and his lack of optimism that the force could be halted. It seems that admission of defeat was not within Schmitt's nature. Instinctively drawn to leaps of faith, both of the religious and political kind, Schmitt clung on to the hope that his worst fears would somehow be averted. He awaited the lightning flash of a new political *Nomos* that would succeed where Nazism had failed in arresting the advance of cosmopolitan dreams. For those who share the same hopes, Schmitt may very well continue to be a source of comfort and inspiration. On his own terms, however, Schmitt the 'diagnostician' was ultimately prevented from crossing the fence and making a real contribution to thinking about how the modern world *ought* to be.

---

[22] Cf. J. Taubes, *The Political Theology of Paul* (trans. D. Hollander), Stanford: Stanford University Press (2004), p. 69.

2 Schmitt's 'international thought'

The 'arrival' of Schmitt as an object of interest to those engaged in the mainstream study of international political theory is hardly a surprise. Chris Brown notes that 'it is striking that there are so few good studies of "the state and IR"'.[1] It is precisely this nexus that dominates Schmitt's political thought as a whole. His interest in the historically conditioned nature of the state, the theoretical grounds of political interaction, the social meaning of warfare and the philosophical basis of political obligation all point towards a basic consideration of the theory of the state. It is impossible to give a full overview of Schmitt's political thought as a whole within these pages, and besides, numerous studies of that nature already exist. Our purpose instead is to sketch out the meaning of 'Schmitt's international thought' and to locate the key concepts and historical interpretations that characterise Schmitt as an international theorist.

In the non-German-speaking world, Schmitt's reputation is largely founded on his work of 1932, *The Concept of the Political*. Although this small, brilliant, polemical work is arguably the most important distillation of Schmitt's political theory, the prominence of this one volume tends to distract from the huge quantity and range of his work over time. As interest in Schmitt has grown, the range of literature available in English has continued to grow, and the recent translations of *The Nomos of the Earth* and *Theory of the Partisan* by Gary Ulmen, and the reissue of George Schwab's translation of *Political Theology* by MIT Press are to be welcomed.[2] In addition, Telos Press continues to publish translated essay pieces by Schmitt, thereby making up for the absence of English translations of Schmitt's collected works such as *Staat, Großraum, Nomos* and *Positionen und Begriffe*. Nevertheless, serious gaps remain in the resources

---

[1] C. Brown, *Understanding International Relations*, p. 63.
[2] C. Schmitt, *The Nomos of the Earth in the International Law of the* Jus Publicum Europeaum (trans. G. Ulmen), New York: Telos Press (2004); C. Schmitt, *Theory of the Partisan* (trans. G. Ulmen), New York: Telos Press (2007); C. Schmitt, *Political Theology* (trans. G. Schwab), Cambridge, MA: MIT Press (2005).

available to English-speaking scholars, and this chapter will attempt to range broadly across Schmitt's oeuvre as a whole in emphasising the key elements of his vision of international order.[3]

Schmitt must be read, of course, as part of a German political tradition centred on Herder's notion of the national community, and Hegel's ethical concept of the state. Yet Schmitt is more apocalypse to, than apotheosis of, this tradition. Schmitt is interested in the problematic aspects of good and stable concepts of state and international law under the conditions of late modernity. This intellectual mileu is, of course, important, and we shall return later in the chapter to consider Schmitt's broad intellectual heritage. However, it is suggested that an attempt to sketch Schmitt's antecedents, and to frame Schmitt in the context of his intellectual heritage should be abandoned for the time being in favour of a straightforward typology of Schmitt's core concepts. Whilst this typology is, to some extent, arbitrary and artificial, such simplification is a necessary prelude to a more detailed consideration of Schmitt's theory of history.

The phrase 'Carl Schmitt's "international thought"' used in the title of this chapter requires explanation. In contrast to certain other twentieth-century political philosophers, who sought to relate theories of the state to issues of international order, it is impossible to point to Schmitt's international work as located in some identifiable source.[4] Whilst *The Nomos of the Earth* is undoubtedly the most important single source of Schmitt's thoughts on world order, it is by no means a distillation of a theory of international order. 'International' concerns are present in Schmitt's political theory from the outset, and his political theory consistently refers itself to the problematic nature of modern global politics. For Schmitt, politics is, by definition, a 'pluriverse' and hence international (or inter-*something*).

As such, our overview of Schmitt's 'international thought' must take account of the inter-penetration of his various fields of investigation. The conjunctive nature of the work under examination is both a source of richness, but also a challenge to the process of sketching an overview. It is therefore proposed to isolate several manageable 'segments' of Schmitt's thought. We will thereby consider the way in which Schmitt's concepts of the political, his account of political theology, his concern for the tension

---

[3] For an excellent short overview of readings of Schmitt, and points of divergence between the German-speaking and English-speaking reception communities, see P. C. Caldwell, 'Controversies over Carl Schmitt: A Review of Recent Literature', *The Journal of Modern History* 77 (June 2005), 357–87.

[4] One might think here of Rawls' *Law of Peoples* as an example of a deliberate 'international' counterpart to a prior theory of the domestic.

between juridical and moral categories, and notions of territoriality inter-relate. The greater objective of this work as a whole will then be to examine how Schmitt's experience of time related to this amalgam.

Aside from the breadth of the literature, several secondary prob-lems attach to this process. The first relates to the conjunctive nature of Schmitt's thought. We have no choice but to follow the contours of Schmitt's thought as accurately and honestly as possible. Yet it is beyond dispute that the connections and intellectual parallels that Schmitt draws are often highly idiosyncratic. One might say that this idiosyncrasy threa-tens to pass the initiative to Schmitt. There is no choice but to confront Schmitt on his own territory, in the complex amalgams he draws. The challenge is to do so without succumbing to 'Schmittitis' (a seemingly common affliction among Schmitt scholars), the principal symptom of which is a rather sycophantic awe for the breadth that his work represents.

The second principal problem to be borne in mind is in the varieties of form that might be termed 'international order'. Schmitt sees world order as problematic, changing and historically conditioned. Such united concept as exists is therefore fairly dynamic in Schmitt's thought. The closest we come to a stable international order composed of like units and possessing a thin, common normative content is the *jus publicum Europaeum* depicted at length in *The Nomos of the Earth*. As depicted in *Nomos*, this is clearly an international society of sorts. But the point of Schmitt's work is that neither does it consist of international society in its entirety (i.e., the society as a whole has a necessary ultimate exterior), nor is it stable over time. Imperial systems, spatial orders based on the premise of trade, *Großräume* and aerial spaces also feature as aspects of a complex global (dis-)order.

Both the 'international' and the 'order' of 'international order' are con-tinually problematised. 'Order' has a particular resonance for Schmitt, who certainly does not associate the concept with peace and security. By con-trast, stable order is characterised by the security of the concept of the political. Good enmity makes good stability, with all of the attendant need for strong concepts of public association, particularism and legiti-mated violence. The ultimate hope that Schmitt holds out is the simul-taneous achievement of order and the political, such that the modern state system had come so close to achieving.

The book as a whole concludes with an overview of the reception of Schmitt into contemporary international relations (IR) theory. This is a useful exercise both in highlighting the potential uses to which Schmitt's work is currently being put, and in highlighting the complexities of Schmitt's reception more broadly. The peculiar paths via which this reception has taken place centre on Schmitt's critique of the hypocrisy and dangers of global liberal hegemony. As such, Schmitt's work has constituted a theoretical resource to those on both the Left and the Right who seek to challenge the logic of a global economic, political and ethical system that, in their view, denies the possibility of local freedom and moral seriousness. As this work as a whole will attempt to show, however, the basis of Schmitt's critique of liberalism has idiosyncratic origins that extend beyond the mere affirmation of the political against universalism, calling into question the validity of attempts to construct a contemporary Schmittian vision of world politics.

The political

Schmitt is most strongly associated with *The Concept of the Political* and the basic definition of politics as enmity. It is no exaggeration to describe this insight as Schmitt's basic theoretical position from which the remainder of his political theory flows, and, as such, we must give due consideration to the true meaning of this observation. The following, oft-repeated remark from *The Concept of the Political* is the essence of Schmitt's definition of politics:

The specific political distinction to which political actions and motives can be reduced is that between friend and enemy.[5]

This theoretical starting point invites several observations. Firstly, this represents politics as a contingent category that reflects the nature of a relationship, and is not a self-referential concept. It defines politics in a sociological or historical sense, and does not represent an attempt to find a basic philosophical account of politics rooted in concepts of the public good. The key referents to this concept of politics are community, power (that can contain and mobilise a community) and war. Schmitt is actively hostile to normative or theoretical definitions of enmity since 'only the participants can correctly recognise, understand and judge the concrete situation and settle the extreme case of conflict'.[6]

Whilst contingent on confrontation, however, Schmitt also regards the political as immutable. He draws sociological assumptions about group behaviour that are reminiscent of questions of the nature of man in classical political theory. Whilst there are men, there will be collectivities of men. Whilst such collectivities exist, war will remain as a basic human possibility. War is the very logic of group existence, since existence would be meaningless without the possibility of existential affirmation. In the extreme instance, this affirmation will involve killing and dying in defence

---

[5] Schmitt, *The Concept of the Political*, p. 26.   [6] *Ibid.*, p. 27.

of the conceptual validity of the group. For Schmitt there is no other possibility, and life will be much easier if we accept and manage these uncomfortable effects of collective life.

Marcuse derided Schmitt's basic political position as 'justification by mere existence', but doubtless Schmitt would have responded by questioning the relevance of 'justification' to his analysis of politics.[7] Schmitt does not claim to be representing a political ideal, but is rather attempting a description of the way the world is. The language of justification in relation to the political only makes sense as an existential, and not a moral assertion: 'There exists no rational purpose, no norm no matter how true, no programme no matter how exemplary, no social ideal no matter how beautiful, no legitimacy or legality that could justify men killing each other in this way.' In short, Schmitt's is a world in which existence is the sole political category. As *The Concept of the Political* makes clear, other disputes that lead to war are mere window dressing for the basic, existential confrontation of one group against another. Once a substantive division is sufficient to create a watershed, and to divide men into 'potentially fighting [collectivities] of men', one has the political.

The category of enemy is thus an existential one, and cannot be reduced to any pre-existing category or norm. Whilst the parameters of enmity will often fall to be realised along, *inter alia*, national, religious, cultural or other such lines, such concepts are autonomous from the fact of enmity:

The distinction of friend and enemy denotes the utmost degree of intensity of a union or separation, of an association or dissociation. It can exist, theoretically and practically, without having simultaneously to draw upon all those other moral, aesthetic, economic or other distinctions. The political enemy need not be morally evil or aesthetically ugly; he need not appear as an economic competitor, and it may even be advantageous to engage with him in a business transaction. But he is, nevertheless, the other, the stranger; and it is sufficient for his nature that he is, in an especially intense way, existentially something different and alien, so that in the extreme case conflicts with him are always possible.[8]

A political world is a world with divisions that have genuine meaning, and which might ultimately result in the requirement to fight or die on the basis of nothing more than the fact of belonging on one side or other of the dividing line. That is not to say that 'the political' emerges only where there is actual war. The essence of the political lies in its potentiality – in the latent potential of the social world to take sides and to fight: 'War is neither the aim nor the purpose nor even the very content of politics. But

---

[7] H. Marcuse, *Negations* (Boston, MA: Beacon, 1968).
[8] Schmitt, *The Concept of the Political*, pp. 26–7.

as an ever present possibility it is the leading presupposition which determines in a characteristic way human action and thinking and thereby creates a specifically political behaviour.'[9] The basic position of enmity as politics is modified by several ancillary observations. Firstly, Schmitt stresses the importance of a *public* dimension to that enmity. Private hatred, or an agonal confrontation between two private citizens will not amount to politics: 'An enemy exists only when, at least potentially, one fighting collectivity of people confronts a similar collectivity. The enemy is solely the public enemy, because everything that has a relationship to such a collectivity of men, particularly to a whole nation, becomes public by virtue of such a relationship.'[10] The political enemy is *hostis* and not *inimicus*, and Schmitt draws on Plato's distinction between the public and private enmity and the corresponding distinction between true war between Hellenes and Barbarians, and mere internal discords between private enemies. Schmitt reads Plato as expressing the thought that 'a people cannot wage war against itself and a civil war is only a self-laceration and does not signify that perhaps a new state or even a new people is being created'.[11]

Schmitt arguably enters difficult conceptual territory here, since he appears to be prejudging the subject matter of the divisions that, according to the view expressed above, cannot be reduced to anything less than the mere fact of adversity. Schmitt has in mind the confrontation of collectives of men who thereby separate the physical existence of the individual from the existential identity and interests of the group.[12] The problem remains, however, of how to determine the stability and continuation of the groupings that give the political its specific character. Why should it be, for instance, that the expression of private hatred in civil war cannot give rise to 'a new state or even a new people'?

This problem of political origins is acute in Schmitt, and nowhere more so than in trying to fit his thought into contemporary international political theory. Leo Strauss dismissed Schmitt's attempt theoretically to separate the political from the theory of the state as a mere polemical device to serve Schmitt's immediate critical goals. 'Following [Schmitt's own general principles], the sentence "the political precedes the state" can manifest the desire to express not an eternal truth but only a present truth ... Thus Schmitt's basic thesis is entirely dependent upon the polemic against liberalism; it is to be understood only qua polemical,

---

[9] *Ibid.*, p. 34.   [10] *Ibid.*, p. 28.   [11] *Ibid.*, p. 28 n. 9.
[12] This distinction between the respective interests of the individual and the political unit is explored in greater depth in the following chapter in the context of Hobbes' concept of the state.

only "in terms of concrete political existence".[13] The precise problem Schmitt encounters is in how to separate logically concepts of the state from concepts of the political, whilst simultaneously retaining his attachment to the state as the sole bearer of, following de Maistre, 'public morality and national character'.[14]

We will return later to the precise relevance of this public content to Schmitt's definition of the political, in the context especially of external recognition of the sovereign decision, and the legal aspects of political identity. For the time being it is sufficient to highlight that politics as conflict need not be inconsistent with a legal framework. On the contrary, true politics will be better sustained by a clear legal recognition of conflict as the basic defining aspect of political life, and a re-emphasis of the existential nature of group life. Such conceptual clarity will allow for a stable *Nomos*, that is to say, stable political units that can act as the locus for political division.

Consideration of these questions takes us beyond the basic political definition, however. It would be a mistake to read Schmitt's definition as advocacy of a belligerent state system. The political could give rise to potentially limitless means of expression. *The Concept of the Political* opens with the assertion that the 'concept of the state presupposes the concept of the political'.[15] Over time, Schmitt moved away from the intimate association of the political with the modern state, and always recognised that the state was a historically contingent form of political expression. In the 1940s and 1950s, Schmitt dedicated considerable energy to contemplating future social configurations that might supersede the state as the dominant basis of public enmity. In this sense, the political is a wholly independent category that seeks to express the most basic manifestation of man in society.

States and their system

For Schmitt, the Westphalian state is the most successful and stable manifestation of the political in world history. That said, in *The Concept of the Political*, the state is not a necessary political concept, and its existence in history is contingent and ephemeral. 'The concept of the state presupposes the concept of the political', and hence is subordinate

---

[13] L. Strauss, 'Notes on Carl Schmitt: *The Concept of the Political*', in H. Meier (ed.), *Carl Schmitt and Leo Strauss: The Hidden Dialogue* (trans. J. H. Lomax), Chicago: University of Chicago Press (1995), pp. 83–4.

[14] C. Schmitt, *Political Romanticism* (trans. G. Oakes), Cambridge, MA: MIT Press (1986), p. 61.

[15] Schmitt, *The Concept of the Political*, p. 13.

to and dependent on the primary friend–enemy distinction.[16] Schmitt has an historical understanding of the state that correlates fairly well with the standard IR interpretation of the emergence of several functioning states at or around the time of the Treaty of Westphalia in 1658. He considers that 'the significance of the state consisted in the overcoming of religious civil wars, which became possible only in the sixteenth century, and the state achieved this task only by a neutralization'.[17]

The precise historical achievement of the state was to achieve the unity of *auctoritas* (traditionally claimed by the emperor) and the *potestas* that had been the preserve of the Papacy throughout the Middle Ages. In achieving this unity, the state perfected its own sovereignty, which, in raw political terms, meant that the state achieved a monopoly of the power to decide on the exceptional situation, and so to name the public enemy. Or, put another way, the precise quality of sovereignty lies in its competence to determine when the normal functions of positive law are inadequate to the circumstances at hand. It is the sovereign who both creates and solves the exceptional situation through the imposition of its will. The essential characteristic of the modern state is that it should form the watershed of the friend–enemy distinction, and so maintain an external–internal divide. After the chaos of the Thirty Years' War, the triumph of the state consisted of its ability to neutralise and overcome civil war. In terms of the basis of conflict, it substituted *raison d'état* for the interminable struggles of religious righteousness.

The two theoretical heroes in the achievement of this neutral concept of sovereignty, Bodin and Hobbes, are again the familiar conceptual 'originators' of the state in IR theory. Schmitt's following account of the historical-theoretical achievement of sovereignty is worth quoting in full:

At least since Bodin, a true jurist would confront [a] sceptical and agnostic disposition with a *decisionist* formulation of the question that is immediately given with the concept of state sovereignty: who then is in a position to decide authoritatively on all the obvious, but impenetrable questions of fact and law pertinent to the question of *justa causa*? The asserted juridical right and moral legitimacy of one's own cause and the alleged injustice of the opponent's cause only sharpen and deepen the belligerent's hostility, surely in the most gruesome way. That we have learned from the feuds of the feudal age and from the creedal civil wars over theological truth and justice. *But state sovereigns ended such murderous assertions of right and questions of guilt.* That was the historical and intellectual accomplishment of the sovereign decision ... A simple question was raised with respect to the interminable legal disputes inherent in every claim to the *justa causa*:

---

[16] *Ibid.*, p. 19.   [17] Schmitt, *Nomos*, p. 61.

Who decides? (the great *Quis judicabit?*). Only the sovereign could decide the question, both within the state and between states.[18]

The authority of the sovereign state is therefore Janus-faced. Internally, the state confers to itself the right to determine all matters of public truth and so denies the potential for internecine struggles over questions of universal truth and justice.[19] Externally, there can be no higher authority than the state, since it must be the state itself that determines the public enemy. As we have already seen, identification of the enemy cannot be subject to any pre-existing norm, and can only be determined in the concrete situation. Therefore, a necessary condition of the truly political state is that it has unfettered discretion to choose whichever enemies, on whatever basis, as it may wish from time to time. The international achievement of the modern state lies in its capacity to recognise and challenge the just enemy.

In intellectual terms, therefore, Schmitt regards the rise of the state as a reaction to the intertwined problems of truth and authority in the Middle Ages. There is an additional spatial dimension to the rise of the state that is less intimately connected to Schmitt's basic theory of decision on the exception, and is rather a matter of historical accident (i.e. the spatial origins of the state do not appear to be logically necessary in order for the state to possess a specifically political character). Whereas the Greeks had envisioned a political world based on twin poles of *polis* and *cosmopolis*, and the Middle Ages had been characterised by religious-intellectual lines of political ordering, the organising logic of the state was its territoriality.[20]

Territory became the dominant basis of the continental state, and the state itself developed a monolithic and absolute notion of a single territorial status. Thus the exercise of legality internally, and the assertion of sovereign right externally, became referable to the territorial possession or extent of a particular state. The process of 'land appropriation' became the very logic of the European state, and with it came the identification of law and authority with the territorial space in which it was exercised. As such, 'the restriction of law to the land and to one's own territory has a long tradition in legal history'. As a result of this, 'it is historically more correct to focus on the relation between order and orientation, and on the spatial context of all laws'.[21]

The precise importance of this territoriality is difficult to quantify, and Schmitt is at pains to ensure that the territorial strengths of the state do not

---

[18] *Ibid.*, pp. 156–7 (my emphasis).
[19] See Chapter 3 for a fuller discussion on Schmitt's reading of Hobbes and the nexus between *auctoritas*, *potestas* and *veritas* in the concept of the modern state.
[20] See Schmitt, *Nomos*, pp. 50–5 and *passim*.   [21] *Ibid.*, p. 98.

end up qualifying the basic political category.[22] Nevertheless, certain advantages of a territorial ordering concept are quite evident. Firstly, territory is consistent with the neutrality of the state vis-à-vis questions of religious truth, ideology or other matters of universal importance. Secondly, and especially in the context of the land battles of modern warfare, territory allows for the unambiguous conduct of hostilities in a regularised, public and self-affirming manner. Furthermore, when looking externally, the concept of territory provides an innate limiting factor to the political ambitions of the state. The ultimately defensive imperative to confront the enemy is strongly affirmed by the identification of the state with a particular, 'telluric' space.[23]

'The ability to recognise a *justus hostis* [just enemy] is the beginning of all international law', Schmitt asserts.[24] The self-assurance of the state with respect to its internal authority creates, in turn, stability in its external visage. The state is allowed the space and moral freedom to examine the external world with a cool and independent eye, and can 'choose' to act in whatever manner it sees fit.[25] The consequence is the Westphalian system of co-existing sovereign states that together mutually create and recreate the terms of the *jus publicum Europaeum*. This is the thin international law that amounts to the mutual recognition of existence that, in Schmitt's scheme, is essential for the validity of the state.

As such, the legal status of sovereign equality is a fact, not a norm. The exercise of sovereignty *is* the international status of the state. Without sovereignty, there can be no state, and so no 'participation' as an international actor. With sovereignty, there is no way to avoid or

---

[22] See Chapter 4 for fuller consideration of the effect of this question of territoriality on Schmitt's historical consciousness and, in particular, the contrast he draws between continental and oceanic concepts of space in *Land und Meer*, Stuttgart: Klett–Cotta (1954).

[23] The loss of the state's basic territorial orientation is one of the elements of the modern malaise with which Schmitt is concerned. In Chapter 6 we consider his *Theorie des Partisanen*, and the idea that modern partisan fighters retain the fundamental link with territory (C. Schmitt, *Theorie des Partisanen: Zwischenbemerkung zum Begriff des Politischen*, Berlin: Duncker and Humblot (1963)).

[24] Schmitt, *Nomos*, p. 52.

[25] In considering the behaviour of the state, Schmitt largely glosses over the question of agency. Perhaps the agency of the state is supposed to be defined in reverse by answering the question *Quis judicabit?* Schmitt is, of course, concerned with the legal possibility of decisive and personal decision making, as evidenced by his advocacy of direct presidential rule under Article 48 of the Weimar Constitution, and his critique of parliamentarism (See C. Schmitt, *The Crisis of Parliamentary Democracy* (trans. E. Kennedy), Cambridge, MA: MIT Press (1985)). Schmitt did develop an early theory of sovereign dictatorship (see C. Schmitt, *Die Diktatur*, Berlin: Duncker and Humblot (1921)), but the decision-making capacity of the state externally is related only implicitly to the need for a single source of internal political authority.

prevent participation as an international actor (and, therefore, member-ship of the international system/society/*jus publicum Europaeum*), since the logic of sovereignty is a latent capacity to exercise the powers of *justus hostis*. A state unable to exercise the power to declare an enemy has ceased to be a state. If there is some other authority capable of making that declaration on behalf of the purported state, then sovereignty has been displaced into the hands of that other party. If no public decision is conceivable, then the politico-legal capability of that group for sover-eignty has been displaced, and presumably civil war ensues.

The unfettered power of the territorial state thus gives rise to a histor-ically distinct system of international law that would be recognisable from realist textbooks on international relations, albeit via an alternative reasoning. International law is the *de facto* collective status of various states that have each reached a comparable settlement of the question of balan-cing *potestas* and *auctoritas*, each having settled on a territorial orientation. The functional similarities of these states give rise to a comparatively stable collective condition that can be *descriptively* characterised as the system of public international law.

> The state had become independent with respect to the question of whether the given state authority was legitimate or illegitimate. Just as state wars became independent of the question of the justice or injustice of the grounds of war in international law, so, too, did the question of *justa causa* become independent *in international law*. All law came to reside in the existential form of the state.[26]

The overall effect, albeit only in a conditional and contingent way, was the limitation of the worst excesses of violence in inter-state war, and the establishment of nominal, social 'rules of the game' in the conduct of relations between sovereigns. By jealously protecting the right to make war, states ended up regularising the conduct of war and, by comparison with the messianic violence of the Thirty Years' War (and the analogous violence of the French Revolutionary Wars), inter-state warfare became increasingly humane.[27] Indeed, 'war in form' is held up as 'the strongest possible rationalisation and humanisation of war'. 'Both belligerents had the same political character and the same rights; both recognised each

---

[26] Schmitt, *Nomos*, p. 204 (emphasis in the original).

[27] Schmitt describes this limitation of warfare as *Hegung des Krieges*. Ulmen translated this as the 'bracketing of war' which is the use we will generally adopt throughout. *Hegen*, however, is a difficult word to translate, and Schmitt's use of it in this context is idiosyn-cratic. *Hegen* is suggestive of a form of benign and protective management of something by a superior and disinterested outsider. Its most natural usage is in the context of forestry, whereby a forester will cultivate, nurture, protect, fell and replant a particular, defined piece of woodland.

other as states. As a result, it was possible to distinguish an enemy from a criminal.'[28]

Anarchy is the key characteristic of this modern European state system, and Schmitt celebrates the existence of such anarchy as the necessary evidence that the political remained intact. Schmitt's account of the ordered world of European politics stresses that anarchy and order are not mutually exclusive categories. In a formulation that Hedley Bull could surely have subscribed to, Schmitt castigates the sloppy conflation of anarchy and disorder: '... [such] use of the word "anarchy" is typical of a perspective not yet advanced enough to distinguish between anarchy and nihilism. For this reason, it should be stressed that, in comparison to nihilism, anarchy is not the worst scenario. Anarchy and law are not mutually exclusive.'[29] For most of its history, the anarchy of the state system has been productive of a form of quasi-legal order. Schmitt's great fear is that the twentieth-century assault on the state system will result in precisely the form of violent chaos that 'liberal' critics erroneously attribute to the state.

The perfectly functioning European state system forms, therefore, something of an historical and conceptual ideal for Schmitt. The fact that the realisation of the European state form, its multiplication, and the style of co-existence were achieved as a result of historical chance does not dent Schmitt's admiration for such achievements. In a fashion typical of his use of historical example, Schmitt paints an idealised notion of the *jus publicum Europaeum* as a system in which the choice between war and neutrality rests with the sovereign, and a proper political dynamic exists unthreatened by universal claims. As such, the state system is worthy of our attachment, and should be defended against rival claims that will dismantle and obstruct this cool functionalism. Although state and politics are not commensurate, the state has done a worthy job, in Schmitt's account, of ensuring the stability and continuation of the political.

Nomos

The modern state exists within a global order that has developed a certain character of its own. The state has generated this order, in Schmitt's account, precisely because the state form so enshrines the 'fundamental process involved in the relation between order and orientation'.[30] Schmitt adopts the word *Nomos* to describe the fundamental territorial ordering of the world. '[N]omos is the immediate form in which the political and social

---

[28] Schmitt, *Nomos*, p. 142.   [29] *Ibid.*, p. 187.   [30] *Ibid.*, p. 67.

order of a people becomes spatially visible … *Nomos* is the measure by which the land in a particular order is divided and situated; *it is also the form of political, social and religious order determined by this process.*'[31]

Schmitt's *Nomos* is a challenging concept precisely because it is taken to encapsulate the fact of a particular set of orientations, and the effect of those orientations on the nature of order. *Nomos* describes the essence of any particular order in its entirety. As such, and as Schmitt makes clear in his consideration of the word's etymology, *Nomos* is a 'fence-word' that can mean 'dwelling place, district, pasturage'.[32] The '*Nomos* of the earth' is therefore intended to convey the conditional and temporally fragile order of things in the world, which, despite this sense of contingency, nevertheless exists as a concrete reality.

The existence of a concrete *Nomos*, whatever its origins and constitutive parts, is a necessary precondition for the possibility of order. Modern Europe, with its constitutive parts and its common awareness of the concrete *fact* of a *jus publicum Europaeum* constituted just such a *Nomos*. Other *Nomoi* based on different concrete spatial realities are theoretically possible, but advocacy of a *Nomos* misses the point that such order and orientation is a reflection in fact of a concrete order, and not an ideal type that adheres to rules of any kind:

As long as the Greek word *Nomos* in the often cited passages of Heraclitus and Pindar is transformed from a spatially concrete, constitutive act of order and orientation – from an *ordo ordinans* [order of ordering] into the mere enactment of acts in line with the *ought* and, consistent with the manner of thinking of the positivistic legal system, translated with the word *law* – all disputes about interpretation are hopeless and all philological acumen is fruitless.[33]

The *Nomos* exists as a constitutive act that is already apparent by the time that anyone could conceive of its outlines. 'The original act is *Nomos*.'[34] Any *Nomos* can be either the fulcrum of history, or subject to historical undermining on its own terms. Whereas the continuing validity of the state depends on the continuing capacity for sovereignty, change in the *Nomos* is determined at a less defined conceptual level. 'All subsequent developments are either results of and expansions of [the original act] or else redistributions (*anadasmoi*) – either a continuation on the same basis or a disintegration of and departure from the constitutive act of the spatial order …'[35]

---

[31] *Ibid.*, p. 70 (my emphasis).
[32] *Ibid.*, p. 75. Schmitt gives a pointed overview of the origins and misuses of the term *Nomos*, and claims to be recovering the Aristotelian meaning from confusion (pp. 67–79).
[33] *Ibid.*, p. 78.   [34] *Ibid.*   [35] *Ibid.*

One possible rendering of *Nomos* would be 'law' in the sense of international law. In *The Nomos of the Earth*, it is clear that the putative international law of the *jus publicum Europaeum* was a *Nomos* – the first global *Nomos*. Alessandro Colombo argues that there is a distinct similarity between Schmitt's notion of common social mores in the *jus publicum Europaeum*, and English School ideas on international society. Far from being an extreme realist with a belief in power politics, Schmitt saw that 'the *jus publicum Europaeum* places international anarchy in a societal and, more importantly, juridical web' and does so via institutions that '[change] the nature of the players, the extent of the playing field, and the rules of the game'.[36] Colombo therefore regards Schmitt as a 'realist institutionalist'.[37]

In the case of the *jus publicum Europaeum* at least, *Nomos* can be meaningfully compared to an idea of international law in the sense of a shared framework of understanding – a shared field in which politics takes place. But the concept of *Nomos* cannot be reduced to law, especially in the way that the latter term has come to be understood. Schmitt specifically rejects the translation of *Nomos* as law because of the array of misunderstandings that would inevitably ensue.[38] The *Nomos* cannot be viewed as a set of rules or norms that somehow 'govern' or 'regulate' the conduct of states. But it does represent a basic level of commonality such that the pluriversal basis of politics can be sustained.

Thalin Zarmanian argues that the concept of *Nomos* is better understood when read in the context of Schmitt's domestically oriented views on the meaning and function of law.[39] He suggests that Schmitt's entire project is motivated by 'the search for an answer to the problem of the *Rechtsverwirklichung* (actualization of the law)'.[40] At the domestic level this search focussed on the tension between a universal principle of law, and the application of principle to the concrete situation. As Zarmanian puts it, Schmitt was searching for 'an Archimedean point – the legal order – in which the tension between the idea of law (*die Rechtsidee*) and empirical reality could converge'.[41]

---

[36] A. Colombo, 'Challenging the State: Carl Schmitt and "Realist Institutionalism"'. Paper Presented to the 5th Pan-European International Relations Conference, The Hague, September 2004, p. 3.

[37] See also A. Colombo, 'L'Europa e la società internazionale: gli aspetti culturali e istituzionale della convivenza internazionale in Raymond Aron, Martin Wight e Carl Schmitt', *Quaderni di scienza politica* 2 (1999), 251–302.

[38] 'In an age such as this, it is inexpedient to Germanize *Nomos* as "law".' Schmitt, *Nomos*, pp. 71–2.

[39] T. Zarmanian, 'Carl Schmitt and the Problem of Legal Order: From Domestic to International', *Leiden Journal of International Law* 19 (2006), 41–67.

[40] *Ibid.*, p. 44.   [41] *Ibid.*, p. 48.

In the domestic context, the most obvious instance in which this tension between norm and concrete reality comes to light is in the state of emergency. The fact that law as a normative set of rules cannot solve the state of emergency is evidence of the fact that the actual content of law as order cannot be determined *a priori*, but is instead a constitutive act rooted in the decision by the sovereign. It is the sovereign decision, in the concrete situation, that produces a legal order, and it is the ability to create order that lends legitimacy to the sovereign decision. In Zarmanian's words, 'legal order is, therefore, according to Schmitt, a particular shape given to empirical reality through a sovereign decision'.[42]

If the sovereign decision is the latent 'solution' to the problem of pluralism in Schmitt's domestic context, the concept of *Nomos* offers a parallel solution to the broader problem of the political pluriverse of groups. The international setting cannot be constituted by an abstract set of rules, since, in the absence of a single culture and a single political community, there will be no means to apply such rules to the concrete situation. What we have instead is the particular arrangement by which the particular political unit is reconciled and embedded in the universal context. In Schmitt's own parlance, any *Nomos* represents the accepted 'structuring combination' of *Ordnung* (order) and *Ortung* (localisation or (in Ulmen's translation) 'orientation').[43] For Schmitt, this is an explicitly spatial accommodation between the particular territory of the political unit, and the widest spatial horizon in which the validity of that political unit is implicated. Following Zarmanian, this use of space is vital for Schmitt's schema in that it 'accounts for the existence and for the co-implication of empirical reality, law, and the political', and secures an environment in which the diverse political units can survive as bearers of specificity or *Lebensmöglichkeit*.[44]

Thus *Nomos* represents a complex mediation between the particular and the universal, through which various political units gain recognition and the ability to project and protect their own concept of collective life. In a similar vein to Zarmanian, Sergio Ortino illustrates the nature of the parallel between *Nomos* and the sovereign decision in a domestic context (*Entscheidung*):

Entscheidung and Nomos share the same substance, because each of them represents the true core of an historical legal event characterized by an absolute and concrete nature capable of founding a new system of law. Entscheidung and Nomos differ from each other because the former refers to a specific legal community, [that] decides to create a new political system upon new principles and new legal norms, while the latter refers to the new way in which humanity decides

---

[42] *Ibid.*, p. 50.   [43] See *ibid.*, p. 55.   [44] *Ibid.*, p. 57.

in a specific epoch of [its] evolution to organize itself into new forms and with new values and principles. When a new holder of the constituent power takes a fundamental decision in favour of a new legal order, we are witnessing a political revolution. When humanity accepts the new Nomos of an emerging new epoch, we are witnessing a space revolution.[45]

The collapse of one *Nomos* and the rise in its place of another seems, therefore, to be nothing less than the transformation of global reality. Only in modern times, of course, is it logically necessary (or even possible) that a *Nomos* would be global. '[N]omos is a matter of the fundamental process of apportioning space that is essential to every historical epoch.'[46] The Greek *Nomos* would have consisted of the Mediterranean world. As Schmitt amply illustrates, the *Nomos* of the modern European state system is, by definition, Eurocentric. A conceptual fence exists around the *Nomos* beyond which there is no social reality, no commonality, no order.

The pre-eminent international problem for Schmitt, therefore, is the attempt to ascertain what will be the new *Nomos* of the earth. Thinking through this task was a breathtaking personal challenge, given that the identification of a new *Nomos* required nothing less than establishing the locus of the political, the determination of the question of orientation, and the unknowable question of the form of order that such orientation would produce. 'Every new age and every new epoch in the coexistence of peoples, empires, and countries, of rulers and power formations of every sort, is founded on new spatial divisions, new enclosures, and new spatial orders of the earth.'[47] Assuming that the old international *Nomos* was witnessing terminal decline, the challenge Schmitt set for himself and for those who subscribed to his basic contention was to observe and theorise the shape of the new *Nomos*.

Style and polemic

Undoubtedly, much of Schmitt's renewed appeal in political theory generally lies in the clarity of the concepts he delivers (his *Begriffsmagie*), and the gently emphatic method of their delivery.[48] In a predictable analogy, the polemical effect of Schmitt's work has been described as akin to *Blitzkrieg*. Ernst Jünger's famous description of Schmitt's thought as a 'mine that explodes silently' neatly encapsulates the dual effect of Schmitt's persuasive style, and the strange intellectual romance that

---

[45] S. Ortino, 'Space Revolution and Legal Order'. Paper presented to the 5th Pan-European International Relations Conference, The Hague, September 2004, p. 1.

[46] Schmitt, *Nomos*, p. 78.   [47] *Ibid.*, p. 79.

[48] G. Kateb, 'Aestheticism and Morality: Their Cooperation and Hostility', *Political Theory* 28:1 (2000), 5–37.

attached to his enforced isolation from post-war intellectual life.[49] Given a general consensus on the literary and polemical impact of Schmitt's work, it is all the more remarkable that a comprehensive study of the aesthetic-polemical nature of Schmitt's work is yet to emerge.[50] More broadly, those who seek to adopt Schmitt in support of contemporary political visions face the tricky task of separating the substance of Schmitt's theory from the aesthetic talent with which he was undoubtedly blessed.

Whilst improving the accessibility of his work to a wider audience, Schmitt's hypnotic style has probably hampered the prospects for temperate and considered reception of his work. His combination of intellectual accessibility, underplayed erudition and sheer readability disturbs Schmitt's critics as much as it delights his fans. Too often, those who seek to criticise Schmitt display an apparent fear of being led into dark labyrinths of mind via a serious engagement with his thought, and this fear results in a reverse polemic of condemnation. The 'dangerous mind' is to be prodded from a distance, avoiding the danger of contagion from those who engage without first 'knowing their Schmitt'. Even William Scheuerman's generally temperate analysis contains the warning that 'it would be a mistake to let Schmitt off the hook too easily *even when his analysis seems most impressive*' (my italics).[51]

The obverse effect of Schmitt's slippery style is that he has been able, as Jan-Werner Müller puts it, to mean 'so *much* and *so many seemingly contradictory things to so many*', such that arguably 'no twentieth-century thinker has had a more diverse range of readers.'[52] This broad appeal and theoretical pliability brings its own dangers, not least the very real possibility that the conceptual core provided by Schmitt is transmogrified by his disciples to the point that putative 'Schmittianism' can have no meaning. This peculiar process of adoption was doubtless aggravated by Schmitt's meddling hand in his supposed years of isolation in Plettenberg after 1947.

---

[49] Andrew Norris takes Jünger's phrase as the title for his review essay 'A Mine that Explodes Silently: Carl Schmitt in Weimar and After', *Political Theory* 33:6 (December 2005), 887–98.

[50] David Pan's short study 'Political Aesthetics: Carl Schmitt on Hamlet', *Telos* 72 (Summer 1987), 153–9 provides a good if esoteric point of departure for consideration of Schmitt as an aesthetic thinker. See also Kateb, 'Aestheticism'; S. Pourciau, 'Bodily Negation: Carl Schmitt on the Meaning of Meaning', *Modern Language Notes* 120:5 (December 2005), 1066–90.

[51] W. Scheuerman, *Carl Schmitt: The End of Law*, Lanham, MD: Rowman and Littlefield (1999), p. 152.

[52] J.-W. Müller, *A Dangerous Mind: Carl Schmitt in Post-War European Thought*, New Haven: Yale University Press (2003), pp. 3, 2 (emphasis in the original).

It goes without saying that Schmitt represents a style of academic writing as far removed from the arcane and intricate forms of typical 'academic German' as it is possible to imagine. Most commentators have engaged at some level with the problematic question of how to comprehend the 'method to Schmitt's stylistic magic'.[53] The process by which Schmitt self-consciously achieves this 'magic' can be described as distillation. He constantly presents the image of a complex and dynamic reality that can be reduced in some instances to a radically pure theoretical proposition, and in other instances is expressed by means of a radically pared down semiotic device. In this vein, the essence of politics is the encounter of between enemies. All of the complexity of non-state violence can be understood through the figure of the partisan. We are asked to believe that these precise, simple, comprehensible devices are the intense residue that remains once all complexity and detail have evaporated away.

The most trite conclusion to all of this is that the attempt to encapsulate such a complex reality with such stylistic precision threatens to render the theory itself inarticulate. All political and social theory is, of course, vulnerable to a charge along these lines. And the fact that theory by its very nature involves the taming of nuance and the ironing out of empirical creases does not, of itself, render theory meaningless. We must often simplify in order to comprehend. But there is little doubt that Schmitt takes this process to extremes. He is driven always to generalise and conceptualise, and to the extent that he relies on empirical research or theoretical insights of others, such extraneous sources are invariably used in order for Schmitt to make a precise and premeditated point, rather than for the purposes of detailed scholarly analysis.

The truth, of course, is that Schmitt was far more than simply an aphorist. The political and social 'reality' that Schmitt posits is developed with ever deeper insight and layers of theoretical and empirical detail. But in terms of Schmitt's style (if not the actual genesis of his ideas), such detail follows on from the basic, pure theoretical device. As such, it transpires that 'enemies' must be 'public'. The enmity between them must resemble *hostis* and not *inimicus*. Such enmity may be latent or overt and its contours may not be obvious at any one time. There are numerous factors that impact on the strength and validity of these relationships of alterity. And these relationships exist within a framework, the *Nomos*, which in turn brings a multitude of theoretical historical factors into the mix. But from a stylistic point of view, all of Schmitt's readers start with the purest, most precise and most persuasive distillation of all this complexity. Rather than reading with

---

[53] *Ibid.*, p. 9.

Schmitt as he moves towards his conclusions, challenging the turns he takes and the interpretations he makes, we instead start at the end, and develop a vested interest in the process of organising reality to fit with the beguiling theoretical starting point.

The problem with Schmitt's style is less that he creates stylish and simple theoretical propositions. The danger lies with his narrative style, which makes critical evaluation of his argument a more than usually onerous task. Many political theorists fear Schmitt because he is widely regarded as a polemnicist. But rather than being of concern as a polemnicist for some dubious Nazi cause, it is more realistic to fear Schmitt for his polemic in the service of his own theoretical conclusions. Isolating and critiquing Schmitt in a fair and impartial way is by no means impossible. But in order to do so, one must penetrate the narrative and isolate the precise and logically distinct choices and intellectual commitments that Schmitt makes in reaching his concepts. One such task that remains decidedly tricky, and that might serve by way of illustration of Schmitt's style, is trying to place Schmitt into intellectual context, both within Germany in the middle of the twentieth century, and more broadly within the context of European political thought.

Schmitt and European political ideas

Earlier in this chapter we remarked on Schmitt's ambiguous relationship to recognisable traditions in German political thought. Indeed, Schmitt has become one of the most persistently difficult figures in twentieth-century political thought to place into an intellectual habitus. It would be an understatement of epic proportions to remark that assembling a credible study of Schmitt's influences, antecedents and intellectual debts would be a mammoth undertaking. Reading Schmitt contextually is an almost uniquely difficult prospect. To be sure, many of the barriers to such an approach are part of the normal process of contextual examination. That Schmitt fails to acknowledge intellectual debts; that his reading is broad, esoteric and ill-disciplined; that he makes random points of connection between ideas and schools of thought; all this is a normal part of any academic endeavour. But Schmitt's is an extreme case in each regard.

Naturally, the fact that this would be a very challenging undertaking does not make it any the less worthwhile. Quite the contrary, in fact. But it is a challenge that must be left to another work. This book will not attempt to provide a comprehensive and detailed contextual reading of Schmitt. In part that is a methodological choice, sacrificing the richness of detail for the sake of clarity of exposition and argument. In part, it is a statement of purpose. Where it is necessary to illuminate shifts in Schmitt's thought, or to highlight themes that clearly derive along certain paths of influence, we will take deep cuts into Schmitt's intellectual milieu. But this is, of course, a fundamentally different exercise from that undertaken by historians of ideas of the Cambridge School. We will start from the text, and look to influence in reverse, rather than isolating the man and building the text alongside him. Indeed, given the very intense interest in Schmitt the man, it may even be refreshing for our starting point to be taking Schmitt at his word.

Nevertheless, before commencing with our substantive study of Schmitt's ideas on world order, it is necessary to make a few general remarks about context. This is obviously a dangerous and awkward exercise, since such remarks must remain general and poorly substantiated. Readers should by all means challenge this overview, and not feel bound by these preliminary conclusions in reading the remainder of the book. Indeed, they are more than welcome to disregard the brief remarks that follow as a facile aside. The intention is to give a brief introduction to the intellectual milieu in which Schmitt operated, and to point out some of the peculiarities that one might not expect of a man in his circumstances. We will focus in turn on Schmitt's relationship with his contemporaries during the course of his long career, before turning to situate Schmitt in the wider and longer context of European political ideas.

Schmitt started his career as a lawyer and a political theorist in the immediate aftermath of the First World War. The first twenty years of Schmitt's career were squarely dominated by themes of legal and political crisis. If the Weimar Republic never attained meaningful stability, it did at least provide a platform for some of the most energetic and open-ended theory about the meaning of political order and the relationship between law and politics. Schmitt's position in this great debate centred around two poles. Firstly, he was committed to concepts of direct and personal authority against those who believed that legal positivism offered a path to neutral and efficient modes of authority.[54] Secondly, in concrete debates about the exercise of power under the constitution, Schmitt argued forcefully for the exercise of presidential power as a means to remedy the indecision of parliamentary politics.[55] As such, Schmitt developed his theory of the exercise of political sovereignty and his concrete arguments

---

[54] Schmitt's position is most famously read in the context of his dispute with the famous legal positivist, Hans Kelsen. See D. Dyzenhaus, *Legality and Legitimacy: Carl Schmitt, Hans Kelsen and Hermann Heller in Weimar*, Oxford: Clarendon Press (1999).

[55] Schmitt was committed to the exercise of direct presidential power from the outset, as made clear in his 1921 work *Die Diktatur*.

about the state of Weimar politics in tandem. The theory of sovereignty that we explore in the following chapter was part and parcel of a practical search to answer the question, 'Who has the power to decide in the emergency situation?'

The political context of Germany forced Schmitt, in other words, to become very comfortable with the question of political emergency as a central fact of political life. Yet there are several other themes of broadly conservative inter-war thought that are far less prominent in Schmitt's thinking than one might have expected. For instance, in contrast to the fervent themes of *ressentiment* that were commonplace at the time, it is rather difficult to make a case for Schmitt as a German nationalist. His study *Political Romanticism*, first published in 1919 and reissued in 1925, constitutes a ferocious attack on the characteristically German failure to solidify an idea of politics in favour of a whimsical, playful idea of the individual spirit and the cultural community. It is a more or less explicit denial of a commonplace nineteenth-century idea of Germany as a land of cultural anti-politics, and shows a rather determined effort to mark a discontinuity with the traditions of Herder and German Romanticism.

If Schmitt is peculiar for his firm rebuttal of unthinking German nationalism, he also stands out in his sensitivity to and admiration for Latin Europe. Although Schmitt was passionately opposed to liberalism, concepts of rights and legal positivism, he never took the step many German theorists before and after took in irretrievably coupling these concepts with France. As we shall explore later, Schmitt had a very nuanced understanding of France. France interested Schmitt for its ambiguities. He often depicts it as grappling between rival destinies: between the religious and the profane, between authority and rights, between land and sea.[56] Schmitt was also very engaged in the politics of Spain, Portugal and Italy, and developed an early admiration for the development of Mediterranean forms of fascism, with their blend, as he saw it, between classical dictatorship, religious renewal and the nudity of their political decision. To a quite remarkable extent, Schmitt retained a very clear perspective on the problem of political power as urgent and, in the sense of being replicated severally, universal to continental Europe.

Infamously, Schmitt rose to the heights of his career in tandem with the ascent and consolidation of Nazi power. There can be no doubt that Schmitt's longstanding advocacy of direct, unaccountable power, his commitment to the exercise of presidential veto, and his visceral dislike of parliamentarism made it predictable that both he and others would see

---

[56] See especially Chapters 4 and 7 below.

this as, in some sense, his moment. So much has been written on this nexus, and on Schmitt's status as 'crown jurist' of the Third Reich, that little more need be added in a superficial study such as this.[57] One might say that the mid 1930s offer a classic tale of hubris and nemesis. Schmitt's greatest fame was followed very rapidly by a slide into political, intellectual and personal insecurity. As we explore in Chapters 5 and 6, the wartime years in particular provoke a loss of clarity and listlessness in Schmitt's writing.

For better or worse, Nazism had come to dominate Schmitt. It became the master of his intellectual productivity and the arbiter of his reputation. This is not to say that such an outcome was not deserved. It is even possible that Schmitt himself recognised that this is the price to be paid for a concept of the political that advocates the fierce restriction of a zone of personal freedom. It is in this respect that Schmitt's relationship to Nazism is most interesting. It is not Schmitt's moral failure, or his enthusiasm for Nazism itself, but rather what the relationship between Schmitt's ideas on the necessary silhouette of politics and his own concrete political choices can tell us.[58]

After 1945, Schmitt would never be rehabilitated within the established intellectual circles of the Federal Republic. What he became, instead, was a cuckoo in the nest of European radicalism. With all the arrogance of his youth, and the recklessness of a man who had already lost more than his disciples would ever possess, Schmitt became a grand political seer for radical thinkers who shared his discontent with what they saw as the emptiness of post-war politics. Schmitt's pessimism of the earlier years blossomed into a sense of the grand twilight of politics as we know it. With his intellectual gamble in favour of Nazism behind him, Schmitt became ever more convinced that the failure to grasp the nettle of political authority left little hope of political renewal from within the horizon of Cold War politics. Although he tried to envisage ways in which the state system could recover its political vitality, the overall sense was one of impending doom.

What follows is an attempt to sketch out Schmitt's own understanding of the historical realisation of this looming disaster, and the way that this historical consciousness affected his ability to theorise beyond the state. It is only by considering Schmitt's specific and idiosyncratic understanding of history that we can begin to understand the uniqueness of

---

[57] The leading such study is Andreas Koenen's meticulously researched *Der Fall Carl Schmitt: Sein Aufstieg zum 'Kronjuristen des Dritten Reiches'*, Darmstadt: Wissenschaftliche Buchgesellschaft (1995).

[58] For more on this, see Chapter 5 below.

the crisis of the state in Schmitt's mind, and the hefty consequences he ascribed to this. Realisation of Schmitt's peculiar pessimism may well leave room for others to develop a Schmittian concept of world order in his stead. To ignore, however, the theological and historiographical aspects of Schmitt's account of modern international relations would be to engage in the kind of selective reading of which Schmitt himself was all too fond.

3   Unravelling sovereignty

Do not concern yourself: the Leviathan – its shadow is long – therefore the Leviathan is already concerned for me. It already holds an honoured place in the barbed wire Prytaneum waiting for me. There it will sustain me with food and drink befitting of the place.   Carl Schmitt[1]

The isolation of stable concepts of power and authority are the hallmarks of Schmitt's theoretical method. As the previous chapter makes clear, the dominant starting point for all of Schmitt's political thinking is the state, and its specific, defining attribute, sovereignty. All of Schmitt's early work was directly or indirectly concerned with accurately defining the state, and making clear the relationship between the state and the political. In theoretical terms, Schmitt rests on a definition of sovereignty as the power to decide on the exception – the pure capacity to impose a coherent ordering decision at the point at which law ends. To act politically is to define enemies. To exercise sovereignty is to decide on the exception. These are the twin poles of Schmitt's familiar, ideal theory of politics in the state.

This lean set of definitions that Schmitt worked out in the 1920s and early 1930s undoubtedly remains as his most distinctive contribution to subsequent political theory. By isolating out the essence of political authority, Schmitt created a powerful descriptive and analytical tool with which to criticise political reality. Yet this slimline approach to theory inevitably left several questions of an historical nature that Schmitt was forced to address in his later work. In situating an ahistoric set of concepts of the state, Schmitt had thus far had comparatively little to say about the existence and persistence of these concepts over time. Moreover, despite logically separating attributes of the political (enmity), from the narrower

---

[1] 'Sorge dich nicht: der Leviathan – lang sei sein Schatten – also der Leviathan wird schon für mich sorgen. Schon hält er eine ehrenvolle Unterkunft in einen Stacheldraht-Prytaneum für mich bereit. Dort wird er mich auch unterhalten mit Speisen und Getränken, die seiner würdig sind.' C. Schmitt, *Glossarium: Aufzeichnungen der Jahre 1947–1951*, Berlin: Duncker and Humblot (1991), 21 July 1948, p. 180.

attributes of sovereignty (a contextual decision), Schmitt fails to exploit the historical relationship of the latter to the former. He famously asserts that 'the concept of the state presupposes the concept of the political', but does not go on to explore the specific attributes and historical experience of statehood.[2] Schmitt's theoretical explorations clearly raise a profound historical question – how, when, and on what basis has the state come to dominate the exercise of the political? And in the shadow there lies an ancillary question – what if this monopoly collapses?

It is evident that Schmitt had always implicitly subscribed to a commonplace understanding of the modern state as a conceptually distinct entity, with its origins in the convulsions of reformation. As early as 1923, Schmitt depicted the European Middle Ages as an era before the state, in which political life was organised as a *complexio oppositorum* – a situation in which the varying enmity of kings, princes, ecclesiastical rulers, republics and dukes all took place within the context of shared commitment to Rome.[3] Assuming, as Schmitt does, that the political is a permanent condition of human life, it is evident that the state can only be a temporary locus of politics. The political history of the state has a beginning, and, presumably, a potential end.

Schmitt's first stop in the conceptual history of the state is Jean Bodin, whom he considers to 'stand at the beginning of the modern theory of the state'.[4] Indeed, the concept of sovereignty that Schmitt develops in *Political Theology* and deploys in *The Concept of the Political*, resonates most strongly with Bodin's methods and typology. Both were concerned to distil a precise and ahistorical *definition* of sovereign power in an attempt to illustrate and secure its conceptual priority over other claims. Bodin was concerned to 'clarify the meaning of sovereign power', and aphoristically settled on a definition of sovereignty as 'the absolute and perpetual power of a commonwealth', which is to say, 'the highest power of command'.[5] Schmitt celebrates Bodin's elevation of command in a single locus – the total and indivisible possession of power – in his own definition of sovereignty as decision on the exception.[6]

---

[2] C. Schmitt, *The Concept of the Political* (trans. G. Schwab), Chicago: University of Chicago Press (1996), p. 19.

[3] See C. Schmitt, *Römischer Katholizmus und politische Form* (2nd edn), Cologne: Klett–Cotta (1925), pp. 11–16.

[4] Schmitt, *Political Theology* (trans. G. Schwab), Cambridge, MA: MIT Press (2005), p. 8.

[5] J. Bodin, *On Sovereignty* (trans. J. H. Franklin), Cambridge: Cambridge University Press (1992), p. 1.

[6] Schmitt suggest that 'by considering sovereignty to be indivisible, [Bodin] finally settled the question of power in the state'. *Political Theology*, p. 8. See also A. Norris, 'Sovereignty, Exception, and Norm', *Journal of Law and Society* 34:1 (March 2007), 31–45 (pp. 42–4).

In his early focus on defining and refining the core elements of sovereign authority, Schmitt has much in common with Bodin. Faced with a
wholly distinct context, Bodin surely produces a more sympathetic and
less necessarily oppressive settled understanding of sovereignty.[7] But in
terms of method, they both seek to produce a stable set of concepts to
characterise sovereignty, and to provide roots. They are both committed
to sovereignty as a principle of order that precedes ideas of justification
or permission. And they both posit a fundamentally ahistorical notion
of sovereignty conceived in terms of its permanence.[8] They both try
to produce an immutable yardstick against which the vagaries of real,
non-ideal political life might be measured.

In time, Schmitt came to recognise the limitations of this stark separation of a concept of sovereignty from the historical manifestations of its
practice. Increasingly during the 1930s, Schmitt turned towards an
examination of the state as an historically conditioned product, situating
the concept of sovereignty in a non-ideal context.[9] Having settled on a
workable set of political definitions, Schmitt turned his concern to the
existence of the state, and the system of states, as a conceptual-historical
reality. Of necessity, this focus combined elements of raw political history
with a more abstract examination of the rise and fall of the state as a
category that monopolised exercise of the political. The starting point to
a reading of Schmitt's history of international order is a closer examination of this reading of the historical survival of the state as the basic unit of
such an order.

Schmitt's curious historical method starts from his pre-formed concept.
He is engaged by the history of the political, the history of the state, the
history of the *jus publicum Europaeum*. Indeed, throughout his oeuvre,
history qua historiography is an under-theorised component of his political thought as a whole. And likewise, the challenge of reading Schmitt as a
historian has been taken up only selectively. Whilst *The Nomos of the Earth*
in particular has been read as an historical work, the interest has focussed

---

[7] For a discussion of points of divergence between Schmitt and Bodin, see G. Harste, 'Jean
Bodin on Sovereignty, State and Central Administration: Unity or Complexity?',
Distinktion: Scandinavian Journal of Social Theory 2 (2001), 33–52.

[8] For both Bodin and Schmitt, historical contingency may attend to the survival of a
particular bearer of sovereignty, but sovereignty itself is 'not limited either in power, or
in function, or in length of time'. Bodin, *On Sovereignty*, p. 3.

[9] One cannot be overly prescriptive in drawing these chronological distinctions. However,
I broadly agree with Ojakangas' characterisation of 1933 as a dividing line between Schmitt's
early work on the decision and a formal definition of sovereignty, and his subsequent
exploration of 'concrete orders and institutions'. See M. Ojakangas, *A Philosophy of
Concrete Life: Carl Schmitt and the Political Thought of Late Modernity*, Bern: Peter Lang
(2006), p. 19.

largely on the way in which Schmitt has appropriated historical phenomena such as the Congress of Vienna or the establishment of the Monroe Doctrine in illuminating his contemporary political theory. Any 'Schmittian' 'theory' of history is somewhat more elusive.

During the Nazi period, Schmitt was condemned and dispossessed on the grounds of his alleged Hegelianism, an accusation brought by Ernst Röhm in connection with supposed progressivism in Schmitt's political work.[10] Certainly, Schmitt is never wholly detached from the German tradition of thinking about the organic and total nature of the state. His critical engagement with Hegelian philosophies of history is worthy of detailed examination, and forms an important element of his wider critique of neutralisation and positivism.[11] However, the purpose of this chapter is to argue that a different form of determinism marks Schmitt's theory of international order. Rather than being characterised by progression, the prospects of the state are coloured instead by a determined process of unravelling and dissolution that can be read into the very content of the state concept itself.

It is Hobbes, rather than Hegel, who emerges as the dominant figure in the formation and explanation of this process of unravelling. It is Hobbes who provides a theoretical peg on which Schmitt hangs his interpretation of the state as a concrete historical entity. Through his reading of Hobbes, Schmitt establishes a historical framework with which to evaluate the fate of the state. By conflating the 'Hobbesian' 'theory' of the state with the emergence of the state as a concrete entity, Schmitt sets about searching for causal clues to the current condition of the state as a bearer of politics.

A note of caution is necessary here. By Chapters 6 and 7 of his 1938 study *The Leviathan in the State Theory of Thomas Hobbes*, it is evident that Schmitt has conflated the Hobbesian theory of the state with the modern state in its concrete manifestation. This conflation seems deliberate and self-conscious, and leads one to conclude that Schmitt read the *actual* modern state as the *product* of Hobbes' concept of the state. Schmitt gives a cursory account, for instance, of how 'Hobbes' important theory of the state did not materialize in England and among the English people but

---

[10] In December 1936, the SS publication *Das schwarze Korps* savaged Schmitt as an opportunist Catholic rooted in a Hegelian concept of the state. It asserted that his avowed anti-Semitism was a mere artifice designed to garner favour with the regime. See J. Bendersky, 'The Expendable Kronjurist: Carl Schmitt and National Socialism, 1933–1936', *Journal of Contemporary History* 14:2 (1979), 309–28.

[11] See Chapter 5 below. For an overview of Schmitt's reading of Hegel, see R. Howse, 'Europe and the New World Order: Lessons from Alexandre Kojève's Engagement with Schmitt's *Nomos of the Earth*', *Leiden Journal of International Law* 19:1 (2006), 93–103.

on the European continent among the land powers'.[12] The Cromwell dictatorship came close to inaugurating a Hobbesian state, but in the end it was the French and Germans who, it is suggested, turned concept into dominating reality.[13]

This notion of materialisation is quite extraordinary. Schmitt appears to be seriously suggesting that, via a process of translation through Pufendorf and others, Hobbes' theory of the state was transformed into political reality. Even by Schmitt's standards of reduction, this appears a remarkably loose notion of causation, and Schmitt declines to elaborate on or justify his bold attempt to read the state concept in reality as more or less identical to Hobbes' idea of Leviathan. One must be in no doubt that the methodology of Schmitt's study of *Leviathan* is entirely self-serving. For our purposes, however, we must tolerate this conflation of conceptual origin and political manifestation, since our interest is in the way in which Schmitt thought about the history of the state. Schmitt's curious study of Hobbes is the clearest exposition of Schmitt's own ideas on the historicity of the state.

In this regard, it is no coincidence that Schmitt's discussion of Hobbes exhibits a growing concern for the interrelationship of political authority and questions of political belief. We will argue for an understanding of Schmitt's historiography as characterised by a problematic form of 'endism'. Grandly determinist in his tone, Schmitt is concerned to portray history in terms of the fate of the state as a bearer of truth. This fatalism, aligned with a fear of universalism that is unmistakably eschatological in character, profoundly impacts Schmitt's understanding of the possibilities inherent in political theory, and his own potential to provide theoretical answers to political problems. It is in his work on Hobbes, and the accompanying account of the unravelling of the state, that Schmitt is most explicit about this unique historical pessimism.

As Morgenthau was to realise with bitterness, Schmitt was extraordinarily reluctant to acknowledge intellectual debt, either to his peers or 'great men' playing a part in the formulation of his thought.[14] In pure intellectual terms, Schmitt presents himself as something of an autodidact.

---

[12] C. Schmitt, *The Leviathan in the State Theory of Thomas Hobbes: Meaning and Failure of a Political Symbol* (trans. G. Schwab), Westport, CT: Greenwood Press (1996), p. 79.

[13] Schmitt's account of the English rejection of Hobbes' state model, and the unique basis of the Anglo-Saxon state, is considered further in Chapter 4 of this work.

[14] After an initially warm relationship, Morgenthau fell out with Schmitt, in part because of Schmitt's failure to acknowledge Morgenthau's clear influence on his redraft of *The Concept of the Political*. See W. Scheuerman, *The End of Law*, Lanham, MD: Rowman and Littlefield (1999), Chapter 11. See also C. Frei, *Hans J. Morgenthau: An Intellectual Biography*, Baton Rouge: Louisiana State University Press (2001), pp. 118–32; and

There is little acknowledgement of the nationalist context provided by Max Weber, and even his important and highly productive confrontation with Leo Strauss was carried out in largely coded form.[15] And although it is clear enough that Schmitt belongs to a recognisable stable of counter-revolutionary, arch-conservative thinkers such as de Bonald and de Maistre, he rejects the status of 'disciple' to any recognisable individual.

Three figures threaten to break through this self-created isolation. In his post-war work especially, Schmitt expresses a fairly uncomplicated admiration for two representatives of European counter-revolution, de Maistre and Donoso Cortes.[16] Although his consideration of the latter, in particular, is of considerable importance in formulating Schmitt's ideas about the Catholic church as a complex and universalising political agent, their position in relation to the history of the state is fairly straightforward. Schmitt admires them both for the zeal of their counter-revolution, the determination with which they pursued an intelligent reformulation of hierarchies of order, and the belief they shared in the possibility of uniting true religious faith with a stable political order. Whilst both are important in Schmitt's impression of the history of the state in the early nineteenth century, neither gives much clue as to Schmitt's deeper sense of the historical fate of the state. For this, we must turn to Hobbes.

One must exercise a degree of caution in considering Schmitt's use of Hobbes in constructing a long view of the history of the state, and this is especially so as regards the nature of the parallels to be drawn. Our primary concern here is with Hobbes' place in the elaboration of Schmitt's peculiar and pessimistic account of modern history. As such, we are interested in Hobbes as the textual figure, seen through Schmitt's eyes. A part of this textual reading concerns Schmitt's own impression that parallels existed between himself and Hobbes, both in terms of the anarchic political situations they both encountered, and in their shared belief in the paramount importance of stable political concepts. Schmitt's own reading of this parallel is important in establishing his reading of time, and in his general account of the time-limited existence of the state.

However, this book is also concerned more broadly with the question of Schmitt's relevance as a political theorist to ongoing questions of international political theory. In this context, it is interesting to draw our own

M. C. Williams, 'Why Ideas Matter in International Relations: Hans Morgenthau, Classical Realism and the Moral Construction of Power Politics', *International Organization* 58 (2004) pp. 633–65.

[15] H. Meier, *Carl Schmitt and Leo Strauss: The Hidden Dialogue* (trans. J. H. Lomax), Chicago: University of Chicago Press (1995).

[16] With the exception of Hobbes, Donoso Cortes is the only thinker whom Schmitt examined in a book-length essay, in his *Donoso Cortes in gesamteuropäischer Interpretation*, Cologne: Greven Verlag (1950).

parallels parenthetically between Hobbes as a political theorist of action, and any attempt that Schmitt may or may not have made to emulate the relative success of Hobbes in formulating and promulgating stable political concepts. This is a more judgemental analysis, and requires clear separation from consideration of the parallels Schmitt himself drew. It is hoped that the separation between these divergent concerns will be maintained as far as is possible, although they will meet, of course, in Schmitt's own interpretation of the weaknesses of Hobbes' political theory of action.

The Leviathan in the State Theory of Thomas Hobbes: Meaning and Failure of a Political Symbol

Whereas his own theory of the political starts with the bald expression of the power to bind, Schmitt sees myth as the starting point of Hobbes' innovation of the state as a new historical category. Starting from the idea of the Leviathan, Schmitt constructs a vision of the state in which the interplay of myth, belief and obedience are the key historical motors. The question of political faith and the link between revelation and political obedience are an increasing theme in Schmitt's work following his study of Hobbes. One need not, in order to recognise this truth, accept in whole Heinrich Meier's thesis that Schmitt is best read as political theologian contra political philosophy as a whole.[17] Indeed, the concern for order that links Schmitt to Hobbes is suggestive of a complex amalgam of philosophy and religion, at exactly the point where 'politics and religion collide'.[18] Both perceived themselves as writing against a background of unprecedented political disorder and uncertainty, and in both cases the origin of this disorder was diagnosed as the destructive 'contrast of *auctoritas* and *veritas*'.[19] Whereas for Hobbes this dissociation manifested itself in the Thirty Years' War and competition between sovereign and papal authority, for Schmitt the separation could be seen in the advance of formless universalisms (liberal, Bolshevik, even (arguably) fascist) at the expense of the sovereign unit.

Schmitt saw parallels between the mid seventeenth and mid twentieth centuries, and regarded himself as driven by similar political imperatives as those that concerned Hobbes. As Meier points out, 'it is certain that no other philosopher is present in a similar way in Schmitt's oeuvre' as a whole.[20] Hobbes' political philosophy presented a challenge to Schmitt.

---

[17] H. Meier, *The Lesson of Carl Schmitt: Four Chapters on the Distinction between Political Theology and Political Philosophy* (trans. M. Brainard), Chicago: University of Chicago Press (1998).
[18] *Ibid.*, p. 101.   [19] Schmitt, *Political Theology*, pp. 33–4.   [20] Meier, *Lesson*, p. 101.

On the one hand, it was Hobbes (beyond even Bodin and Erastus) who created the theoretical underpinning of the modern state structure, and, in turn, the modern international system. It was Hobbes who ensured that the sovereign state would become the 'ultimate concrete deciding instance', and thus *created* the extra-legal international system to which Schmitt is so attached.[21] Thus to Hobbes is attributed a crucial historical role in the creation of a new and stable political order. Schmitt observes that 'the distance that separates a technically neutral state from a medieval community is enormous', and there is little doubt that the modern state represents unprecedented success in uniting authority and truth under one roof.[22]

Schmitt's conclusion on the value of Hobbes as political philosopher is worth quoting in full:

[H]e restored the old and eternal relationships between protection and obedience, command and assumption of emergency action, power and responsibility against distinctions and pseudoconcepts of a *potestas indirecta* that demands obedience without being able to protect, that wants to command without assuming responsibility for the possibility of political peril, and exercise power by way of indirect powers on which it devolves responsibility.[23]

However, as the subtitle of the 1938 work reveals (*Meaning and Failure of a Political Symbol*), Hobbes is by no means the hero of the piece. In his study of Hobbes, Schmitt is attempting to explain how the successful Hobbesian state has met (in Schmitt's view) with such an ignominious end in the twentieth century. Having achieved the goal of a secure, *staatlichen* condition, why has the modern state eaten itself away from the inside through a series of neutralisations and abandonment of its mythical force? Schmitt's depiction of this historical process is, it is submitted, typically eschatological in its scope. He seeks the seeds of political destruction in the very origins of the concept of the state. Rather than attributing the decline of the Hobbesian state to historical accident or exterior force, Schmitt reads this decline as a product of the concept itself.

Schmitt wrote this short but significant work during 1938, at the beginning of his period of enforced exclusion from the mainstream intellectual life of the Third Reich. It is unique among Schmitt's works in several respects. First, it outwardly resembles a normal academic thesis more closely than any of his other works, with the predictable exception of his subsequently published doctoral thesis, and his legal treatises. The work is thick with cross-references and acknowledgements to Hobbes scholars, and shows that Schmitt was remarkably conversant with English-language scholarship on Hobbes. Schmitt also acknowledges the degree to which

[21] Schmitt, *Political Theology*, p. 47.   [22] Schmitt, *The Leviathan*, p. 46.   [23] *Ibid.*, p. 83.

Tönnies and Strauss had shaped his thinking on the content of Hobbes' work.

The outward appearance of the work as a thoroughly researched treatise on the content of Hobbes' theory of the state is, however, little more than a smokescreen. As Schmitt makes clear, his work on Hobbes is primarily 'directed at ascertaining the influence of the political myth [of the Leviathan] as an arbitrary historical force'.[24] Hobbes is being read in the work as the creator of a political myth that comes to interpenetrate the state as a concrete reality. And although Schmitt suggests that the 'last word on where the political fate of the mythical image [lies]' has not yet been written, he nevertheless considers the concrete reality of the state to be in crisis. As such his concern is to examine how myth and reality were brought together, and the consequences of that association for the future of the concrete reality. Schmitt starts, therefore, from the premise that the myth of Leviathan is flawed in its historical manifestation. The purpose of *The Leviathan in the State Theory of Thomas Hobbes* is therefore to account for the 'failure' of the symbol in its very conception.

The critique of Hobbes contained within this work takes on a typically Schmittian seriousness precisely because of the success of the Hobbesian conceptual framework. In tying Hobbes' mythical concept of the state to the concrete history of that concept over time, Schmitt comes to conflate the origin of the concept into its consequences. Schmitt undoubtedly considered Hobbes' mythology of the dominance of the state to be the single most important early modern attempt to restore some form of unity to politics. Schmitt agreed with Strauss and Schelsky that Hobbes wrote *The Leviathan* as a form of political action, in an attempt to counteract 'the anarchy brought about by the religious fanaticism and sectarianism that destroyed the English Commonwealth during the Puritan Revolution'.[25] But the concern for Hobbes is dynamic and referable to contemporary conceptual problems. Under such conditions, confusion can easily arise as to the particular target Schmitt has in mind at any one time.

The work begins with consideration of Hobbes' choice of the 'Leviathan' as the mythical symbol used to characterise the state. Schmitt explores the various meanings attached to 'Leviathan' over time. Whilst endless variations on the myth appear to have existed over time, Schmitt focusses on the contrast of Christian and Jewish imagery of the Leviathan. In Christian theology, he suggests, the Leviathan is read as a demonic sea-creature that is caught and tamed by Christ, using the cross as fish-hook, and so symbolising the triumph of Christianity over heathen power. By contrast,

[24] *Ibid.*, p. 26.   [25] *Ibid.*, pp. 10–11, 21.

Schmitt presents the supposed Jewish-Cabbalist myth in typically anti-Semitic terms as a 'Jewish battle myth' in which Leviathan and Behemoth represent the heathen earthly powers, with Jews standing in a position of innate superiority to the violence of their political battle.[26]

Given such richness of mythical background, Schmitt goes on to criticise Hobbes' appropriation of the Leviathan myth for the thinness of its mythical content. Whereas the rich symbolic imagery of the famous copperplate frontispiece to *Leviathan* seems to offer so much, the actual text of the work disappoints in its failure to account for the importance of the mythical image itself. On the one hand, Schmitt argues, Hobbes was writing in a period in which demonic mythology had lost all seriousness, and the depiction of demonic myths such as Leviathan and Behemoth has become tools of irony rather than serious theological content. Schmitt illustrates the point by drawing a contrast between the serious demonology in the paintings of Hieronymus Bosch and the playful and ironic depiction of demons in Bruegel the Elder and Pieter Brueghel the Younger. 'Between the demonology of Hieronymus Bosch and the hell of Bruegel the notion of worldly realism arose', and so the force of demonic imagery is reduced.[27] Thus on the one hand, Hobbes' use of Leviathan can be read as a merely playful depiction of hugeness and power, and could increasingly be read as such by those subject to the power of the state.

The immediate impression of the Leviathan myth, Schmitt argues, is one of irony. At most, the Leviathan is depicted as a colourful and somewhat playful metaphor for the concentration of power in the state. Yet Schmitt still clings to the belief that Hobbes did, in fact, *intend* that the Leviathan should have real mythical force. 'Like all great thinkers of his time', Schmitt suggests, 'Hobbes had a taste for esoteric cover-ups'.[28] The suggestion is that the selective reference Hobbes makes to the meaning of the Leviathan myth is revealing in its parsimony. Despite insisting that clarification of this meaning would require 'biographical and individual psychological inquiries' beyond the scope of his study, Schmitt does nevertheless seek to draw out the content of Hobbes' Leviathan myth beyond this mere allegory of power.[29] Schmitt suggests that Hobbes draws three links between the Leviathan myth and the state as reality, namely in the covenant of men, the state as machine and the Leviathan as an object of awe.[30] Schmitt's suggestion seems to be that the key to Hobbes' mythical representation of the state lies in the relationship of these three components.[31]

Schmitt immediately appears to be grappling with the gap between an original mythical and conceptual unity in the idea of the Leviathan, and its

---

[26] *Ibid.*, pp. 8–9. [27] *Ibid.*, p. 24. [28] *Ibid.*, p. 26.
[29] *Ibid.* [30] *Ibid.*, Chapter 3. [31] See below, p. 45.

evident vulnerability to the ravages of irony and individualism. If Hobbes did intend the mythical image of Leviathan to represent the harmonious relationship of political association, executive power and representative majesty, the key question is the competence of the myth to achieve its task. Or, put another way, how do these core elements of concrete politics – elements, it must be stressed, that had existed in alternative configurations in the medieval *complexio oppositorum* – fare when configured with the device of Hobbes' state? Without the universal faith of Rome, the state itself becomes a highly concentrated source of truth and belief.

Schmitt illustrates the potential impact of time on the concrete meaning of the elements Hobbes brings together. In Chapter 4 of the work, he examines the changing meaning of mechanisation over time, and seeks to explain that, in contrast to the inanimate concept of machine created by German idealism, Hobbes' machine was perfectly capable of possessing mythical and organic content.[32] There is no irony or contradiction in the dual imagery of personal and mechanical sovereign in Hobbes' *Leviathan*. Both the organic and the mechanical aspects of this sovereignty could be objects of awe and myth. In spite of this coherent starting point, Schmitt suggests that the adoption of a mechanical image lent itself to gradual attack by rationalism. As Schmitt puts it, 'Because of [the confrontation between rationalism and a mechanistic mythology], Hobbes' concept of the state became an essential factor in the four-hundred-year-long process of mechanization, a process that, with the aid of technical developments, brought about the general "neutralization" and especially the transformation of the state into a technically neutral instrument.'[33] Schmitt then presents an illustration of this technically neutral, mechanised state that is familiar from his earlier work on the process of neutralisation in the modern state. Specifically, in its very neutrality, the state comes to associate 'its values, its truth and justice', in its technical perfection, and so gives rise to the formlessness of juristic positivism.[34] The laws of the state become independent of subjective content, and the state itself 'derives its esteem and dignity from its organised inclusiveness and the calculability with which it functions rationally as a mechanism of command'.[35]

In this mechanised and ordered entity, we arrive at the perfectly functioning modern state that Schmitt will later depict as the constituent unit

---

[32] In an earlier essay, Schmitt had focussed on the effect of the mechanical image of the state in creating a mechanised image of man. As Schmitt notes, 'the mechanisation of the concept of the state thus completed the mechanisation of the anthropological image of man ... Just as a mechanism is incapable of any totality, the here and now of an individual's existence cannot attain any meaningful totality'. C. Schmitt, 'The State as Mechanism in Hobbes und Descartes', in *The Leviathan*, pp. 91–104 (pp. 99–100).
[33] Schmitt, *The Leviathan*, p. 42.   [34] *Ibid.*, p. 45.   [35] *Ibid.*, pp. 46–8.

of the *jus publicum Europaeum*. The mechanism of the state refers itself to its internal order. International questions are thus affairs of state, and are removed from questions of truth, myth or faith. Since the rationale of the machine is its own technical perfection, the question of justice cannot penetrate confrontations between states. 'In contrast to religious, civil, and factional wars, wars between states cannot be measured with the yardsticks of truth and justice.'[36]

It is the mechanism that finally removes questions of justice from the realm of international relations. 'It used to be observed that even though there are just wars, there are no just armies. That observation can be made of the state as a mechanism.'[37] But alongside this bald mechanical content, attempts are still made to conceive of the state in mythical terms. Schmitt ranges widely to illustrate the continuing force of animal metaphors in describing the state. He also cites with approval Ernst Jünger's analogy between the modern warship and the mechanism of the state. Both possess centralised command and immense power, and become the object of awe and wonder. Thus it is 'in its mixture of huge animal and huge machine [that] the image of the Leviathan attains the highest level of mythical force'.[38] A purely positivist, mechanical vision of the state as a functional entity immediately loses the original integrity that Hobbes intended. Yet it is Hobbes himself who inadvertently presages that process by stressing the mechanical nature of the state.

The mechanical state depicted in *The Leviathan* is clearly recognisable from the ideal-type state presented in Schmitt's *Concept of the Political*. The purely political form presented there is characterised by its unchallenged capacity to make political decisions, its competence in binding citizens to the validity of those decisions, and the absence of any normative basis (whether moral, religious, economic or ideological) that serves to determine those decisions. In the short term, therefore, the mechanical neutrality of *The Leviathan* achieves an ideal *staatlichen* condition. It is Schmitt's intention to illustrate the unsustainability of this order in the very basis of the order itself.

It is in Chapters 5 and 6 of his work that we come to our principal object of interest – Schmitt's account of the preordained unravelling of the Leviathan concept. Schmitt takes up the earlier theme of the place of the individual in Hobbes' state, but this time casts the individual as the bearer of capacity for faith. Hobbes' fatal error, according to Schmitt, was in his conceptual separation of privately held belief and public confession of faith. He points to Hobbes' concern for the subject of miracles as evidence

---

[36] *Ibid.*, p. 47.   [37] *Ibid.*   [38] *Ibid.*, p. 49.

that Hobbes was acutely aware of the political importance of private belief.[39] For Hobbes (whom Schmitt describes as 'agnostic' in relation to actual belief in miracles), the key political question is that the state should have power to enforce public confession of faith. It is for the sovereign to choose between truth and falsehood. But Hobbes will not extend this compulsion to private reason, which he considers to be beyond the reach of politics.[40]

It is this distinction between public and private that Schmitt regards as the 'rupture of the otherwise so complete, so overpowering unity'.[41] The acknowledgement that public truth need not actually be believed, and the resultant hollowness of the 'truth' of the state, are, for Schmitt, the fatal error in Hobbes' state concept. Schmitt is emphatic in his criticism of this step:

At precisely the moment when the distinction between inner and outer is recognised, the superiority of the inner over the outer and thereby that of the private over the public is resolved.[42]

[Hobbes underscores] the importance of absorbing this right of private freedom of thought and belief into the political system. This contained the seed of death that destroyed the mighty leviathan from within and brought about the end of the mortal god.[43]

Whilst the distinction is extremely limited within Hobbes' theory of the state itself, Schmitt suggests that the fatal error lay in drawing the distinction in the first place. The Hobbesian concept of the state is doomed by the creation of a private sphere that is not incorporated into the concept of the state. This 'barely visible crack' is then exploited on all sides by those who seek to advance a private and particular interpretation of truth. In a process he attributes to figures and forces as diverse as Spinoza, Pufendorf, Thomasius, Frederick the Great, Kant, Moses Mendelssohn and Freemasonry, the relationship between public and private is inverted, and the essential power of the state to determine truth is lost. Private freedom becomes the form-giving principle, and the 'public' as a whole becomes contingent on how well it coheres with private notions of truth and right.[44]

Leaving aside problems of tone, Schmitt's central contention is unmistakable. The very concept of the state fails to achieve the degree of totality required to sustain itself in its monopoly of the political. Schmitt concedes

---

[39] As Schmitt points out, the miracle continued to be a very direct and evident source of political authority in Stuart England. He observes that Charles II carried out around 23,000 healings between May 1660 and September 1664. *Ibid.*, p. 54.

[40] *Ibid.*, pp. 53–6.   [41] *Ibid.*, p. 56.   [42] *Ibid.*, p. 61.

[43] *Ibid.*, p. 57.   [44] *Ibid.*, Chapter 5 *passim*.

that the state has an exceptional and unparalleled capacity to contain the totality of political life within its own conceptual boundaries. It creates a stark division of outside and inside. As the locus of decision and the arbiter of the friend–enemy distinction, the modern state has largely made itself the bearer of politics. However, Schmitt is determined that in basing the authority of the state on thin *auctoritas*, and not properly contesting true *veritas*, the state has mortgaged itself to the individual. Hobbes as 'individualist' has created a political form that seeks justification in its own technical perfection, that bases the exercise of power on authority without truth, and that has only 'the *simulacra* of divinity on its side'.[45] The historicised Hobbes falls into an overview of history that profoundly shapes Schmitt's political theory as a whole.[46]

Hobbes in Schmitt's political eschatology

> Carl Schmitt thinks apocalyptically, but from the top down, from the domain of the powers, whereas I think from the bottom up. But we both share the experience of time and history as a delay. And this was, originally, the Christian experience of time.   Jacob Taubes[47]

Schmitt argues that Hobbes' concept of the state included a grievous error that 'contained the seed of death that destroyed the mighty leviathan from within and brought about the end of the mortal god'.[48] We have already considered the role confession of faith played in ensuring the authority of the state. In Chapter 37 of *Leviathan*, Hobbes argues for the importance of sovereign authority over the truth of revelation. Man must be compelled to make a confession of faith in accordance with the concept of truth determined by public authority. However, as Hobbes acknowledges in Chapter 26, 'it is easier to bind a man to obey law as miracle than it is to bind a man to believe it'.[49] As such, Hobbes opened up a conceptual space between public confession and private faith. Man is free to believe whatever he likes, provided his confession of faith accords with public doctrine.

It is this 'lip-service confession' that Schmitt holds responsible for the erosion of the concept of the state. The 'barely visible crack' in Hobbes' structure provided an inroad for liberalism to undermine the authority of

---

[45] *Ibid.*, p. 61.
[46] Heinrich Meier gives an excellent account of this historicisation of Hobbes in *Lesson*, pp. 122–32.
[47] J. Taubes, *The Political Theology of Paul* (trans. D. Hollander), Stanford: Stanford University Press (2004), p. 32.
[48] Schmitt, *The Leviathan*, p. 57.
[49] Hobbes, *Leviathan*, Oxford: Oxford World's Classics (1998), p. 190.

the sovereign.[50] In a process he attributes firstly to Spinoza, the concept of the state is inverted.[51] Whereas Hobbes had envisaged a total authority in which freedom of thought remained a private indulgence, for Spinoza 'freedom of thought is the form giving principle'.[52] Over time, therefore, the distinction between public and private became concrete, and liberalism acted to assert the primacy of private emancipation over public authority. Inadvertently, then, Hobbes had created a system in which *auctoritas* and *veritas* were bound to unravel again.

As such, Schmitt's study of Hobbes combines despair for the prospects of the state in the twentieth century with a teleological-eschatological account of how this crisis has come about. Schmitt's entire historical consciousness is geared around this concern for the prospects of the state, to be read in the context of its origins. The story of modern politics becomes a story of dissolution. Admittedly, there are several aspects to this story, and Schmitt explores several sub-plots throughout his oeuvre. At times Schmitt is primarily concerned with the internal dissolution of the authority of the state, as, for instance, in *The Crisis of Parliamentary Democracy*. At other times, the concern is with the effects of this neutralisation on public international law, as in *The Nomos of the Earth*. And in still other works, Schmitt peers into the abyss, and considers the parameters of the apolitical world – the possibility that the failings of the state might spell the end of the political. What all these concerns have in common, however, is that they are fleshed out in the ultimate context of this history of dissolution of the state as the modern bearer of politics.

If the language of this study is uncomfortable within mainstream theories of international politics, the focus of concern is nevertheless familiar. How has man's disenchantment with the state, and the erosion of the latter's capacity for political action affected the underlying world order? Can there be a new basis for political organisation and a new fabric for world order that combines the mechanism of the state with a broader form of association, allowing both for protection of the citizen and a less abusive source of *veritas*? It is all well and good that Schmitt had previously distinguished the political from the state. Here, he is acknowledging that the dominance of the state in the modern period creates its own historical logic, and has a feedback relationship with the political. Hobbes' state does not simply represent a particular solution to the problem of the

---

[50] Schmitt, *The Leviathan*, pp. 56–63.
[51] It should be noted that *The Leviathan* is one of Schmitt's most aggressively anti-Semitic works, and nowhere is this more apparent than in his attack on Jews such as Spinoza, Moses Mendelsohn and Stahl-Jolson as responsible for this erosion of the state. Fuller consideration of Schmitt's anti-Semitism follows below.
[52] Schmitt, *The Leviathan*, p. 58.

political; it dominates all discourse. It superimposes its own historical trends on the fate of the political. The history of the state therefore transcends its own boundaries, and affects the very capacity to exist politically.

In this sense, Schmitt's history of the concept of the state is constructed against the background fear of the apolitical – against the fear that man might cease to exist politically. If Hobbes' state progressively dissolves its own political instincts, then surely we are required to look elsewhere for political renewal. It is here that Schmitt's language of Christological history comes to the fore. The avoidance of an apolitical existence is an historical task that emerges in every generation. More or less actively, the pluriverse of friends and enemies must be maintained. The task of the state, and the task of statesmen, is to act as historical restrainers: to hold back the advance of universalism, to delay the realisation of world unity. The state, to be sure, might be an effective structure for exercising this task. But if it is possessed of its own conceptual-historical dynamic towards unity and towards mechanical perfection, then at what point does it threaten to accelerate the process of universal pacification?

Drawing on St Paul's Second Letter to the Thessalonians, Schmitt occasionally depicts this projected pacified world as the reign of the Antichrist – that is, as a false paradise imposed on earth. An unpolitical world would, on this account, spell the end of history, and the final stage before apocalypse. On one level, the notion of the pluriverse of states as 'restrainer' of the coming Antichrist could be read as an elaborate metaphor for the dangers of world unity.[53] To a certain extent, Schmitt is not demanding that we share a literal interpretation of apocalyptic theology. He invites us to share his fear that a world without politics would be a world without serious meaning, and, as such, a life not worth living. According to this perspective, it might fairly be stated that Schmitt's demonic language, if taken seriously, simply opens the position up to ridicule.

Yet the language of the Antichrist is, *for Schmitt*, more than an unfortunately anachronistic choice of language. Rather, it represents a key element in his criticism of the failings of the modern state. The dangers of the unified world are not simply those of abuse of the protective function of the state. More basically, world unity would be characterised by a form of peace and security that Schmitt, in common with Leo Strauss, regards as a negation of politics by means of technology. As Meier points out, 'for Schmitt's own expectations ... the Antichrist's slogan *pax et securitas*, which originates in 1 Thessalonians, is determinative'.[54] Moreover, with

---

[53] Any cursory glance through realist international relations texts will yield comparable warnings about the despotic dangers of world unity.

[54] Meier, *Lesson*, p. 164.

the state's effective absorption of the fabric of Christian truth, comes the danger that, as the state collapses, faith itself will also disappear.[55] Instead of living according to a unique, revealed political truth, man would face a nihilistic life in a world where there may be 'competitions and intrigues of every kind,' but where all seriousness would be lost.[56] It would constitute a perpetual 'Sunday of life'.[57]

This Antichrist is therefore presented as the potential destination of the state, or, more accurately, the coming negation of the state. In its individualism, in its abdication of truth and in missing the opportunity to create a political totality, the concept of the state is actually accelerating the process of universalism that Schmitt so fears. This historical dynamic lies at the heart of every attempt Schmitt makes to theorise contemporary politics, and it is impossible to understand the true nature of these unfamiliar concepts without examining in more detail the linkage that Schmitt draws between politics, history and theology. As Heinrich Meier has convincingly argued, nothing in Schmitt's work 'escapes the fundamental jurisdiction of political theology'.[58]

Meier relies in large part on a little-known essay written by Schmitt in 1950, entitled 'Drei Möglichkeiten eines christlichen Geschichtsbildes' ['Three Possibilities of a Christian Historical Perspective'] in which Schmitt sets out his views on the historical reaction of Christianity to the posited coming of the Antichrist.[59] Schmitt here suggests that the prospect of apocalypse allows for three authentically Christian historical understandings. The first is eschatological, which accepts or embraces the coming dissolution in the hope of witnessing the second coming of Christ. Schmitt has no hesitation in agreeing with Karl Löwith that Enlightenment positivism and its progressive philosophy of history 'was only a secularized Judaism and Christianity and derived its *eschata* from them'.[60] Indeed, once Schmitt's theological concerns come to the surface, it is difficult not to read his concern for the modern loss of moral seriousness through

---

[55] Judith Shklar attributes the same eschatological pessimism to Schmitt's two other heroes, de Maistre and Donoso Cortes: 'the identification of Christianity with a dying social order meant that faith itself was about to disappear from the world, and in this calamity they saw the very end of the world, the approach of the prophesised coming of the Anti-Christ' (*After Utopia: The Decline of Political Faith*, Princeton: Princeton University Press (1969), p. 106).

[56] Schmitt, *The Concept of the Political*, p. 35.

[57] See J.-W. Müller, *A Dangerous Mind: Carl Schmitt in Post-War European Thought*, New Haven: Yale University Press (2003), p. 94.

[58] Meier, *Lesson*, p. 72.

[59] 'Drei Möglichkeiten eines christlichen Geschichtsbildes', *Universitas* 5:8 (August 1950), 927–31; cf. Meier, *Lesson*, p. 20 n. 56.

[60] Schmitt, 'Drei Möglichkeiten', p. 928.

depoliticisation in tandem with Löwith's thesis of the loss of moral serious-ness in secularisation.[61]

Such a standpoint is unacceptable to Schmitt, and so he demands a choice between the two alternative standpoints that seek to postpone or avoid apocalypse. These both centre on the idea that worldly political power acts to 'restrain' the coming unity of the world, and so accords with Schmitt's basic belief in the importance of the political universe. Where they diverge is in their view of the degree of activism required to maintain the political. The doctrine of the Christian Epimetheus holds that a defensive stance is insufficient, and that fear of apocalypse should be a spur to political action. In discussing the work of Konrad Weiß, Schmitt reflects on the argument that 'the simply restraining forces are insuffi-cient'. For the Christian Epimetheus, 'historical conditions are always more to be gained than preserved'.[62]

By contrast, Schmitt appears to prefer a view of human history that has a more passive confidence in the capacity of politics to 'restrain' world unity. This passive, confident, *katechontical* view of history focusses on the occasional and unpredictable *emergence* of world powers that prevent the much feared world unity. It is this confidence that a Katechon will emerge at moments of great danger that comes to be characterised by a curious amalgam of anxiety and optimism. We cannot follow Hobbes' example and design the Katechon, but we should be confident that such a Katechon will emerge from an unknown source. Schmitt 'believes in the uninterrupted succession of historical bearers' of the Katechon, and it is this belief that explains why, on his account, 'we have yet to reach the end of history'.[63]

In Schmitt's despairing account of the failings of the state, the only remedy to a meaningless, non-political world (the realm of the Antichrist) is the recognition of, and unequivocal obedience to, the restrainer (Katechon). Throughout the modern period, the nation state has more or less adequately fulfilled this role. However, as Meier points out, Schmitt's account of the political Katechon leaves little room for political design. The entire logic of Schmitt's theory of the state means that there can be no criteria for deciding to whom this obedience should be granted, since such a decision must be based on faith (through revelation) rather than reason.[64] The imminent arrival of a non-political world creates an

---

[61] It seems that Schmitt even had a hand in the translation of Löwith's *Meaning in History* into German, having successfully recommended his pupil Hanno Kesting for the job (see J.-W. Müller, *A Dangerous Mind*, p. 109).
[62] Schmitt, 'Drei Möglichkeiten', p. 931.
[63] Meier, *Lesson*, pp. 160–1.   [64] Cf. *ibid.*, p. 43.

imperative to discover a new pluriversal order, but order by design is, on Schmitt's account, an oxymoron.

This observation returns us to Schmitt's ambivalent attitude towards Hobbes' state system. Certainly, the pluriverse of states looks very much like a successful encapsulation of Schmitt's core political principles as expressed in *The Concept of the Political*. The state system creates a form or order that nonetheless possesses the inherent potential for war. In so far as this is the case, the state offers protection in return for obedience, and guards against global unity by means of its existential status. Hence the modern state system.

The mounting problem of the state is that it has increasingly confused form and content. At times and in places, the state might provide a suitable form for the exercise of restraint. Although Schmitt does not claim to be able to identify the Katechon for every era, he does suggest a few historical candidates, including modern statesmen. For instance, he suggests that the last Habsburg Emperor Franz Joseph could be considered a restrainer, and even two presidents of Central European states, Masaryk of Czechoslovakia and Piłsudski of Poland.[65] One cannot say, however, that state = Katechon. One cannot rely on the state to represent political division. The dominance of the state form (especially once the form had escaped Europe, and become a *prêt à porter* form of political organisation) has obscured this fact, and generated a sloppy ignorance of the real contours of political history.

One could say that Hobbes has been too successful. He has contained the political within an ordered structure. Yet the structure itself is so powerful as to obscure real politics. This is a theme we shall return to later, but it is worth observing that Schmitt's definition of the political always involves a point of rupture with the existing order. Mika Ojakangas points out that Schmitt's own theory of real politics always focusses on 'events that introduce rupture in the self-enclosed rationalistic systems immanent to themselves'.[66] Hence the sovereign decision in *Political Theology*, the determination of the enemy in *The Concept of the Political*, or the foundational act of land appropriation in *The Nomos of the Earth*. The idea of real politics within a contained system (the state system) seems at first glance a non sequitur – or at least, as something akin to shadow boxing. It always threatens to become a sanitised version of the acts of discontinuity and rupture that are the hallmark of real politics.[67]

Just as the confession of faith in Hobbes' state is a 'lip-service confession', so too can the state constitute a false Katechon. As Meier forcefully

---

[65] See *ibid.*, p. 161.   [66] Ojakangas, *Concrete Life*, p. 35.   [67] See Chapter 5 below.

argues, the core of Schmitt's critique of the Hobbesian state is that it is 'the work of man' and not of 'divine provenance'.[68] Whilst Hobbes had achieved enormous success in shaping the foundations of politics, his failings (the 'barely visible crack') illustrate the dangers of substituting man-made political structures for the revealed Katechon. Hobbes may have produced a workable solution that sufficed for 400 years. However, Schmitt appears to believe that in so doing Hobbes encouraged the ascendance of a mechanical rationality that has actually hastened the coming of the Antichrist.[69]

Faced with a modern crisis comparable to that in the seventeenth century, yet aggravated by the solutions sought at that time, Schmitt clearly observes a modern imperative to discover new political forms that will prevent the dangers of world unity. Stymied as he is, however, by the critique of human political design, Schmitt seems helpless to envisage a new political order that could replace the compromised state form. Despite his clear inclinations towards political involvement, Schmitt is reduced to simply commentating on decline, and stressing the need to realise the revealed Katechon where and when it reveals itself.

This essentially diagnostic position is reflected in the general poverty of Schmitt's imagination about new political forms. Rather than seeking to shape them, Schmitt instead looks out for evidence that new political forms may emerge. His approach is suggestive and detached, rather than dynamic and innovative. As Meier points out, his peculiarly Christian notion of revelation, with its anti-Judaic overtones, was perhaps one element in his cautious belief that Nazism may be the revealed answer to the modern political crisis.[70] Elsewhere, Schmitt considers the possibility that political phenomena such as the growth of large territorial spaces[71] or the violence of partisan warfare[72] may become successors to the state. In each case, however, Schmitt's approach is passive. There is no attempt to shape a new political order, but instead a hopeless watchfulness for the 'revelation' of the order to come.

This, it might be argued, is the essence of an eschatological political perspective that is saved from nihilism only by the hope that a new political order will emerge from the ether. Sovereignty represents an inexorable path towards lost clarity, mechanical stasis and the collapse of politics.

---

[68] Ojakangas, *Concrete Life*, p. 105.   [69] *Ibid.*, p. 104.   [70] *Ibid.*, p. 153.

[71] C. Schmitt, 'Völkerrechtliche Großraumordnung mit Interventionsverbot für raumfremde Mächte', in *Staat, Großraum, Nomos: Arbeiten aus den Jahren 1916–1969* (ed. G. Maschke), pp. 184–203.

[72] C. Schmitt, *Theorie des Partisanen: Zwischenbemerkung zum Begriff des Politischen*, Berlin: Duncker and Humblot (1963).

Whatever its original achievements, the form has been allowed to overcome its political content. Schmitt's critique of the vulnerability of the state system's capacity to ensure world order is arguably as uniquely challenging and invigorating as his critique of liberalism. In both cases, however, his sense of historical inevitability and his scepticism of the capacity of human ideas to make a telling difference to man's political condition limit his theory to a critical perspective.

Eschatology and anti-Semitism

Schmitt's work on Hobbes also forms the most obvious point of departure for consideration of Schmitt's alleged anti-Semitism. Not only is *The Leviathan* Schmitt's most evidently anti-Semitic work, it can also be read in tandem with contemporaneous entries in the vast diaries, published posthumously as *Glossarium*. The question of the nature, extent and political manifestations of Schmitt's anti-Semitism has been perhaps the most hotly, and the most poorly debated aspect of Schmitt interpretation. Above all other areas of interpretation, evaluation of this question has produced mutually reinforcing polarisation.

On the one side it is argued that Schmitt was at most a private, temperate anti-Semite in the general nineteenth-century German tradition (whatever that might exactly consist of), whose overt anti-Semitism of the 1930s was clearly opportunism run wild. The clearest exponent of this view was George Schwab in *The Challenge of the Exception*, where he argues that Schmitt's wartime publications are inherently unreliable in light of the competitive and protective pressures of academic life under the Nazi regime.[73] Works such as *Über die drei Arten des rechtswissenschaftlichen Denkens* (1934) and *The Leviathan* (1938) offered up gratuitous anti-Semitism in a culpable but simplistic attempt to ride the rhetoric of the age. It represents, according to this view, the defensive attempts of the *Kronjurist* of the Reich to defend his position.

Certainly Schmitt was no stranger to opportunism of this sort. It seems plausible, for instance, that Schmitt would substitute one target of an argument for another according to the impact it would have on its audience. In the second and third German editions of *The Concept of the Political*, for instance, Schmitt removes a critical statement on Marx, Lenin and Lukács, and replaces it with an overtly anti-Semitic remark about F. J. Stahl. Karl Löwith points to this change as clear evidence that

---

[73] G. Schwab, *The Challenge of the Exception: An Introduction to the Political Ideas of Carl Schmitt between 1921 and 1936* (2nd edn), Westport, CT: Greenwood Press (1989).

Schmitt's Nazi-era anti-Semitism amounted to little more than gratui-tously 'toeing the [Nazi] party line'.[74]

Indeed, it is argued by some that it may have been mere self-preservation, and not the more base motive of self-advancement, that motivated Schmitt. Gottfried is especially generous in his interpretation of Schmitt's behaviour in the mid 1930s: 'He was trying to cover up for his own record as an outspoken anti-Nazi; and – like his beloved Hobbes who supported, each in its own time, Cromwell's Commonwealth and the Stuart Monarchy – he was coming to terms with an established power, however distasteful he might have found it.'[75] Under such pressure, it is argued, Schmitt's submission to Nazi rhetoric is an unreliable guide to his own views. According to such a view, the project is to disentangle the important works of this era from their context. This, Gottfried suggests, is a task made easier by the clear 'impression of insincerity' that such remarks give.[76]

Such an argument has been somewhat undermined by the posthumous publication of the *Glossarium*. Schmitt's diaries of 1947–51 were pub-lished in Berlin in 1991 and show him to have been consistently and intensely preoccupied with an aggressive critique of Judaism. The entries provide a sometimes startling and distasteful insight into a vehement and politically oriented hostility to Judaism, sufficiently strong to distort Schmitt's cool political calculus. The apparently unavoidable conclusion is that Schmitt held real, private, vehement and (even within the context of commonplace contemporary German prejudice) abnormally forceful anti-Jewish views. The *Glossarium* thus erodes the argument that the prejudice expressed in *The Leviathan* towards the political project of Jewish emancipation, or the influence of 'liberal' Jewish theorists of the state from Spinoza to Mendelsohn, were merely gratuitous additions designed to spice up the work for a Nazi audience.

The publication of the *Glossarium* in no way settles, however, the ques-tion of the political relevance of Schmitt's opinions on Judaism, and the way in which it relates to his theory of politics overall. The argument of Schwab, Gottfried *et al.* remains in modified form. Schmitt's anti-Semitism is criticised as distasteful and reprehensible. It even, to some extent, explains why Schmitt was susceptible to the allure of Nazism. If anti-Jewish sentiment dovetailed with Schmitt's contempt for liberalism, then both instincts come together in a weakness that 'allowed his notion of

[74] K. Löwith, 'Der okkasionelle Dezisionismus von Carl Schmitt', in *Saemtliche Schriften*, 9 vols., Vol. VIII (ed. K. Stichweh and M. B. de Launay), Stuttgart: Metzler Verlag (1984), pp. 93–127 (p. 119).
[75] P. Gottfried, *Carl Schmitt*, London: The Claridge Press (1990), p. 36.   [76] *Ibid.*, p. 37.

enemy to generate his idea of friend'.[77] The argument continues to maintain that whatever anti-Semitism Schmitt might have felt was irrelevant to his political thought, and should not be an object of scholarly concern.

Even if one were to accept this view, there would nevertheless be much to say about 'Schmitt's uninhibitedness' in '[catching] the infection of national uprising and [going] crazy for one or two years'.[78] Schmitt's collaboration with Nazism was far deeper and more committed than that of other German intellectuals such as Jünger and Heidegger. Not only did Schmitt intensify the anti-Semitic tone of his publications, he also applied his considerable experience as an advocate in providing (or attempting to provide) legal justification for the discriminatory policies of the Nazi government. Those who continue to hold that Schmitt's antipathy towards Judaism was politically irrelevant are left simply to castigate Schmitt as a rotten opportunist.

Taking Schmitt's concern for the political importance of the Katechon seriously might offer one avenue of explanation. Firstly, Schmitt's concern for the Katechon displays a familiarity with many of the mythological aspects of medieval anti-Judaicism, alongside the mythology of the Leviathan. We simply cannot know, given Schmitt's half-ironic playfulness with concepts, the degree to which he took such concepts seriously. What is more certain, when one examines the pattern of his work as a whole, is that a deep concern for such *potentially* anti-Semitic imagery emerged under the shadow of Nazism, but was never really abandoned in the post-war years. The concept of the Katechon also holds out the prospect of the kind of messianic delivery from danger that the Nazi party may have appeared to offer. The Katechon is revelatory, absolute and infinite – all familiar Nazi themes.

All of this is not to say that Schmitt's status as a specifically Christian or Catholic thinker condemns him to the status of anti-Semite. The point rather is that Schmitt showed a remarkable and apparently natural propensity to apply the conceptual tools of Christian apocalyptic thought in the service of Nazi propaganda. One need only look, for instance, at Schmitt's 1943 article in *Der Reich* entitled 'Beschleuniger wider Willen, oder: Die Problematik der westlichen Hemisphäre' ('Hastener against His Will; or, The Problem of the Western World') for a deliberate and

---

[77] T. B. Strong, 'Foreword' to Schmitt, *The Concept of the Political*, pp. ix–xxviii (p. xxiv).

[78] Taubes, *The Political Theology of Paul*, p. 101. Taubes considers Schmitt's lack of inhibition as perhaps the most compelling feature of his character, and ascribes Schmitt's use of Nazi rhetoric to an almost child-like propensity to get caught up in the mood of the moment: '[Schmitt] adopted not a text, but a tradition, that is, the folk traditions of church anti-Semitism, onto which he, in 1933–36, in his uninhibited fashion, went on to graft the racist theozoology' (p. 51).

polemical association of the concepts of Katechon and *Führerprinzip*.[79] What hope would the Jews have in Schmitt's account if one is truly supposed to believe that the Führer represents the defence of God's will on earth, and that absolute obedience to his will is the sole duty of the German people?

More prosaically, Schmitt made the same customary identifications of Jews with international socialism and extreme liberalism that were commonplace in early twentieth-century Europe. In Schmitt's study of *Leviathan*, Spinoza is condemned for his exploitative liberalism. He is condemned because, in Schmitt's account, he used the language of individual human freedom as a weapon against the integrity and solidity of the Hobbesian state. For Schmitt, the campaign for Jewish emancipation is a selfish and destructive movement that fraudulently phrases the particular and selfish wishes of its adherents in a universalised language of rights and human freedom. Judaism irks Schmitt from a political perspective because it resolutely stands outside the authority structure of modern European statehood, and refuses to engage in the ironic double loyalty that the Hobbesian state requires. It is therefore a hostility born as much of political as truly religious sentiment, and reflects the degree of intersection between politics and theology in Schmitt's work.

It seems clear that consideration of Schmitt's views on Judaism requires some degree of conceptual separation between prejudice based on race, and prejudice based on religious, theological, political and cultural grounds. Those seeking to rehabilitate Schmitt are quite right to point out that the racially tinged language of Schmitt's Nazi-era publications does not seem characteristic either of his other works, or of his private reflections. Race, in a biological or eugenic sense, does not appear to have interested Schmitt as a political category. For instance, his international legal writings of the 1930s make no mention of ethnic divisions within Europe, and contain no racial perspective on the 'superiority' of Germans.[80] Schmitt had huge admiration for Serbia (both of his wives were Serbian), and must presumably have felt uncomfortable with the racial categorisation of Slavs as subhuman.[81] As with his attitude to Slavs, it would be hard to substantiate a claim that Schmitt was a fervent anti-Semite in a racial or eugenic sense.

---

[79] See Chapter 5 below.   [80] See Chapter 6 below.

[81] Schmitt's sympathetic attitude towards Slavs during the war in the East is captured in a national myth he recalls being told by his Serbian friend Ivo Andric:

Marko Kraljevic, the hero of a Serbian saga, fought the entire day long against a powerful Turk, finally defeating him in a bitter struggle. When he had killed the defeated enemy, a snake that had been sleeping in the dead man's heart awoke and spoke to Marko: 'You were lucky that I was sleeping during your fight.' At this, the hero cried out: 'Woe is me, I have defeated a man who was stronger than me!' (C. Schmitt, *Ex captivitate salus*, Cologne: Greven Verlag (1950), pp. 32–3).

It is perhaps more accurate, therefore, to refer to Schmitt as anti-Judaic rather than anti-Semitic. Both his published and private writings betray an implacable hostility to Jews qua Jews – that is to say, it is their cultural and religious status that generates Schmitt's antipathy. He clearly regards Jews as standing in a dangerously ambiguous position in respect of modern, Christian European states. He regards them as existentially not belonging to the structures of authority, public truth and unconditional obedience that he sees as fundamental to the success of the body politic. For Schmitt, Jews have always stood outside the unified whole of the state. They are not within the body of men composing the Leviathan, but instead constitute an external and (most importantly) radically *individual* and *individualist* standpoint. For Schmitt, Judaism = liberal universalism.

If this interpretation of Schmitt's antipathy to Judaism is correct, then one can no longer sustain the argument that these views are politically irrelevant. Rather, they are part and parcel of Schmitt's overriding critique of liberalism and his dominant fear of universalism. He readily blames Jews, individually and collectively, for accelerating the dissolution of the state and for promoting a formless and apocalyptic extreme individualism. Therefore he selects Jewish figures as emblematic of the pursuit of philosophical individualism (as with Spinoza) and of legal positivism (as with Kelsen). Schmitt is especially animated by the latter association, bolstering his view of legal positivism as a refuge for a form of scandalous, anti-political rootlessness:

The Jews as an elite in comparison with the Christians: as more or less faithful administrators once the Christian elite sinks into legalism. Then, armed with the logic, tactics and practice of a formless legalism [*leergewordenen Legalität*], the Jews understand reality far better than Christian peoples who cannot stop believing in the capacity of power and charisma to counteract the law.[82]

Clearly these are politically pregnant views, and it would be crass to try to argue whether they are more or less reprehensible than racially tinged prejudice. Certainly, Schmitt never apologised for his views, made no attempt to explain them away as febrile opportunism and, as the publication of the *Glossarium* shows, continued to hold firm to his hostility even when faced by the horrific consequences of Nazi racial policy. Criticism on moral grounds is, one feels, no longer necessary. The relevant point for us is that there is a strong relationship between Schmitt's anti-liberalism and his anti-Judaicism. The intersection lies in his interest in Hobbes and the question of political faith and authority. For our purposes, Schmitt's attitudes to Judaism are interesting in so far as they amplify and

[82] Schmitt, *Glossarium*, 24 May 1948.

underscore his understanding of the state and its history, and because they form a part of his critique of the modern malaise. We cannot know how decisive this perspective was in predisposing Schmitt towards his dalliance with Nazism.

The tripartite structure of the state

Schmitt basically identified with Hobbes' sense of the intangible unity of politics. Both struggled to find a conceptual apparatus to understand the majesty of politics – the unique force of the political union to compel and inspire its citizens. The sum of the political union is clearly more than the sum of its constituent parts, and a parsimonious depiction of the logic of the *polis* is necessarily unsatisfactory. In their own ways, both Schmitt and Hobbes drew a line around their political theory, beyond which was the real but impenetrable *Dasein* of politics.

In *The Leviathan*, Schmitt stresses the mysterious tripartite nature of the Leviathan figure. It is the political covenant. It is the competent machinery of action and compulsion. And it is the mysterious object of awe and obedience. The co-existence of these three facets of the state may be, for all we know, historical accident. Schmitt himself, as we have explored, makes the extraordinary claim that Hobbes' theory was somehow made flesh in the European state form. Whichever line we follow, the claim is that the interaction between these three poles of meaning is self-reinforcing and logically consistent. In an arrangement that is immediately reminiscent of Clausewitz's theory of war, Schmitt argues for the integral complexity of the state concept.[83] The exact nature of the sovereign is the result of the continuing interaction and competition of the three elements.

---

[83] Along with Hobbes, Clausewitz is one of the few figures to whom Schmitt acknowledges an intellectual debt. He reads Clausewitz as arguing that war is not an instrument of politics but, instead, 'the ultima ratio of the friend–enemy distinction', according to which 'politics remains [the] brain' of war (*The Concept of the Political*, p. 34 n. 14). Schmitt is also impressed by Clausewitz's recognition of the Prussian partisan fighters against Napoleon as bearers of true political spirit. Through Clausewitz, the partisans were 'philosophically accredited' in a conservative fashion, before the world revolutionary version of the partisan theory under Lenin (*Theorie des Partisanen*, p. 51). In many respects, Schmitt reads Clausewitz with a good deal of sympathy and accuracy, and was especially attracted by the sense of inherent restraint he conveyed. This is a point entirely missed by Beatrice Heuser in her study of the reception of Clausewitz when she describes Schmitt as criticising Clausewitz for 'focussing so much on inter-state war, which he called a "conventional game" compared with true war, war inspired by intense hatred'. Her conclusion that 'for Carl Schmitt [in contrast to Clausewitz], the desire to annihilate the opponent was intrinsic to his definition of true war' is fallacious, and overlooks the great value

Just as Clausewitz's war is composed of design, aggression and chance, Schmitt's (Hobbesian) state is composed of representative, authoritative and mystical elements. In Schmitt's account, such a conception is distinctly modern, as it was only the post-Reformation state that could conclusively abrogate mystical and authoritative functions to itself. This perhaps explains Schmitt's determination to hang this concept so firmly on Hobbes' shoulders. Having glimpsed the abyss of hyper-politics without order, it fell naturally to Hobbes to theorise the emergence of a new Commonwealth that could restore the old unities. In a clear analogy to Schmitt's concept of his own role, Hobbes was the prescient mind who presaged a new order. Thus the state supersedes the church as the conclusive political entity (although, as we have seen, Schmitt cannot credit the modern state with the same political integrity as the *complexio oppositorum* of the medieval Catholic church).

It is precisely this internal dynamism of Hobbes' state concept that gives rise to the need to craft and re-craft the balance. Political theory is a fundamentally different exercise for Schmitt depending on whether or not he is assuming the basic harmony of these three elements of the state. Schmitt's *Concept of the Political* represents a basic analysis of the political logic of sovereigns that maintain an adequate balance of these functions – representative, authoritative and mystical. Such an exercise is easy in comparison to theorising the unravelling and potential reassembly of the tripartite structure in modern politics. Schmitt's study of Hobbes, and the accompanying turn towards Christological history, seem to represent a recognition that one must engage in exactly this kind of historicity, if one is to recognise and restore true political authority.

Once authority or mysticism are lost, the state's inherent logic is changed. It becomes merely representative in the way, presumably, that liberal theory would anticipate and welcome. Again, Hobbes proves to be the vehicle by which Schmitt embeds this argument in historical context. The great flaw, or 'crack', in Hobbes' theory was in the way in which he phrased the conventional basis of the state. In describing the contract as the foundation of the Commonwealth, Hobbes allowed for interpretation of his state theory as privileging representation above the other two poles

---

Schmitt derived from a Clausewitzian sense of military regularity and conventional enmity between states. See B. Heuser, *Reading Clausewitz*, London: Pimlico (2002), p. 48. Raymond Aron offers a far more sympathetic appraisal of Schmitt's reading of Clausewitz, although he disputes the theoretical lessons Schmitt draws. See R. Aron, *Clausewitz: Philosopher of War* (trans. C. Booker and N. Stone), London: Routledge and Kegan Paul (1983), pp. 363–70. See generally Chapter 7 below on Clausewitz in Schmitt's theory of the partisan.

of the state. As Clausewitz could have told us, once one element of the three-pole structure is privileged, the entire edifice becomes dysfunctional.

Schmitt attributes the exploitation of this 'barely visible crack' to Spinoza and other Jewish philosophers. In so doing, they purportedly reversed the basic structure of the state by making authority contingent on consent, which Schmitt regards as a paradox. By separating out the two elements and placing them in a hierarchy, this nascent liberal theory removed the basic possibility of political authority and, with it, the logic of the state. If authority is contingent on consent, we would all require the insight of Dostoevsky to will our own vulnerability, mortgage our own resistance and submit willingly to the power of the state. We would have to consent to our own powerlessness – an idea of consent that is logically unsustainable. It is only when mediated through the feedback of the triangular structure that true authority can appear as something that belongs to the citizen. The maxim, after all, is *protego et obligo*, and not *protego ergo obligo*. The great flaw of these humanist theorists was to make man vulnerable again, by reasoning authority too rationally and axiomatically.

Schmitt thus has an integral vision of the relationship between protection and obedience. In one of his earliest works, he gives a lengthy account of the 'incompatibility of law [*Recht*] and power'.[84] Whilst Schmitt's early concern was with stressing the distinction between the function of law and the concept of authority (in a foreshadow of his famous distinction of legality and legitimacy), his insistence on law and authority as logically inconsistent concepts reinforces the argument for an integral view of their relationship. Representation and authority, right and power, the law and the state, can only speak to each other through the medium of the mystical sovereign. Otherwise, they do not have anything directly to say to one another. 'Law is not will, but a norm, [it is] not a command, but a rule.'[85] As such, privileging of the covenant over authority cannot amount to the replacement of authority, since the covenant, simply put, *is not*, nor ever could be, authoritative. It needs its obverse part.

Political design and political revelation

Schmitt's challenge, then, both to himself and to us, is to bring the historical contingency of the state form into clarity. It is to clarify the fact that sovereignty is a particular social institution that is not reducible to the exercise of politics itself, but rather represents one possible vehicle for

---

[84] C. Schmitt, *Der Wert des Staates und die Bedeutung des Einzelnen*, Tübingen: Paul Siebeck (1914), pp. 22–44 *passim*.
[85] *Ibid.*, p. 42.

the political. And indeed, given that the political cannot, by definition, have any prior normative character, the state can only ever be an accidental and derivative political form. Unlike the political, which is immutable, the state is a vulnerable entity. It is possible to envisage its end. And this end, Schmitt argues, is a product of the very concept itself. The question remains – what comes next, and how will we be able to identify true politics without the comfortable contours of the state to which our lazy minds have become accustomed?

Christological themes in Schmitt's work are relevant to us in two related respects. Firstly, they colour his historical account of the state and the international system, and shape his historical understanding. Secondly, they open up a limited mode for thinking about the future order. Schmitt invites us, it seems, to await some Damascene moment in which the true locus of contemporary politics will be found. Yet this aspect of Schmitt's account of political authority and its prospects for future renewal remains strangely absent from most debate about the suggested 'relevance' of Schmitt to debates on international politics. In the English-speaking world, debate on a theological reading of Schmitt has been almost totally absent. By contrast, among German scholars, the reading of Schmitt as a profoundly anti-modern, theological thinker gained widespread currency, and became a source of great consternation to those who championed Schmitt as a potential answer to eternal political dilemmas. Little debate has taken place across this divide. The former group tend to characterise Schmitt's more theological work as part of his idiosyncratic private life and something that they are happy to dismiss as irrelevant, along with his political choices. The latter group have tended towards tight academic containment, and tend to eschew any attempt to 'apply' Schmitt's thought in engaging with broader questions of future order and organisation. As Müller puts it, '[t]hought on Schmitt was safely contained within the universities. Yet Schmittian thought was not.'[86]

The absence of a comparable debate outside Germany will doubtless be of little concern to self-proclaimed Schmittians.[87] The fear is that taking Schmitt's theological concerns seriously will result in the characterisation of Schmitt as obscure and illogical and, hence, of limited interest to contemporary debates. The prospects of serious debate are further

---

[86] Müller, *A Dangerous Mind*, p. 206.

[87] In his 312-page 'intellectual portrait' of Schmitt, Gopal Balakrishnan dedicates just one page to consideration of the secularisation thesis, and two pages to the concept of Katechon. He concludes somewhat unsatisfactorily that the concept formed part of an oscillation that Schmitt experienced between the conservative impulses of the Katechon and a contrasting radical tendency in 'a restless movement without synthesis'. (G. Balakrishnan, *The Enemy: An Intellectual Portrait of Carl Schmitt*, London: Verso, (2000), pp. 221–5.)

hampered by the challenge of addressing the contours of the fore-running debate in Germany.

Furthermore, the 'Schmittian' response to the question of Schmitt's basic theological concern might be dismissed as something ephemeral. We have already seen enough of Schmitt's broad appeal to disparate groups to suggest that Schmittians would have resilience enough to overcome such a debate. Indeed, for Right Schmittians such concerns would appear to confirm Schmitt's basic concern for the righteousness of the international order, the historical uniqueness of Europe and the policy applications that de Benoist *et al*. envision. As Müller dryly notes, at least those who are sceptical of the relevance of the wider relevance of the Katechon can productively debate the possible role to be ascribed to it. By contrast, 'every fervent reassertion of the "theology thesis" seemed to be caught in a performative contradiction: if Schmitt was *only* an obscurantist theologian, why was it so important to have yet another treatise on him?'.[88]

The problem, of course, is that Schmitt was in no way an 'obscurantist theologian'. The Katechon is of very direct relevance to Schmitt's hugely influential interpretation of the European state and to his concept of political authority. Consideration of the role of Katechon involves far more than mere historical-psychological speculation regarding Schmitt's irrelevant private motives. The intensity of Schmitt's schematic attachment to the European order as an object of faith must affect our reading of him as an international theorist. In particular, if he was truly motivated by eschatological concerns that outstripped a subordinate opposition to liberal cosmopolitanism on its own terms, a reading of Schmitt as providing a clarion call to continue the assault on the liberal order must confront the question of whether or not to adopt his more fundamental opposition to unity per se.

Hobbes as international theorist

> … we are not every one, to make our own private reason, or conscience, but the public reason, that is, the reason of God's supreme lieutenant, judge; and indeed we have made him judge already, if we have given him sovereign power, to do all that is necessary for our peace and defence.
>
> Hobbes[89]

Evidently, Schmitt's treatment of Hobbes has rather less to do with Hobbes, and far more to do with Schmitt's own theoretical and political concerns. The reading of Hobbes is an element in several ancillary

---

[88] *Ibid*., p. 205.   [89] Hobbes, *Leviathan*, p. 296.

concerns including the 'secret dialogue' with Leo Strauss, as a way of illustrating the shortcomings of political philosophy, and in Schmitt's need to provide a theoretical peg for his own depiction of European history.[90] Schmitt posits Hobbes as an idealised theoretical starting point for the modern state and the modern system of states, and conflates theory and empirical reality through the somewhat bizarre notion of the 'concretisation' of Hobbes' ideas. As Scheuerman accurately observes, 'A common argumentative strategy in Schmitt's political and legal theory is to describe historical reality by focussing on the theoretical arguments of a paradigmatic theorist or theoretical tradition, before proceeding to contrast sad present-day realities with a fictional golden age based more on some set of stylised ideas than social reality itself.'[91] By any standards, Schmitt's reading of Hobbes is historically inaccurate. Yet as a work of political attribution, and in the way it elides Hobbes' reputation as a theorist of power with the Westphalian system, there are interesting and illuminating parallels between Schmitt's Hobbes, and the 'canonical' Hobbes of IR theory.

Schmitt himself might be termed a proto-constructivist in the way in which he saw the coming-together of intangible conceptual components (fear, authority, violence, 'the public', faith) in the formation of dominating concepts of sovereignty, war and legality. He read Hobbes with the same eye, and recognised the same conceptual amalgamations in Hobbes' 'theory of international relations'. In this respect, it might be argued that Schmitt prefigured the new reading of Hobbes in international relations, emphasising the extremely complex way in which the state mediates between the universal, the particular and the individual.

The figure of Thomas Hobbes has always loomed large in IR. Sadly, for the most part he has been a misused figure. For Morgenthau, Hobbes was a prop in support of his basic contention that there can be no objective morality in the international system since such a concept cannot have meaning outside the state.[92] More commonly, Hobbes has been the straw man extreme realist and 'peer of Machiavelli' used by numerous scholars to illustrate the dubious and dangerous roots of thoroughgoing realism.[93]

---

[90] Meier, *Carl Schmitt and Leo Strauss*.
[91] W. E. Scheuerman, 'International Law as Historical Myth', *Constellations* 11:4 (2004), 537–50, p. 539. As Scheuerman points out, Schmitt is 'uninterested in the nuances of Hobbes's account of the difference between morals and law or, alternately, sin and crime', and instead focusses wholly on those aspects of Hobbes' thought that give misleading evidence of Hobbes as a 'decisionist' thinker.
[92] H. Morgenthau, *Politics among Nations* (5th edn), New York: Knopf (1978), p. 53 n.
[93] M. Wight, *International Theory: The Three Traditions*, London: Leicester University Press (1991), p. 17.

This abuse has been compounded by the relative lack of interest shown by traditional Hobbes scholars in IR debates. A feedback relationship seems to have emerged, whereby 'serious' Hobbes scholars look at the generalisations and misinterpretations in IR theory with almost total disdain.

In this context, the work of Hobbes scholars such as Noel Malcolm and international political theorists such as Michael Williams is to be welcomed. Malcolm's critique of traditional understandings of Hobbes in IR is particularly compelling. In contrast to the view of Hobbes as amoral, Malcolm draws the distinction between a jural standard of morality (qua 'justice') that pertains within the state, and natural morality that subsists as an objective standard, and was referable in the state context to an obligation to protect the life of the citizen. Armed with this distinction, Malcolm performs a textual analysis to show that Hobbes considered these moral rules to be instrumental in nature.

Certain examples in support of the revisionist view of Hobbes are worth repeating. For instance, in *De cive* Hobbes points out that, in contrast to the example of Athens and Rome, aggressive, imperialist war in the name of profit runs contrary to the logic of the state, '[f]or the militia, in order to profit, is like a die, wherewith many lose their estates, but few improve them'.[94] Since, for the citizen, the sole rationale for obedience to the state is that it better protects the citizen's life than the fragile state of nature, it makes no sense for the state gratuitously to endanger citizens' lives.[95] Accordingly, peace and trade, as circumstances conducive to the physical protection of the citizen, are part and parcel of the logic of the state.

Certainly, Hobbes accepts that offensive war may result from necessity or insecurity. The picture of Hobbes' international system is further confused by the fact that it makes little sense to use the language of justification when discussing the aggression of the state. It is not so much that imperialist aggression is not justified. Rather, as Malcolm illustrates, gratuitous aggression or cruelty undermine the logic of the state as it is not referable to the moral duty of self-preservation and can, in fact, only jeopardise the security of the citizen.[96] As Schmitt himself notes, 'if protection ceases, the state too

---

[94] T. Hobbes, *Man and Citizen*, p. 174 para. 22.

[95] This aspect of Hobbes' account of the state resonates strongly with Schmitt, for whom '*protego et obligo* is the *cogito ergo sum* of the state'. Schmitt, *The Concept of the Political*, p. 52.

[96] N. Malcolm, *Aspects of Hobbes*, Oxford: Clarendon Press (2002), p. 445. Curiously, the revisionist view of the integral tension between the state's capacity for war and its tendency towards limitation is, in some respects, an echo of Schmitt's account of the modern, Hobbesian state as expressed most clearly in *The Nomos of the Earth* (although it seems unlikely that Malcolm's account is influenced by Schmitt). Schmitt's basic account of international order centres on the contention that strongly constituted states with no higher authority serve the best interests of human security. It is the absence of an international legal order, and so the state attribute of *ius hostis* (the quasi-legal 'right' to go to war,

ceases, and every obligation to obey ceases'.[97] Thus the traditional image of the inherently bellicose state fails to take into account the origins of the state in protecting its citizens from violence.

Williams perhaps goes further than Malcolm in his admiration of Hobbes' achievement. For Williams, Hobbes' 'political sensibilities are far too subtle to rest with the idea that fear – the most basic and potentially destabilising of the passions – provides a simple or straightforward resolution to the difficulties of constructing and maintaining a political order'.[98] Instead, on Williams' reading, the twin fears of the state of nature and the power of the Leviathan are transformed by Hobbes in a more humane, more individualistic and more 'liberal' direction through the device of the state:

Rather than valorising fear as the basis of a rigid absolutism, or denying it in the name of a politics of transparency, [Hobbes] seeks to manage a politics of fear in order to construct a political order which can minimise its necessity and to create a recognisably liberal political society in which fear plays a minor but positive role in a politics of self- and sovereign-limitation.[99]

Our point of departure, therefore, is the modern state with an inherent logic of peaceful protection, but the inevitable capacity for violence. The unpredictability of this international order is heightened by the fact that aggression may, at times, be the best moral choice for statesmen with reference to protection of their citizens. This accords with the traditional association of Hobbes with the state's disposition towards pre-emptive violence. As the historical record in *De cive* illustrates, imperialist aggression may be the correct moral choice where circumstances so demand. It is for the statesmen to use the tools of modern rationality (including espionage and scientific calculation) to determine that moral choice.[100] This, it is submitted, is a preferable summary of Hobbes' state as international actor to the more bellicose caricature.

without objective justification) that results in amoral harmony under the constant potential for violence. The dangerous modern alternative is a discriminatory, legalist concept of war in which one party is characterised as an aggressor and hence a total enemy without the existential right of statehood (as explored in Schmitt's *Die Wendung zum diskriminierenden Kriegsbegriff*, Berlin: Duncker and Humblot (1938)).

[97] Schmitt, *The Leviathan*, p. 72. Some commentators interpret this aspect of Schmitt's 1938 work as a veiled protest against the Nazi state. Since death at the hands of the state had become arbitrary, the state had become a vehicle of obligation, with no recompense in terms of protection. For an elaboration of this argument see George Schwab's introduction to Schmitt's *Leviathan*.

[98] M. C. Williams (ed.), *The Realist Tradition and the Limits of International Relations*, Cambridge: Cambridge University Press (2005), p. 38.

[99] *Ibid.*

[100] Hobbes expands on the issue of scientific calculation and the moral choice of statesmen in *A Dialogue between a Philosopher and a Student of the Common Laws of England* (ed. J. Cropsey), Chicago: University of Chicago Press (1997).

Indeed, it is precisely these references to the logic of the state to the protection of the individual that Schmitt seeks to criticise. The very elements that Malcolm and Williams hold up as evidence that Hobbes was not as bad as once thought are the same elements that Schmitt condemns as fatal to the coherence of the state concept. In Schmitt's account, the meaningfulness of political authority is lost at precisely the point at which state and society penetrate one another. In making the exercise of power directly (rather than abstractly) referable to the protection of individual life, the whole edifice of the state becomes contingent. In moral terms, therefore, it is Schmitt rather than Hobbes who resembles the straw man extreme realist.

Less familiar in IR is the argument that Hobbes be read in a religious context. On the one hand the relationship between protection and obedience can be read as a contractarian issue. A certain body of individuals is bound to the sovereign as a result of the imagined or actual political pact via which they have traded the insecurity of nature for regulated existence in the state. Of course, this covenant is an explicit and highly prominent aspect of Hobbes' *Leviathan*. Nowhere is it symbolised more powerfully than in the famous frontispiece to the 1651 edition, where the mythical beast is composed of the bodies of men.

Beyond the juristic covenant, the Leviathan is also, in Schmitt's account, a Cartesian-mechanical sovereign, capable of 'acting' internationally in a meaningful way and, moreover, a mythical unifying symbol of biblical origin.[101] In the successful state, the tripartite nature of the Leviathan (covenant, machine and object of faith/fear) remains seamless and assumed. As such, the question of the relationship between protection and obedience remains unproblematic and, in a sense, preternatural. Belief in the state makes sense to the eighteenth-century man as belief in a Catholic God did to the thirteenth-century man. As such, the modern state possesses a power as an object of belief that goes beyond its function as bearer of the covenant. '[T]he sovereign-representative person does not come about as a result of but because of this consensus.'[102]

In this context the role of political faith is more than simply another way of expressing the mechanics of obedience. Hobbes' maxim *auctoritas, non veritas facit legem* points towards a form of political faith. It is the state's possession of political truth that pulls together the three strands of the Leviathan metaphor. One often overlooked instance of such reasoning in *Leviathan* is to be found in Hobbes' discussion of miracle in the modern state. Hobbes asserts the private right of individuals to decide for themselves whether or not to believe. However, 'when it comes to confession of

---

[101] Schmitt, *The Leviathan*, p. 31.   [102] *Ibid.*, p. 33

that faith, the private reason must submit to the public'.[103] The public order thus rests on the capacity of the sovereign to determine 'truth' in the public sphere.

The stable modern state thus possesses a complex inherent logic that attains stability through its mythical representative function. The state demands a certain confession of faith, amounting to a confession of political faith. The citizen obliges either because his political faith is genuine, or else because the protective-coercive capacity of the state exceeds any alternative form of confession. In such an arrangement, the relationship between protection and obedience remains latent. Individual instances may arise in which some failure of the state's protective function raises the issue of the individual's right to resist. One might imagine, for instance, a miscarriage of civil justice, in which a wronged citizen faces judicial death. As an isolated instance in an otherwise functioning state, such an example seems a minor lacuna in Hobbes' system. As A .P. Martinich puts it, 'Hobbes would abhor this consequence, but, given his principles, it is not clear how he can avoid it.'[104] Certainly, the individual context does not give rise to a general right of resistance to the state – a notion that Schmitt rejects as 'factually and legally nonsensical and absurd'.[105]

However, when viewed in historical perspective, and in the context of the question of political faith, the relationship between protection and obedience takes on a different mantle. When the issue of political faith is examined as an historically conditioned product, the unravelling of the relationship of *protego et obligo* becomes a more realistic prospect. If the mythical premise of *Leviathan* is taken as something more than mere allegory, it becomes necessary to question how changes in modern consciousness of the state as an object of belief affect the contractarian basis of Hobbes' state. This concern for the erosion of political belief and the unravelling of the modern state constitute one aspect of Schmitt's intellectual project. Thus the hollowing-out of the modern state and the unravelling of the three-tiered Hobbesian sovereign became, for Schmitt, both a political and a religious crisis. Whereas the crisis of order in the twentieth-century world exercised political theorists of all persuasions, for Schmitt there is an eschatological aspect to this crisis that fundamentally affects his capacity to imagine a new world order. Nowhere is this eschatological angst more apparent than in his study of Hobbes.

---

[103] Hobbes, *Leviathan*, p. 296.
[104] A. P. Martinich, *The Two Gods of Leviathan: Thomas Hobbes on Religion and Politics*, Cambridge: Cambridge University Press (2003), p. 48.
[105] *Ibid.*, p. 46.

4   Histories of space

If one peculiarity of the state is its emphatic claim to truth and authority, the other is its unique configuration of space. In the previous chapter we explored Schmitt's ideas on the history of political authority, and the slow process by which the particular order enshrined by the 'Westphalian' state was unravelled from within by the privileging of the individual. In so doing, we have relied heavily on aspects of Schmitt's work that stress religious and eschatological themes, as well as his more conventional engagement with political theories of the state. We turn now to the second historical dynamic that Schmitt creates in his work – the history of spatial consciousness. According to Schmitt, changes to the nature of spatial consciousness over time both made the state form possible in the first place, and then came to pose a mounting challenge to the continuing coherence of the state concept in late modernity. A clear parallel therefore exists between the internal process of unravelling outlined previously, and a second historical dynamic that effectively challenges the state form from the outside by undermining one of its key characteristics – territoriality.

Although handy as shorthand, the characterisation of these histories as 'internal' and 'external' threatens all kind of confusion and obfuscation. A note of caution is required. Both processes implicate the historical existence of the state as an effective political unit, and involve consideration of a complex web of normative phenomena. The 'domestic' themes of the previous chapter largely concern the *constitutive social* phenomena that make the state possible, and in turn impact the prospects for the state. In the first instance, then, it concerns *this* (whichever) state and *its* (internal) social arrangements. The 'external' phenomena under examination in this chapter concern the specifically *spatial* ordering of states. Since such space is all about boundaries with the outside, it naturally draws our attention to the relational position of the state.[1] It implicates *other* states, and the wider experiences of land.

---

[1] Although ultimately, on Schmitt's terms, the establishment of the political community via a sovereign act is already, of course, all about other communities – the enemy. In the end, therefore, both historical processes take the exterior as their logical starting point.

Whereas the 'domestic' historical dynamic is characterised by the slow widening of the 'barely visible crack' in Hobbes' state, and the triumph of the individual over sovereign power, the international historical dynamic is fundamentally shaped by the historical dynamic of 'land' and 'sea.' This elemental dialectic is, for Schmitt, an entirely modern phenomenon, rooted in the opening up of the oceans, and cemented by the 'real decision in favour of the element of the sea' made by certain states (most importantly England, but also the Netherlands, perhaps Portugal, abortively by France, and later by the United States).[2] Much of this chapter will explore the vast content that Schmitt inserts into this elemental dynamic, incorporating a whole myriad of mythical, religious, technological, legal and geographical elements. He argues that 'each time in history that a power has made a new advance into the sphere of human consciousness (through the unleashing of new energies, new lands and seas), they also change the spaces of human existence'.[3] The astonishing outcome, as drawn out in *Land und Meer* and *The Nomos of the Earth*, is an idea of 'world history [as] the history of the conflict of sea-powers against land-powers, and of land-powers against sea powers',[4] that is, a kind of elemental determinism.

Given the great interconnections throughout Schmitt's work, and his tendency to draw compound concepts across works on varying themes, the clarity of this separation of internal and external challenges to the state is quite remarkable.[5] Schmitt recognises, of course, that such a clean separation between two logically connected historical processes cannot be wholly sustained, and acknowledges the feedback relationship between the two. In particular, Schmitt is acutely aware of the various nuances that come together to create 'spatial consciousness', and the fact that such nuances stand in a relationship with other, internal factors (including questions of political authority).[6]

Nevertheless, Schmitt developed wholly distinct historical architecture to explore the 'internal' constitutive and 'external' spatial processes. Despite the evident crossover points between internal and external, the

---

[2] C. Schmitt, *Land und Meer*, Stuttgart: Klett–Cotta (1954), p. 21.

[3] *Ibid.*, p. 56.   [4] *Ibid.*, p. 16.

[5] As Zarmanian correctly notes, '[Schmitt's] key concepts were disseminated in numerous short texts, none of which is complete in itself and which often make an implicit reference to concepts discussed elsewhere.' T. Zarmanian, 'Carl Schmitt and the Problem of Legal Order: From Domestic to International', *Leiden Journal of International Law* 19 (2006), 41–67 (p. 43).

[6] Schmitt asserts linkages between individual perspectives, collective life and understandings of space. He argues, for instance, that the growth of Calvinism and its doctrine of predestination created the opportunity for whole new forms of spatial understanding in the sixteenth and seventeenth centuries. See pp. 89–93 below.

two historical dynamics are basically concerned with different questions, as we see if we place them in the context of the political dynamic expressed in *The Concept of the Political*. On the one hand, the unravelling of the state from within threatens the very possibility of the 'group', and as such, presents a threat to the political per se. This is the very essence of its dangerousness. The widening Hobbesian crack not only erodes the state as a coherent organisational concept, but further undermines the very concept of the group decision, of authority, of collectivity and of war. This is the basis of the *eschatological* crisis, because the end point of the historical dynamic Schmitt posits does not appear to be the realisation of some new organising principle but, rather, the erosion of the very possibility of organising principles.

The confrontation of land and sea, by contrast, can be isolated out into a question of *Nomos*. As the discussion of the concept in Chapter 2 makes clear, confusion and change in a *Nomos* constitute a highly dangerous and unpredictable phenomenon, and should not be welcomed or taken lightly. In contrast to the unravelling process, however, the changing of the *Nomos* at least holds out the possibility of a new order without the removal of politics per se. As such, Schmitt can retain a degree of excitement (zeal, even) in contemplating the new possibilities of territorial space with the advent, for instance, of aeronautical technologies. The history of Atlanticism, although dangerous in its globalising and homogenising tendencies, is less necessarily teleological than that of the unravelling of the state. Schmitt is thus much closer to mainstream international relations (IR) in his analysis of Atlanticism than in the unfamiliar territory of Hobbesian determinism.

Of course, there is a third and much less penetrable historical dynamic at work – the interaction of the Hobbesian dynamic with the land–sea dynamic. This is the most dangerous facet of all for Schmitt. He admires the great force of Atlanticist globalism and its capacity to establish a new *Nomos* that can transcend the European space. Indeed, he looks to the example of the American continent as the prime historical example in support of his suggested *Großraum* concept. However, the greatest danger lies in the innate association of Atlanticism with the liberal privileging of human independence to the detriment of political action. It is for this reason, in light of the great potential of the United States to shape the coming *Nomos*, that Schmitt attached such importance to the examination of these phenomena as conceptually distinct. The third dynamic, that of their interaction, is nothing less than world history itself – Schmitt's great synthesis of syntheses that was to provide answers to his concerns about the future viability of the political.

Nomos and land

In Chapter 2 we introduced the concept of *Nomos* in Schmitt's work as an idea related to the fundamental order and orientation of human life in a spatial context.[7] As Schmitt writes, '*Nomos* is the measure by which the land in a particular order is divided and situated; it is also the form of political, social and religious order determined by this process. Here, measure, order, and form constitute a spatially concrete unity.'[8] The specific *Nomos* characterises and, in some sense, organises the continuance of politics in a largely self-contained area or 'world'.

One way of thinking about a *Nomos*, therefore, is to think of it as the coherence of multiple, simultaneous understandings of political space. Politics is possible within a coherent *Nomos* because, in the shared understanding of space, it is possible to recognise a relationship of alterity between 'us' and 'them' – between 'our space' and 'their space'. Politics is possible *within* the *Nomos* since the various political units understand the existence of a zone in which interaction can take place. One might suggest that since the enmity that Schmitt regards as vital to the existence of politics must contain a degree of mutuality, the individual states require a common grammar with which to express their hostility. This grammar is provided by the *Nomos*.

As such, the idea of *Nomos* immediately brings forward a notion of epochal history, with each epoch characterised by its fundamental and distinct orientation of man to the land – the specific relationship of *Ortung* to *Ordnung*. Indeed, the fundamental coherence of a single period of history only makes sense in terms of the coherence and endurance of its *Nomos*. In this sense, the terms epoch, era, age, *Nomos* and 'world' are interchangeable in so far as they relate to the temporal endurance of a certain set of shared understandings about human spatial interaction. Thus ancient Greece was characterised by a single *Nomos* that ordered the affairs of Greeks and gave a sense of the universal that overarched the interactions of the territorial units that interacted politically in the Greek 'world'. Likewise, the 'Roman world', and the medieval age in Europe are each characterised by their own peculiar *Nomos*.

In our previous discussion of *Nomos*, we explored the act of land appropriation as the foundational act of any comprehensive territorial order. Schmitt stresses that '[e]very autonomous and ontological judgement derives from the land.'[9] It is the original act of dividing, fencing,

---

[7] See above, pp. 22–26. See C. Schmitt, *The Nomos of the Earth in the International Law of the Jus Publicum Europaeum* (trans. G. Ulmen), New York: Telos Press (2004), pp. 42–83.
[8] *Ibid.*, p. 70.   [9] *Ibid.*, p. 45.

distributing and organising the land that makes the creation of order possible. This implication of the land creates the *Ortung* that may then stand in its specific and peculiar relationship to *Ordnung* in a way that cannot be achieved without the foundational division. It is this that creates character – both inwardly, and in the orientation of the 'fenced' land towards the outside. Schmitt clearly understands the original, physical meaning of character – '[t]he sea has no character, in the original sense of the word, which comes from the Greek *charassein*, meaning to engrave, to scratch, to imprint'.[10] Each epoch – each *Nomos* – has its origins in a distinctive form of land appropriation.

Epochal change is therefore the product of a change in the collective conception of space that underlies a certain spatial order. A new form of land organisation is the motor of change from one epoch to another – the putative spatial revolution that Sergio Ortino compares to the equivalent domestic revolution when one locus of domestic authority is superseded by another.[11] Schmitt is therefore wedded to a geographically informed view of history at a macro level, in which the particular possibility of order is derived from the particular form of spatial arrangement. The particular contours of a land appropriation, from the ground up, precede and create all other elements in an historical order. The act of appropriation 'constitutes the original spatial order, the source of all further concrete order and all further law. It is the reproductive root in the normative order of history'.[12]

Pre-modern orders

World history has therefore witnessed numerous *Nomoi* existing both simultaneously and consecutively, but never overlapping. A *Nomos* is not universal in a scientific sense. There need not be a provable extension to the outer bounds of known human existence. But it must cast the *shadow of universality* over those people and those political units that operate within its *universe*. In the pre-modern world, therefore, the shadow of other worlds at the fringes of various *Nomoi* did not fundamentally disturb the sense that a particular *Nomos* represented a comprehensive and complete spatial order. The *Nomos* of the ancient Greek world, for instance, was never conceptually or existentially challenged by the known reality of a Persian universe predicated on an incompatible sense of the spatial world.

---

[10] *Ibid.*, p. 43.   [11] See above, pp. 25–26.   [12] Schmitt, *Nomos*, p. 48.

In the pre-modern era, 'interconnections [between power complexes] lacked a global character'.[13] Where confrontations occurred between such power complexes, the absence of a common spatial consciousness was starkly reflected by the lack of any highly self-conscious and public form of specifically political interaction in the sense of that depicted in *The Concept of the Political*. When Greeks confronted Persians, or Romans confronted Germanic tribes, the confrontation fell outside the coherent boundaries of a single spatial universe. The Persians did not present Greeks with the 'ever-present possibility of conflict', but rather with an exceptional, extraordinary and existential discontinuity with the Greek world.[14] As such, where the orbits of ancient *Nomoi* clashed, the result was extreme, existential violence, and the urge towards annihilation that is definitively precluded by the controlled version of enmity that exists within a *Nomos*.

All pre-modern *Nomoi* therefore lacked the global character that would enable the political recognition of enmity in all instances.

All the great political power complexes that emerged in the high cultural areas of antiquity and the Middle Ages, in both the Orient and the Occident, were either purely continental cultures, river (*potamic*) cultures, or at most inland sea (*thalassic*) cultures. Consequently, the *Nomos* of their spatial order was not determined either by the antithesis of land and sea as two orders, as in traditional European law, or (still less) by an overcoming of this antithesis ... The common law that arose from such a pre-global division of the earth could not be a comprehensive and coherent system, because it could not be an encompassing spatial order.[15]

This absence of a common spatial order made it virtually impossible for empires (each with its own *orbis*) to recognise the *justus hostis* of other empires. As a result, wars between such 'worlds' would invariably be 'waged as wars of annihilation'.[16] The only agent of restraint in such circumstances was the simple empirical fact that the low level of pre-modern communication and technology kept such interactions to a bare minimum. To a large extent, each *Nomos* sustained the illusion that it was a world unto itself.

Given his attachment to the original Greek etymology of *Nomos*, Schmitt pays surprisingly little attention to the ancient world as a concrete instance of pre-modern, non-global *Nomoi*. He does go some way to creating a broad typology of pre-modern spatial cultures, and in so doing emphasises the highly particular form of spatial awareness that underlies these mini-universalisms. In *Land und Meer* Schmitt relies on Ernst Kapp to offer a

---

[13] *Ibid.*, p. 51.
[14] C. Schmitt, *The Concept of the Political* (trans. G. Scwhab), Chicago: University of Chicago Press (1996), p. 32.
[15] Schmitt, *Nomos* pp. 53–4. See also Schmitt, *Land und Meer*, pp. 23–8.
[16] Schmitt, *Nomos*, p. 55.

three-stage view of the types of relationship of the *Nomos* to the land.[17] In the first instance there are the ancient river cultures around the Nile, Tigris and Euphrates, including the Egyptians, the Babylonians and the Assyrians. In such *potamic* cultures, the obvious orientating spatial relationship is between the land and the river. Greece, by contrast, represents a *thalassic Nomos* centred on the Mediterranean, and with elements in common with ancient Rome, and the Mediterranean Middle Ages.

Although *thalassic* cultures were evidently characterised by their relationship to the inland sea, Schmitt is at pains to point out that these were still *essentially territorial* orders that were oriented to a certain notion of *land* appropriation. In the pre-modern world, 'the great primeval acts of law remained terrestrial orientations; appropriating land, founding cities, and establishing colonies'.[18] Therefore, whilst *thalassic* cultures stood in a relationship to the sea, this relationship was 'characterised' by the idea of coast as a boundary, and as one element in the act of land appropriation. The primary element continued to be the land. The point is made most clearly in Schmitt's discussion of Venice as a medieval *thalassic* culture, in which all of the ceremonial and symbolic acts of Venetian life point towards a culture of coasts and camps, rather than a maritime existence. Venice represents a *Küstenreich* that treated its mastery of the sea as part of the formative process of its fundamental concept of the land.[19]

Schmitt is far more interested in the historical example of medieval Christian Europe as the last pre-modern *Nomos*. To a certain extent the focus on medieval Europe in Parts I and II of *The Nomos of the Earth* is motivated by the search for seeds of the spatial revolution that led to the first global *Nomos* in world history – the system of European states. Schmitt therefore focusses to a great extent on the way in which scholastic theories of 'international law' developed in late medieval Europe (and especially the reaction of Vitoria to the discovery of the New World) are properly understood in the context of the medieval political order from which they originated.[20] The objective is polemical to a certain extent, and

---

[17] Schmitt, *Land und Meer*, p. 23.   [18] Schmitt, *Nomos*, p. 44.
[19] Schmitt, *Land und Meer*, pp. 24–5.
[20] Schmitt explicitly predicates his discussion of the medieval international order on the need to rescue medieval concepts from the artificial history of their reception:

In scholarly discussions of international law today, especially concerning the question of just war, the international law of the Christian-European Middle Ages is invoked and utilized in a peculiar and contradictory manner … [This is true of] numerous arguments and constructions in which, for example, League of Nations theorists in Geneva and American jurists and politicians have endeavoured to utilize medieval theories, above all those concerning just war, for their own ends. (Schmitt, *Nomos*, p. 56)

it soon becomes clear that Schmitt wishes to attack those contemporary legal positivists who fail to recognise that Vitoria's language of justice 'must be judged in terms of the *jus gentium* of the *respublica Christiana* of the Christian Middle Ages – not in terms of present-day international or interstate law'.[21] Schmitt stresses the spatial and conceptual uniqueness of the European Christian order so as to rubbish contemporary attempts to decontextualise medieval doctrines of the just war, and reapply them to radically different modern conditions.[22]

Nevertheless, even if Schmitt's objectives are polemical, he is drawn towards a fuller explication of the medieval order than he offers for Greek or Roman spatial orders. The fundamental characteristic of European Christendom is that it displays an essential unity between order and orientation – that is, between the local and the universal, between *Ortung* and *Ordnung*. As early as 1923 Schmitt was developing a theory of the possible political relationship between the universal church and the particular state (or political unit). In *Römischer Katholizmus und politische Form* (*Roman Catholicism and Political Form*), Schmitt had depicted the Catholic church as a potential common point of mediation among European powers that could dispel the worst effects of their antipathy.[23] The great strength of the Catholic church, in this account, was its ability to survive as a *complexio oppositorum* (a set of complex oppositions) and so to provide a political form to the diverse political pluriverse of European civilisation. Put baldy, the 'universal' church could offer an order that is compatible with the inward orientation of the political units.

Although Schmitt's concern in *Römischer Katholizismus* lay mainly in arguing for the possible mediating potential of the church in contemporary Europe (an idea he quickly abandoned), the vision of a Christian order expressed is clearly that of a re-creation of the *complexio oppositorum* of medieval Europe. The medieval church stood as the superior source of religious authority, external to, but enveloping, the anarchical relations between 'secular' powers. 'No difference [*Gegensatz*] emerged that it could not encomapass.'[24] Rome formed the cardinal orienting point for all of European civilisation, such that all language of legitimacy and justification was expressed in terms of the ultimate orientation towards

---

[21] *Ibid.*, p. 111.

[22] For a discussion of Schmitt's wider appeal to medieval historical examples as a tactic in his critique of just war, see G. Slomp, 'Carl Schmitt's Five Arguments against Just War', *Cambridge Review of International Affairs* 19:3 (2006), 435–57 (pp. 437–40).

[23] C. Schmitt, *Römischer Katholizismus und politische Form* (2nd edn), Cologne: Klett–Cotta (1925).

[24] *Ibid.*, p. 11.

the universal church. 'The history of the Middle Ages is thus a history of the struggle *for*, not against Rome.'[25]

Schmitt stresses the conceptual distinction between the order contained in the idea of European Christendom, and the political dynamic expressed in the power relations of the princes and emperors. 'Thus, the antitheses of emperor and pope were not absolute, but rather *diversi ordines* [diverse orders], in which the order of the *respublicana Christiana* resided.'[26] Any idea of a fundamental rivalry between the Papacy and the Christian princes derives, in Schmitt's account, from a failure to recognise the fact that these institutions constituted logically distinct and mutually reinforcing elements of the same overall order. The 'unity of *imperium* and *sacredotium*' relied at all times on 'the distinction between *potestas* [power] and *auctoritas* [authority] as two distinct lines of order of the same encompassing unity'.[27] This unity of order and orientation meant that all roads of authority led to Rome.

At the local level (in the various *Ortungen* of medieval Europe) political power was possessed and deployed according to the will of sovereign princes, in accordance with the logic of their political power. Whilst perhaps less firmly defined territorially than the sovereign state that was to follow in the modern era, the power of political units was nevertheless inscribed on the land. The foundational acts of the European spatial order were those that fundamentally challenged the territorial logic of the preceding spatial order. In Schmitt's account, the foundational land appropriations of the medieval European order were those acts of conquest and adverse possession by migratory peoples such as the Vandals in Spain and the Lombards in Italy. The vital character of these land appropriations is that 'they exceeded the limits of the existing order of the [Roman] empire', and thereby placed the spatial logic of the Roman order into question.[28]

Politics was territorial, and the possibility of reciprocal politics (i.e. warfare) rested on the fact that medieval Europe possessed a common historical point of departure – a certain act of land appropriation that gave rise to the possibility of the *Nomos*. Europe in the Middle Ages was therefore anarchic in the sense that it was a political pluriverse, and the

---

[25] Schmitt, *Nomos*, p. 59.   [26] *Ibid.*, p. 59.   [27] *Ibid.*, p. 61.

[28] See *ibid.*, p. 57. Schmitt distinguishes between those acts of conquest by the Vandals and Lombards that challenged the order of the Roman Empire, and early acts of land appropriation by Germanic tribes such as the Odoacer, the Ostrogoths and the Burgundians that occurred in accordance with the Roman spatial order, and so reinforced the existing *Nomos*. See below, p. 80 for discussion on the difference between land appropriation that supports an existing spatial order, and those land appropriations (such as those discussed here) that place the logic of an existing order in doubt.

potential of princes to engage in war against one another was never put into question. Nevertheless, such conflict as did take place between Christian princes (over the usual political matters of rights, power and defence) took place within the overall context of the *respublica christiana* and, as such, they were 'bracketed wars' that 'were distinguished from wars against non-Christian princes and peoples' (i.e. wars that took place outside the boundaries of the *Nomos*).[29]

The component parts of the *respublica christiana* therefore exist within the context of the universal shadow of the church. The unity of order and orientation resulted in a restraint of history in the subtle co-existence of order and diversity. As such, in the midst of this complex order of opposites, one might say that the Katechon was here at work, restraining the possibility of meaninglessness and total disorder. The anarchy of the Christian Middle Ages acted as a barrier against historical stasis, whilst at the same time avoiding a headlong historical rush to some empty *telos*. As Taubes might have put it, the Christian Middle Ages embraced history as delay.[30] As such, this medieval order was not static to the point that the possibility of its own collapse was impossible (a situation that would have been ahistorical and hence nihilistic), and yet it nevertheless achieved a very high degree of stability.[31] As Schmitt puts it, the European Middle Ages experienced a tension between great historical continuity and a specifically Christian sense that 'the Christian empire was not eternal'.[32]

Spatial revolution

Before one can witness a historical dynamic within a spatially normative order, Schmitt demands that there must be a foundational act that brings that order into existence in the first place. Just as the sovereign decision lies with the determination of law in the exceptional situation, a spatial order comes about by an act of puncture. The modern system of European states did not, on Schmitt's account, come about through some gradual and piecemeal process of reform. Rather, it involved a radical shift in spatial consciousness, destroying the old spatial order and erecting a new vision of spatial orientation in its place. The decaying medieval ideas of space, Schmitt contends, were swept away in a revolution of collective consciousness.

---

[29] *Ibid.*, p. 58.   [30] See above, p. 47.
[31] See the following chapter for detailed discussion on this idea of static, dynamic and accelerating history.
[32] Schmitt, *Nomos*, p. 59.

Schmitt's account of the political conditions of medieval Europe coheres in many respects with an understanding of pre-Westphalian order that is common in contemporary IR theory. It is meaningless to talk of the medieval princes, emperors and city republics as if they were 'states' in the modern meaning of the word. The universal power of the Roman church, as yet unchallenged by Reformation particularism, presented an overwhelming context and orientation for the conduct of political life. European Christendom represented a complex and coherent 'order' in which the particular *Ortung* of the political unit is counterbalanced by the universal *Ordnung* of the Papacy. Schmitt could surely have subscribed, for instance, to Chris Brown's account of the medieval political order;

Within medieval Christendom there were borders between the various political authorities, but these borders existed in a context where the overriding identity was, in principle, universal and religious. Individuals were discouraged from thinking of their secondary identities as natural, or as conveying more than limited and conditional moral obligations. Rulers ruled where they could, often through violence, but the influence of the church – which was material as well as spiritual, since religious foundations owned much of the wealth of the continent – was, for the most part, exercised to limit the scope of the resulting conflict, and sometimes successfully.[33]

The contrast drawn here between the coherently oriented politics of medieval Europe and the starker, modern landscape of sovereignty and non-intervention coheres with the traditional use of the Westphalian myth in the history of IR. Schmitt touches on the common themes that are deployed to explain the collapse of the medieval order and the rise of the state system in terms of the radical changes of the 'long sixteenth century'. In particular, the Reformation punctured the capacity of Rome to bracket war, and to act as an external point of orientation and restraint among European powers. The scale of violence exhibited in the 'creedal civil wars' made it clear that the bracketing of wars by means of the concept of just cause could only cause instability, violence and an acceleration of history under conditions where the authority of the church was divided. Following the blood-letting of the Thirty Years' War, European powers finally started to achieve a new order based on the personification of the political unit; the new public character of sovereigns; and a new, intensely spatial order. Such changes finally dismantled the old unities of the *respublicana christiana*, replacing it with a much less coherently ordered

---

[33] C. Brown, *Sovereignty, Rights and Justice*, Cambridge: Polity (2002), pp. 20–1.

(but nevertheless rooted) *Nomos*.[34] The state was created as 'the agency of a new, interstate, Eurocentric spatial order of the earth'.[35]

The sectarian violence that emerged from the Reformation in Europe could clearly not be bracketed and contained by the existing European order. As Schmitt puts it, a confrontation, war or territorial challenge is 'bracketed' to the extent that it 'do[es] not jeopardise the comprehensive spatial order as a whole'. If one considers Schmitt's use of the term 'bracketing' (*Hegung*), one is struck instantly by its basic applicability to the medieval order. An agricultural or forestry word, *Hegung* refers to the safe containment and management of livestock or trees within a contained, safe and ordered space.[36] The challenge posed by rival spatial understandings inherent in certain strands of the Reformation clearly emanated from outside this contained Roman space, and challenged the coherence of its spatial concept. The impact of this challenge was therefore revolutionary in a spatial sense.

The difference between a spatial change that takes place within an existing order, and a spatial change that jeopardises that order, may not be easily discerned in certain instances. Wars, of course, do not challenge the coherence of a *Nomos* per se. The whole point about the medieval order that Schmitt depicts is that it was a comprehensive order that contained genuine conflict within it. The multiple confrontations of the Peloponnesian Wars did not destroy the comprehensive spatial logic of the Greek world. Anarchy does not pose a challenge to the survival of a spatial order (but is often rather a sign of its health and coherence).

Indeed, Schmitt regards the ability to reconstitute one's sense of being in space as a core human characteristic. '[Man] has the power to overcome his historical being and consciousness. He knows not only birth but also the possibility of rebirth.'[37] Accordingly, man possesses the choice to exist and live within spatial horizons that are, in some sense, of his own construction. For the most part such choices and distinctions do not constitute revolutionary alterations to the generalised spatial consciousness, but are instead latent evidence of man's capacity to cope with differing spatial categories. At a localised level, this capacity for variant spatial experience simply described the profound differences between different kinds of people and their existence in space: 'A city dweller thinks of the world differently than a farmer; a whaler has a different *Lebensraum* than an opera singer, and a pilot experiences the world and life not only in a different light, but also in different matter, depths and horizons.'[38] But

---

[34] See Schmitt, *Nomos*, pp. 140–51.   [35] This is the title to *ibid.*, Chapter 1, Part III.
[36] On the translation of *Hegung* see above, p. 21 n. 27.
[37] Schmitt, *Land und Meer*, p. 14.   [38] *Ibid.*, p. 55.

beyond such personalised distinctions, it is the generalised capacity for changing existence in space that forms the essence of Schmitt's notion of spatial revolution. There are clearly certain instances in which the overall collective understanding of space – the understanding of space that has political consequences – is radically altered.

In Chapters 10 to 12 of *Land und Meer*, Schmitt uses theoretical and historical reasoning to answer the question 'What is a spatial revolution?'.[39] He suggests that people in the long sixteenth century 'had a particular understanding that their "space" was subject to great historical changes', and considers whether this consciousness amounts to a spatial revolution.[40]

Each time in history that a power has made a new advance into the sphere of human consciousness [*in den Geschichtskreis des menschlichen Gesamtbewußtseins eintrete*] (through the unleashing of new energies, new lands and seas), they also change the spaces of human existence ...

The change can be so deep and so unexpected that it not only changes distances and scale, not only changes the external horizon of man, but also changes the very structure of spatial consciousness itself. Then one can talk of a spatial revolution.[41]

Schmitt provides only two detailed instances of such spatial revolutions. The first – the shift from a comprehensive medieval order to the Westphalia system of sovereign states – appears, at first glance, to be less about the concept of space, and rather more about ideological or authoritative principles of politics. After all, the immediate territorial basis of the emergent states was, in very many cases, virtually identical to the immediate spatial claims of preceding princes and kings. France or England, for instance, continued to be recognisable notions on either side of the historical watershed. If anything, one might suggest that the revolutionary aspect was a question of degree rather than extent. Westphalia was revolutionary because it represented the political charge of territory as a foundational political fact, rather than as a contingent and subordinate fact of a wider and looser order. It represents a decision in favour of territory – in favour of the element of land – as the primary ordering principle of politics. In this respect, the experience of the Thirty Years' War might be said to have created a higher degree of self-consciousness about the possible political effect of territoriality. It helped to situate territory as an historical concept, rather than as an assumed fact of political existence as it had been in every previous *Nomos*.

If the shift to a modern Europe of states marked the conceptual realisation of land, the second instance of spatial revolution of concern to

---

[39] *Ibid.*   [40] *Ibid.*   [41] *Ibid.*, pp. 56–7.

Schmitt marks the conceptual discovery of its antipode – the sea. This present, ongoing alteration of spatial consciousness is doubtless the most radical spatial revolution. In its very nature, maritime life rejects all fixity, all permanence, all rootedness. It conceives of order only in terms of the ultimate coherence of its own references. A concept without limits, the sea engulfs everything. It knows only temporal difference, and at the micro level – in the momentary position of a ship, or the breaking of a wave. And it can only conceive of order in terms of the coherence of its entirety. In the development of sea-power, global commerce, extra-European expansion and the emergence of the United States, Schmitt senses precisely this decision against the political premises of land, and in favour of a maritime form of existence. To a great extent, *Land und Meer* and *The Nomos of the Earth* are engaged in an attempt to analyse the conceptual-historical effect of this ongoing discontinuity between terrestrial and maritime modes of situating political existence.

The element of land

Before we go on to consider Schmitt's depiction of the modern historical dynamic between firm land and free sea, it is worth pausing a moment to consider the status of the primary element, land. Land is clearly the natural human habitat. In the beginning, therefore, man knew only the land. Simply put, 'since man is not a fish and not a bird', he is a 'creature of the land'.[42] The firm land is man's ordained domain, and every pre-modern spatial order was predicated solely on the land as the form-giving element. Any relationship to the sea or to the air was merely by means of a boundary to the land, as evidenced in Schmitt's discussion of the Venetian *Kustkultur*.

Schmitt's turn towards the elements as the key to historical under-standing is a characteristically esoteric move. In *Land und Meer* Schmitt stresses his understanding of elements in terms of the ancient division between land, sea, air and fire, as drawn from Thales.[43] Schmitt clearly arrives at the device of an elemental history via his prior emphasis on the centrality of land to the ordering of any existence. In Schmitt's thought, as in his theory of human organisation, land is both the point of origin and the form-giving element. Schmitt's concept of elemental history grows out of the status of land as man's natural element, and is so geared to a discussion of the *disturbance* of this terra firma by the historical *activation* of other elements.

---

[42] *Ibid.*, pp. 7–8.   [43] *Ibid.*, pp. 12–15.

As our previous discussion of the *Nomos* concept illustrates, firm land is vital to the realisation of a spatial order, since it is only land that has character – that can be inscribed, appropriated, owned and divided. In *The Nomos of the Earth*, land is depicted as the tripartite source of all law and order:

(i) First in the inner measure of man's toil in the earth,
(ii) Second, in the fact that soil cleared for work manifests clear lines (that is to say, divisions),
(iii) Third, it is in the fences and walls that grow up around these divisions that 'the orders and orientations of human social life become apparent'.[44]

Thus the land is not only man's 'natural' habitat, but also offers the physical and ontological fixity required to create meaningful order.

Schmitt argues that man's orientation to the land is the source of the original distinction between public and private, and that it mutually implicates ideas of private ownership and public protection. In this he is by no means unique among political theorists in looking to the land as the original basis of legal divisions. He applauds Kant for having recognised that 'supreme proprietorship of the soil [is the] main precondition for the possibility of ownership and all further law, public as well as private'.[45] But Schmitt rejects Kant's formalism, and the reduction of the fact of land ownership to a categorical theory. He stresses instead the concrete fact of land appropriation as an historical event that in itself precedes the possibility of all other distinctions between public and private, or between authority and ownership. The very force of a land appropriation comes not from any normative status as a new order, but rather from its historical character as a point of rupture, and the foreshadow of a new order.[46] The land appropriation is the defining act of a new historical era – '[at] the start of every great epoch there is a great act of land appropriation'.[47]

As such, Schmitt's ideas on land as the concrete source of order implicitly repudiate Lockean ideas on property as the product of human energies. Famously, for Locke, property is to be viewed as that which man removes from nature by his labour, and since 'this *Labour* [is] the unquestionable Property of the Labourer, no man but he can have a right to that what is once joyned to ...'.[48] For Schmitt, the foundational act of proprietorship is not labour, but force. Appropriation is a violent act that

---

[44] Schmitt, *Nomos*, pp. 42–3.
[45] I. Kant, *The Philosophy of Law: An Exposition of the Fundamental Principles of Jurisprudence as the Science of Right* (trans. W. Hastie), Edinburgh: T. & T. Clark (1887), p. 182. See Schmitt, *Nomos*, p. 46.
[46] Schmitt, *Nomos*, pp. 45–8.   [47] Schmitt, *Land und Meer*, p. 71.
[48] J. Locke, 'The Second Treatise on Government', in *Two Treatises of Government* (ed. p. Laslett), Cambridge: Cambridge University Press (1988), pp. 265–428, para. 27 (p. 288).

establishes the future possibility of ownership. To talk of man's labour, his use of the soil, the content of his social life – all of this, for Schmitt, is to avoid the arbitrary historical fact of appropriation that must necessarily precede the social order. Property, for Schmitt, is a contingent social fact that hinges on an arbitrary original event of appropriation.[49]

The act of land appropriation is primary in Schmitt's thinking about the foundation of law for three main reasons:

(i) Land appropriation is the foundational act, and it is theoretically impossible to think about the creation of law in any other order. All other aspects of social order necessarily derive from the original, concrete act of appropriation, and any attempt to avoid this harsh, real, unjust fact is delusional. In his essay 'Appropriation/ Distribution/Production', Schmitt sought to attack the narrowness of political economic debates in contemporary liberalism and Marxism by stressing the primacy of the act of appropriation. Schmitt argued that it is impossible to discuss acts of distribution and production without first having ascertained the act of original appropriation.[50]

(ii) The act of land appropriation is the only means by which the ruler of a political unit can achieve a secure separation of a zone of peace from a zone of conflict. The boundary creation involved in a land appropriation involves the exclusion of enemies to the zone on the exterior, and the neutralisation of the interior as a single order. Thus the land appropriation is the foundational separation between domestic and international law.

(iii) In creating an internal zone of peace, the act of land appropriation cements the amity of the particular political community. The particular political community is predicated on a certain understanding of land ownership, and is therefore existentially committed to the maintenance of that spatial arrangement. As such, individual interests in land ownership dovetail with the spatial logic of the political community itself. The very self-interest of citizens compels them to act together in the maintenance of the spatial status quo.[51]

---

[49] This insistence of the logical priority of appropriation is also the basis of Schmitt's rejection of Alexandre Kojève's conclusion that a stable future order could be based on production alone. See M. Ojakangas, *A Philosophy of Concrete Life: Carl Schmitt and the Political Thought of Late Modernity*, Bern: Peter Lang (2006), p. 161.

[50] C. Schmitt, 'Appropriation/Distribution/Production: Towards a Proper Formulation of the Basic Questions of any Social and Economic Order' (trans. G. Ulmen), *Telos* 95 (Spring 1993), 52–64.

[51] See also Zarmanian, 'Carl Schmitt', p. 56.

This latter point clearly coheres with the logic of *protego et obligo*, which we explored in the previous chapter. One measure of the degree to which a sovereign succeeds in his protective role lies in the degree to which he maintains the internal spatial order and the security of formative instances of land rights. In *Die Diktatur* Schmitt displays an interest in the classical definition of despotism, and the relation of this concept to the disruption of common understandings of property rights. His argument that there is a basic connection between the territorial status of the political unit and the maintenance of a certain concept of territory within the political unit could doubtless be illustrated by numerous historical examples.[52]

There is a natural stability to the concept of territory then, that derives from the permanence of the land. Changes to the concrete element are either *de minimus* (as in the case of landslips or changing vegetation), or else are imperceptibly slow (as with erosion or glaciation). In the context of the firm land, therefore, a spatial revolution will entail either an alteration of scale, or a change in the intensity of association with the land. In other words, as with the changes wrought by Westphalia, it will involve changes in perception rather than being driven by changes in the substance of the land. The emergence of the sea as a politically charged element changed this.

The element of sea

In all antiquity, Schmitt suggests, man has only had an elemental relationship with the land. All order is territorial, all ownership derives from the land, and all orientation is in accordance with the division of land. The most significant historical departure of the modern era (the one that distinguishes it from every previous political order) is the emergence of the sea as a real and total element in human existence. Of importance here is the difference between relationships to the sea as a boundary in *thalassic* societies, and the modern decision in favour of the sea that was total, elemental and irreversible. In Schmitt's account, certain modern states made an elemental decision in favour of the sea that radically changed the very basis of their orientation. As such, a radical dichotomy between sea-

---

[52] See C. Schmitt, *Die Diktatur*, Berlin: Duncker and Humblot (1921). Consider, for instance, the delicate territorial balance of the Habsburg empire in the early seventeenth century. The disappropriation of the duchy of Mecklenburg, and the replacement of the duke with a Bohemian commoner was clearly an unsustainable disturbance of the common understanding of the relationship between the overall territorial structure of the empire, and the particular property and ownership concerns of local agents. See A. Osiander, *The States System of Europe, 1640–1990*, Oxford: Oxford University Press (1994), Chapter 2.

power and land-powers emerged as a basic motor of modern history. In the Westphalian era, Schmitt argues for an understanding of world history as the dialectical relationship of land and sea.

Schmitt acknowledges that the sea has always exerted a curious pull on humankind. He remarks on the prominence of the sea in myths of creation in which the sea 'features as the ancestor of mankind'.[53] From ancient Greece and the legends of peoples of the south Pacific, right up to Darwin's theory of evolution, man has always (Schmitt argues) had some form of Romantic attachment to the sea as a source of origins and mysticism. 'It is curious that when men stand on a coastline, they naturally stare out from the land over the sea, and do not look back over the land from the sea.'[54]

We have already seen that pre-modern societies such as medieval Venice often lived according to a coastal disposition. Schmitt is also interested in pre-modern attempts to appropriate areas of sea as an adjunct to land appropriations. Such attempts to extend terrestrial authority over areas of the sea relied on a far higher degree 'of human means of power and human consciousness of space' than is necessary for the original and primary land appropriation.[55] Moreover, in the pre-modern era, such appropriations were fundamentally limited by the corollary of the land-appropriation out of which they grew. Thus the great Mediterranean societies of Assyria, Greece, Rome and Carthage, and arguably also the Hanse in the Baltic, are instances of prototypical sea-appropriations that nevertheless relied fundamentally on the terrestrial limits of the inland seas to which they related. The defining characteristic of such appropriations continued to be a basic terrestrial consciousness.

Despite their limited nature, these early attempts to inscribe law and order onto the sea already point to some of the fundamental differences between the possibilities of fixity inherent in the land element, and the fluidity of the sea. For each of the *thalassic* cultures mentioned above, the sea remained an area of contestation at the outer limits of the grounded *Nomos* within the particular empire or society. It was never possible to achieve the same status of law (or normative order) on the sea as could be achieved on land. The sea was a realm of piracy that could never be made subject to the same intensity of political orientation as could firm land. The absence of boundaries made it impossible to separate a zone of peace from a zone of war, and so there appeared a seamless continuum between trade, political power and piracy. 'On the sea, fields cannot be planted and firm lines cannot be engraved.'[56] The sea was a zone of constant and

---

[53] Schmitt, *Land und Meer*, p. 10.   [54] *Ibid.*, p. 9.
[55] Schmitt, *Nomos*, p. 44.   [56] *Ibid*, p. 42.

immutable conceptual challenge to any order.[57] Those powers that ventured into the sea are best seen as land-powers with ships.[58]

This huge indeterminacy of the sea in contrast to the fixed land meant that, for the most part, the sea continued to be an object of fear in the pre-modern world. 'Many peoples kept to the mountains, far from the coasts, and never lost the old, pious fear of the sea.'[59] In Schmitt's account, the sea was present as an elemental force in human life only as a supra-boundary concept. The sea represented an unknown, inhuman and uncontrollable exterior that stood as antithesis to the very fabric of ordered human existence. For the most part it was shunned and avoided, and history continued to be constituted by the slow-moving tensions within the terrestrial unity of order and orientation.

The elemental decision in favour of the sea

For most of human history, therefore, land has been the hegemonic element of human existence. It is only during the long sixteenth century, and the transformation of Europe from a unified *respublica christiana* to a system of sovereign states, that the sea comes to play a world-historical role. In our discussion of spatial revolution, we have already seen that one factor in the destruction of the old order and the foundational act of a new order lay in the consequences of Reformation. The key spatial characteristic of this new order was in the unprecedented decision of certain states to reorder their spatial self-consciousness along maritime rather than terrestrial lines.

Most of the content of *Land und Meer* concerns itself with the factors that encouraged and enabled certain peoples to take this elemental leap into total maritime existence; that is, the structural changes that allowed people to break the elemental bonds with the land that had characterised all previous human existence. Schmitt points to a myriad of changes in technology, innovation, religion, forms of trade, notions of commodity and the growth of capital that coalesced with changes in the perception of space and adventure. Certain societies fundamentally resisted this draw to a maritime existence, and concentrated on fleshing out the primary territorial consequences of the new *staatlichen* political order.[60] And in this

---

[57] *Ibid.*, pp. 42–6.   [58] Schmitt, *Land und Meer*, p. 26.   [59] Schmitt, *Nomos*, p. 43.
[60] Recall Schmitt's remark that Hobbes' idea of the territorial state only became actualised in continental Europe, whilst the English attachment to the freedom of the sea negated the idea of the centralised territorial space to which Hobbes' state theory naturally led. See above, pp. 37–38.

combination of embrace and resistance, a new bipolar historical dynamic started to emerge.

Schmitt's great prototypical symbol of the elemental decision in favour of the sea is the image of whalers (*Waljäger*).[61] Enabled by the great advances in English and, more particularly, Dutch ship-building in the period from 1450, the practice of whaling gradually opened up the horizon of the open ocean, and stimulated a form of interaction with the sea that cut loose of its territorial boundaries. Whilst the ordered world of the Doge focussed only on the inland sea, the ramshackle Dutch gradually turned their eyes to the meaning of maritime existence. A productive dynamic thus emerged between ship technology and the practice of whaling that drew Englishmen and Dutchmen ever more into the orbit of the sea. Whaling was a conduit to adventure and discovery. 'The whale tempted them out onto the oceans, and emancipated them from the coasts. Through the whale man discovered the ocean currents and found the northern passage. The whale led us.'[62]

Here, as elsewhere, the whale is an important symbol for Schmitt in its original biblical role. In *The Leviathan* Schmitt discussed the Cabbalistic myth of the great battles between the sea-creature Leviathan, and the great land beast, the Behemoth. Schmitt revisits this theological mysticism in *Land und Meer*, and the prominence of the whale as the symbol of the new maritime existence is no accident in this respect. Schmitt explicitly endorses the value of reading the world-historical dynamic through the lens of this mythical confrontation, and shows admiration for the prescience of Isaac Abravanel's fifteenth-century linkage of the Leviathan–Behemoth myth to the political situation of Portugal, Castille and Venice.[63] In both a practical and symbolic sense, therefore, the whale serves Schmitt as cause and also symbol of the shift towards a maritime existence.

In terms of the more tangible historical forces encouraging a shift towards the maritime existence (such as technology and new forms of capitalism) Schmitt characteristically conflates causation and outcome, all under the banner of elemental change. Therefore the discovery of the Americas, the development of navigation equipment, the invention of ships capable of sailing to windward, the foundation of chartered trading companies, the encouragement of privateering and the opposition of Catholicism and Protestantism, '[all belong] to the elemental change from land to sea which constitutes our subject here'.[64] Whilst this scatter-gun picture of the structural changes of the sixteenth century may fail to

---

[61] See Schmitt, *Land und Meer*, Chapter 5.   [62] *Ibid.*, p. 34.
[63] *Ibid.*, p. 17.   [64] *Ibid.*, p. 46.

satisfy from a causal perspective, Schmitt is nevertheless effective in presenting an image of this as a concrete, momentous, historical point of rupture. His point appears to be that *something* is happening that is opening a historical cleavage between the conception of space as fixed land and the conception of space as free sea.

In a twist on the familiar Weberian thesis of the Protestant origins of capitalism, Schmitt looks to religion as one of the sources of variant spatial horizons.[65] Alongside Europe's growing capacity to engage with oceanic space, the new theology of predestination encouraged, in Schmitt's account, a new detachment from the concrete orientations of the dry land. It is no accident, Schmitt argues, that Calvinism was the faith of the most adventurous and territorially detached of Europe's peoples in the sixteenth century – the Huguenots, Dutch freedom fighters and sea beggars, and the English Puritans. Schmitt sees the doctrine of predestination as the highest expression of self-confidence by an elite, and as a natural conduit to both 'devil-may-care' adventurism, and a lofty self-elevation from the concrete orders of the terrestrial world. Calvinism saw its opportunity in the opening possibility of maritime existence, and in turn reinforced the depth of the revolution in favour of the sea. To a great extent, therefore, the adoption of the sea was the product of a 'world historical brotherhood that was cemented between political Calvinism and Europe's emergent maritime energy'.[66]

This decision of certain European peoples in favour of maritime existence is the revolutionary event in the creation of a new *Nomos*. Schmitt argues that the comparison of medieval Venice with early modern England or the Netherlands firmly establishes the revolutionary substance of the latter's relationship with the sea:

However, when we pose the question of whether [Venice] is an example of pure maritime existence, and represents a real decision in favour of the sea, we are struck by how narrow the Adriatic, and, indeed, the Mediterranean as a whole were, when compared with the unforeseeable expanses that the world's oceans would come to offer.[67]

[The whalers] were the first born members of a new elemental existence – the first new, genuine, 'children of the sea'.[68]

What, then, is the substance of this 'decision' supposedly made by England and the Netherlands? In some respects, as Schmitt points out, the English were late starters in realising the full planetary potential of

---

[65] See, especially, *ibid.*, Chapter 15.
[66] '… die weltgeschichtliche Brüderschaft, die den politischen Calvinismus mit den aufbrechenden maritimen Energien Europas verbindet'. *Ibid.*, pp. 84–5.
[67] *Ibid.*, pp. 21–2.   [68] *Ibid.*, p. 35.

oceanic space. Schmitt argues that their starting point was the founding of the Muscovy Company in 1553 (fully sixty years after Columbus sailed) and claims that the English first ventured south of the equator as late as 1570. Moreover, English advances at this time were largely based on technological advances achieved in the Netherlands, which remained the leading innovator in ship design.[69] The English 'decision' certainly did not lie, therefore, in some status as a trailblazer, or in some unique technical capacity to embrace maritime life.

England's status as an island was clearly one factor in its predisposition to the maritime decision, and yet, as Schmitt points out, there were many island peoples who specifically did not decide in favour of a maritime existence in the early modern period. Nevertheless, he does regard England's self-conscious identity as an island nation as causally important. It gave the English a head start in grasping the ocean as an independent, absorbing element. For continental people, the sea forms one of several boundaries in which land is the primary element. Schmitt argues that island people tend to look on land as coast with a 'hinterland'. The sea is the sole meaningful boundary. One might say that it is the land that is the oddity – a point of interruption. Whereas continental peoples are predisposed to think about the sea in terms of shipping 'lanes' between territorial points, the English (Schmitt argues) had some conception of themselves as implicated by the sea, and as inhabiting a ship or the back of a whale – i.e. inhabiting a space defined by the sea.[70]

Yet all such structural predispositions towards a maritime existence do not of themselves explain the substance of the decision that Schmitt is talking about. This is not a decision in the political sense, in that it does not represent a process of political distinction and enforcement. 'Decision' in this context refers rather to a form of sociological shift in perception, via which the English and Dutch came to define their spatial consciousness on radically different lines to the rest of Europe. The 'decision' in question is the full embrace of the possibilities of maritime life, the adoption of a new concept of spatial freedom, the extension of global adventure, and the transformation and expansion of society in reflection of these newly found freedoms.

In Schmitt's schema, the unique factor in the English and Dutch relationship to the sea was in their readiness to regard the sea as empty, lawless and free. Whilst other European powers attempted to comprehend the dawning oceanic age from within the context of the European spatial order, these northern Europeans embraced the possibilities of the sea as

---

[69] *Ibid.*, p. 51.   [70] See *ibid.*, pp. 90–5.

a separate element. This elemental distinction is best illustrated, in Schmitt's account, by the officially sanctioned growth of privateering in Tudor England. The free marine corsair capitalism – or piracy by another name – encapsulated the distinction between the free sea, and the ordered territory of land in which law and order applied.[71] Whilst the English and Dutch embraced the full possibilities of this maritime existence, other states held firm to strict territoriality.

The notion of an 'elemental decision' in favour of the sea allows Schmitt to skirt around the problem that numerous European powers, both Catholic and Protestant, were fully engaged in the opening-up of oceanic space and the 'New World'. The early prominence of Spain and Portugal in this area is self-evident, but Schmitt continues to regard these early modern states as wedded to the land as their foundational element (and especially so Spain). France likewise strikes Schmitt as an interesting example of the failure to make a decisive change in favour of maritime existence – a decision he again attributes to religious determinism: 'France failed to follow through on its promising attempts at the sea, such as were primarily associated with the Protestant Huguenots … [the decision] against the Huguenots and in favour of Catholicism was also, in the final analysis, a decision against the sea and in favour of the land.'[72] The substance of a decision in favour of the sea clearly consists of more than the mere fact of oceanic reach and maritime capability – for Schmitt it represents an existential departure.

This conclusion on the fate of French maritime existence also points to the conclusion that the leap into a maritime form of existence is culturally mediated. As with changes in territorial consciousness, the initial decision for or against the sea only makes sense as an expression of certain pre-existing aspects of culture. The turn towards a maritime existence is not historically inevitable, but rather represents a form of boldness and adventurism – a radicalism that could be resisted and restrained by conservative sovereigns in Europe who acted to bolster their territorial status, and clamped down on domestic forces that pushed for an opening-up of these new indeterminate spaces. The great Catholic powers of early

---

[71] Schmitt illustrates this conceptual difference with the historical example of the Killigrew family of Cornish pirates. The legality or otherwise of their behaviour is entirely determined by whether or not it occurs within the element of land or sea. The two represent separate realms, each capable of total human occupation. *Ibid.*, pp. 46–50.

[72] 'Frankreich hat den großen Anlauf zum Meer, der mit dem hugenottischen Protestantismus verbunden war, nicht durchgehalten … [dem Übertritt] gegen die Hugenotten und für den Katholizismus entscheiden hatte, war damit, im letzten Endergebnis, auch die Entscheidung gegen das Meer und für das Land gefallen.' *Ibid.*, pp. 52–3.

modern Europe sought, therefore, to extend absolute political control over the growing maritime sphere, and to make seafaring a limited adjunct of their terrestrial power base.

Spain and Portugal attempted to benefit from the new opportunities of seafaring, whilst at the same time protecting the land-oriented order of Europe from any disturbance from the great new oceanic space. In the first instance, the response to the realisation of great oceanic space was an attempt to extend the form of sea-appropriations that had characterised *thalassic* attempts to organise maritime space. This was pursued in an attempt to organise a form of sea-appropriation from within the existing order that merely extended their respective territorial conceptions of themselves. As such, they negotiated *raya* – great lines projected across the sea that would divide the rule of Spain from the rule of Portugal. The most famous of these, of course, is that enshrined in the Treaty of Tordesillas of 1494.[73]

The other geopolitical response of firmly 'territorial' states against the emergence of the sea was via the use of so-called amity lines.[74] These lines reflected an awareness among territorial states that they could not evade the reality of huge oceanic space by merely ignoring its existence. At the same time, however, the new space clearly presented a challenge to the territorial orientation of the metropole. Amity lines, whereby states agreed to the geographical limits of the European order, represented an attempt to externalise oceanic space, and thereby to neutralise its potential effect on the foundations of European order. 'Beyond the line' there lay another world, in which Europeans would explore, conquer and fight as aliens unconnected to the order and orientation of metropolitan Europe. Such a concept was insufficient, however, to neutralise the dialectic effect of the sea on the land, since of itself it recognised the relationship of two distinct spaces in an historical relationship with one another.[75]

Germany, meanwhile, remained virtually isolated from the fact of oceanic expansion and the dynamics of New World colonisation. The states of Germany continued to represent the highest point of terrestrial orientation. Schmitt remarks with interest that Lutheranism – the dominant Protestant doctrine in Germanic Europe – was territorially conservative in contrast to Calvinism. German Lutheranism was doctrinally content with a territorial framework for history and the persistence of small states.[76] Where continental Calvinism did persist, it either sought an oceanic outlet

---

[73] See Schmitt, *Nomos*, pp. 86–92.

[74] Amity lines are an important aspect of Schmitt's view of the dynamic between land and sea, and will be discussed in more detail later.

[75] See Schmitt, *Nomos*, pp. 92–9.   [76] See Schmitt, *Land und Meer*, p. 84.

(as with the princes of Brandenburg, who were among the few German princes with an instinct for sea power) or, in the case of Swiss and Hungarian Calvinism, was rendered historically meaningless as a result of the failure to express its expansive energy.[77]

The sea and 'emptiness'

In point of fact, the opening up of oceanic space during the 'first planetary spatial revolution' was as much about new land as it was about the dominance and mastery of the sea by whale hunters and pirates. The 'land-appropriation of the new world' by European powers was therefore the final component of the new global *Nomos*, and constituted the new foundational act on which a territorial order of the globe could be founded. '[T]he basic event in the history of European international law [is] the land appropriation of the new world.'[78] But as Schmitt is quick to point out, this process of appropriation is by no means as well-oriented as previous, uncontested territorial appropriations. The territory of the New World fell into a conceptual no-man's land, best categorised as somewhere on the boundary of free sea and fixed land.

All European powers could agree on the conceptual distinction of European and non-European land. The land of European states acquired a special territorial status rooted in mutual recognition. Colonial land was regarded as free space that was not subject to the same normative framework as the European space. As such, the new global *Nomos* was rooted in the distinction of three spheres – European land, non-European land and the sea – each with varying tendencies towards the definition of enemy, property and authority.[79] This conceptual distinction suited all European powers (both 'territorial' and 'maritime') as it allowed the distinction of a stable European space in which the basic territorial logic of the home states was not challenged. The logic via which each reached the notion of free spaces varied, however. As we have seen, 'territorial' powers were already well used to the idea of amity lines that served the practical purpose of neutralising the new horizon of conflict.[80] For the maritime powers, however, the free continental space of the New World came to be seen as made of the same substance as the free sea.

In both cases, the most significant characterisation of the New World was that it represented an area 'free' for discovery and occupation. In *Nomos* Schmitt considered the sixteenth- and seventeenth-century debate

---

[77] *Ibid.*, p. 83.   [78] Schmitt, *Nomos*, p. 83.   [79] See *ibid.*, pp. 183–4.
[80] Schmitt identifies the first such amity line as having been included as a secret clause in the Treaty of Cateau-Cambrésis (1559). See *ibid.*, p. 92.

on whether the New World should be regarded as *res nullius* or *res omnium*. The lands of the Americas and the Far East were, of course, 'land'. But in truth, their territoriality was not now implicated in the creation of order. They were not appropriated as territory so much as concepts. The lands of the New World were situated as an abstract idea – that which lay beyond the line, in a zone of indeterminacy. They were not part of the order, but conceived of instead as a theoretical category subordinate to the European order. In a sense, the territory of the New World was treated with irony, as a plaything.

For the first time, the entire earth was comprehensible as a single unit. And this realisation immediately generated a shift away from the concrete and towards the abstract. Man started to contemplate the relationship of the earth to the sun. The Enlightenment philosophers revelled in the pregnancy of 'emptiness' – the *horror vacui* of the New World – as a philosophical idea. The enormity of the global space invited an intimacy between the individual subject and the seductive universalism of the new age. Renaissance painters – 'barometers of the changing spatial concepts' – started to depict the human subject 'in a space that gave a perspective of emptiness'.[81] Whereas Gothic architecture had 'angled' people in a heavy context, emergent geometric styles sought to replicate the idea of free space.[82] In short, the realisation of an incomprehensible global space invited personal transcendence. It took man outside the concrete context of his existence in a place, a community and a political order.

What better way to characterise this aesthetically clean escape from the concrete realities than through Thomas More's idea of Utopia. That is to say, *U-topos* – the negation of *topos*, the negation of place. 'Such a word would have been unthinkable in the mouth of anyone in antiquity.'[83] Without the medieval avenues of belief and the promise of Roman salvation, man started to create his own fantasy worlds from the confines of his own mind. In the Hobbesian state, the individual was to be allowed the space to dream his own dreams of paradise. And in the embrace of an oceanic existence, the individual could find substance for those dreams – desert islands, tropical shores, u-topias. Although he declines to bring the two historical stories together, it is abundantly clear how Schmitt understood their relationship, and that they were pulling together towards formlessness. 'Each *horror vacui* brought much joy for the philosophers of the Enlightenment. But maybe this was just an understandable shuddering in the face of the nothingness and emptiness of death, before a nihilistic idea and, above all, nihilism itself.'[84]

---

[81] Schmitt, *Land und Meer*, p. 68.   [82] *Ibid.*, p. 69.
[83] Schmitt, *Nomos*, p. 178.   [84] Schmitt, *Land und Meer*, p. 67.

All was not lost at this stage, of course. Within Europe, conscious efforts were made to sustain a highly normative, terrestrial order of states. Here, land continued to dominate. Politics continued to be a terrestrial affair. But even if it had wished to, Europe could not, and did not wish to, incorporate the new wide-open spaces as part of the territorial order. In contrast to the unity of order and orientation in medieval Europe, the *Nomos* of the *jus publicum Europaeum* was instead founded on the fundamental opposition of and tension between land and sea. Whereas the coherence of universal and particular in the medieval world had 'slowed down' history, Schmitt presents the confrontation of land and sea as an almost Hegelian dialectic. Here we have two forces that threaten to negate each other. It constituted an explanatory framework into which Schmitt was able to pour all the various points of divergence between the conservatism of terrestrial Europe and the spatial radicalism of the Anglo-Saxon world. Accordingly, much of Schmitt's international history of the period following 1500 is reducible to the idea of world history in the confrontation of land and sea.

On the one hand there are the terrestrial accommodations of continental Europe. On the other we have the detached English – 'of Europe, but not in Europe'.[85] Added to this was the uncertain position of non-European lands in relation to this division. Colonial land-appropriations muddied the waters, since 'they were neither international interstate nor international private law matters, but even so they were not purely intrastate matters'.[86] Within the context of the world-historical dialectic of land and sea, non-European territory was to constitute a unique source of conceptual contest. The sea represented the pregnant possibility of disorder – u-topos, formlessness, nihilism – and there was no apparent way to contain this possibility within an order of territory.

Geopolitics and history

Against the backdrop of Schmitt's constitutional and political theory of the 1920s and early 1930s, this turn to geopolitics seems curious. Schmitt had displayed comparatively little interest in the geopolitical movement in German politics during that period, despite the relative prominence of such ideas in popular discourse during the 1920s and, increasingly, in the

---

[85] Schmitt, *Nomos*, p. 173. Any observer of recent debates about British Euroscepticism would be amused by Schmitt's use of this formulation.
[86] *Ibid.*, p. 199.

early 1930s.[87] Moreover, through figures such as Manfred Langhans-Ratzeburg and Otto Köllreuter and their ideas of 'geojurisprudence', geopolitical ideas had entered the academy as a significant branch of anti-positivist legal theory.[88] With his focus on the content of sovereignty and the intricacies of constitutional law, however, Schmitt seems to have made certain assumptions about territoriality that he only now called into question.

The distinction between Schmitt's preoccupation with juridical analysis and the trends in geopolitical thought are perhaps most evident in the varying intellectual responses to the legal and political status of the Rhineland under the Versailles settlement. Schmitt's concern had always been primarily with the sovereign-constitutional ramifications of this international indeterminacy.[89] The key prompt for his concern was the Rhineland as a problem of sovereign authority, rather than some geographically principled question of a specifically 'German' right to that territory. By contrast, the geopolitical disciples of Rudolf Kjellen and Friedrich Ratzel addressed the problem in the language of 'natural' borders and a providential German space stretching from the Rhine to the Vistula. In a sense their concern was more specific and concrete, and less intellectually abstract than Schmitt's. Walther Vogel, for instance, argued that the internationalisation of the Rhine would be unsustainable because France was an alien power in the Rhineland. German control of the Rhine was geopolitically determined, and any attempt to prevent it by means of international law was historically unsustainable.[90] Elsewhere, Adolf Grabowsky was concerned with the distinction between 'mere treaty

[87] For a comprehensive overview of the German geopolitical movement in the Weimar period, see D. T. Murphy, *The Heroic Earth: Geopolitical Thought in Weimar Germany 1918–1933*, London: Kent State University Press (1997).

[88] Langhans-Ratzeburg's major study, *Begriff und Aufgaben der Geographischen Rechtswissenschaft (Geojurisprudenz)* [The Concept and Application of a Geographic Science of Law (Geojurisprudence)] was published in 1928 (Berlin: Vowinckel), advocating the importance of geographical understanding to the reality of international law. Apparently in line with Schmitt's ideas on the distinction between real and artifical sovereignty, one of Langhans-Ratzeburg's innovations was the creation of maps of real, *de facto* power in contrast to the artificial borders of *de jure* state power. Köllreuter popularised the idea of a 'community of destiny' (an idea that he partly derived from his study of Japan in *Das politische Geschicht Japans*, Berlin: Heymann (1940)), and also engaged in public debate with Schmitt through the *Deutsche Juristenzeitung* in April 1933.

[89] See Schmitt's 1928 essay, 'Die Rheinlande als Objekt internationaler Politik', in *Positionen und Begriffe im Kampf mit Weimar–Genf–Versailles, 1923–1939*, Berlin: Duncker and Humblot (1994), pp. 29–37.

[90] See Vogel's essay 'Rhein und Donau als Staatenbilder', *Zeitschrift für Geopolitik* 1 (1924), 63–78.

borders' such as those imposed by Versailles, and 'natural' borders based on territory and ethnicity.[91]

Schmitt was a latecomer, therefore, to geopolitical and geohistorical modes of thinking from within the context of theorising on the problems of contemporary German geopolitics. Characteristically, Schmitt skirted around the large body of literature already in existence about the problem of geographic determinism and the role of geography in sustaining and shaping political formations. *Land und Meer* makes absolutely no reference to Kjellen, Ratzel, Haushofer or Langhans-Ratzeburg, despite (or perhaps because of) the fact that his 'application of Raum concepts to international law and state relations had been prefigured in the 1920s [and earlier] by [such] geopolitical thinkers'.[92] Despite its obvious debt to an ongoing tradition of geopolitical thought – a debt cagily acknowledged by reference to Halford Mackinder and Alfred Thayer Mahan – Schmitt is clearly seeking to present a different perspective from the ongoing and increasingly programmatic debates in German geopolitics and geojurisprudence. Two key distinctions are apparent.

Firstly, German geopolitics in the 1920s and 1930s was pre-eminently concerned with the 'problem' of Germany's position, and the search for a programmatic policy response to solve its geopolitical vulnerability. As David Murphy carefully illustrates, German geopolitics was constantly caught between a pessimistic appraisal of Germany's geopolitical disadvantages, and the optimistic proposal of ideas on spatial expansion and *Lebensraum* designed to remedy this position.[93] Despite drawing thinkers from differing backgrounds of law, academic geography, demography and journalism, publications such as the *Zeitschrift für Geopolitik* were constantly engaged in the search for purposive theories that could help to address the immediate situation in Germany. Alongside its pretensions to scientific status, German geopolitcs was self-consciously political in the sense of proposing and pursuing tight policy ideas, and bolstering a broader set of foreign policy ideas (particularly on the political right). It was also unashamedly nationalistic.

Despite its own political motivations, Schmitt's *Land und Meer* simply does not engage in the specific question of Germany's geopolitical

---

[91] See J. Klein, 'Adolf Grabowsky: ein vergessener Politikwissenschaftler', in B. Hafeneger and W. Schäfer (eds.), *Aufbruch zwischen Mangel und Verweigerung*, Marburg: Marburg Rathaus Verlag (2000), pp. 393–410.

[92] Murphy, *The Heroic Earth*, p. 29.

[93] It was Karl Haushofer who coined the phrase *Lebensraum* and introduced it to Hitler as early as 1924 through their mutual friend Rudolf Hess. See Murphy, *The Heroic Earth*, pp. 106–10.

position, and the prospects for a future realignment of its spatial conditions.[94] Overtly, at least, Schmitt is not writing a specifically *German* meditation on the problems of geodeterminism and the political ramifications of spatial consciousness. Indeed, his clear objective is to situate Germany as one among several traditional, territorial, European states-in-form that are together conceptually challenged by the turn towards a maritime mode of spatial thinking. Mainstream German geopolitics sought to stress the uniqueness of Germany contra France and Italy on the one hand, and Russia on the other. Infused with Romantic themes, Karl Haushofer *et al.* tended towards an assertion of Germany's territorial uniqueness as a bridge between East and West – that is, as a specifically non-western state.[95] In stark contrast, Schmitt's depiction of a geopolitical dynamic between land and sea clearly rehabilitates Germany as a traditional European state pitted against a rival Anglo-American understanding of space.

There is much that could be said about Schmitt's determination to write and think in terms of the historic European experience of statehood rather than reverting to a particular concern for the specific geopolitical problems of Germany. It is a tendency that persists broadly within Schmitt's work, and that distinguishes him significantly from most other conservative German political and geopolitical theorists of the inter-war years.[96] His Catholicism, his deep grounding in French history and language, his engagement with Donoso Cortes and de Maistre, and his marriage to a Serbian wife all perhaps play a part in drawing Schmitt away from an overtly nationalist theoretical language. But beyond this, it also re-emphasises Schmitt's concept of a certain, special, plural, political-territorial arrangement in the process of erosion. It represents his idealised commitment to a particularly European territorial state that is struggling to survive the pressure of Atlanticism.

For most geopolitical theorists, the problem of maritime space and naval power was one of simple tactics and orientation. Much debate in German geopolitics centred around the question of whether or not Germany might be able to assert itself as a maritime power, and latterly

---

[94] In this respect, Schmitt's later work on *Großraum* is far more in keeping with the German geopolitical tradition. See Chapter 6 below.

[95] See M. W. Lewis and K. E. Wigen, *The Myth of Continents: A Critique of Metageography*, Berkeley: University of California Press (1997), p. 59.

[96] The most obvious distinction is from Max Weber for whom, as Wilhelm Mommsen has amply illustrated, the purpose of political theory was always first and foremost the creation of specific answers to the concrete and particular problems of German politics. See W. J. Mommsen, *Max Weber and German Politics, 1890–1920* (trans. M. S. Steinberg), Chicago: University of Chicago Press (1990).

challenge the imperial and oceanic power of Great Britain and the United States. Under the influence of Mahan, theorists such as Haushofer and Josef März grappled with the realisation that maritime power was now a prerequisite of world power, and tried to address the challenge this posed to Germany in policy terms.[97] 'The key geographic fact confronting Germany', März concluded, 'is that it has no free access to the world's oceans and that its links to overseas colonies can always be blocked by the power that controls the English Channel and the North Sea'.[98] The lesson derived from Mahan is that Germany would have either to achieve authentic maritime power, or else to radically restructure its terrestrial power to such a height as to obviate the imperative to maritime existence – that is to say, it would have to achieve a maritime form of power on the continent.

For Schmitt, the lesson from Mahan is less axiomatic, less positive, and in many respects more subtle. The maritime mode of power that Mahan identifies represents a form of spatial orientation that is so totally at odds with the terrestrial foundations of the state as to represent a wholly distinct mode of being. Schmitt would doubtless have recognised the possibility that a 'maritime' mode of orientation might be possible within a continental context – that is to say, that the formlessness, unrootedness, ideologically universal form of (anti-) spatial politics represented by Mahan's Atlanticism might supplant traditional terrestrial political arrangements and, as a result, that politics might become despatialised. But for Schmitt, this was hardly a policy challenge to be embraced and acted upon. Instead, it represented a meta-historical challenge to the coherence of a terrestrial way of living politically. The challenge posed by the sea to the land is less to do with the mechanics of power, and has far more to do with the limits of historical consciousness.

This realisation leads us to the second key distinction between Schmitt and those geopolitical theorists engaged in the hunt for a geographic response to Germany's political circumstances – their differing comprehension of the interaction of history and geography. Walther Vogel presents a good example of ideas on geopolitically determined history. Similarly to Schmitt in *Land und Meer*, his avowed project in *Das Neue*

---

[97] Mahan's seminal work, *The Influence of Sea Power upon History 1660–1783*, Boston, MA: Little, Brown and Co. (1890), enjoyed a high profile in Germany even before its translation in 1896, and became a key resource in debates about the development of German naval power during the Weimar period. See H. H. Herwig, 'The Influence of A. T. Mahan upon German Sea Power', in J. B. Hattendorf (ed.), *The Influence of History upon Mahan: The Proceedings of a Conference Marking the Centenary of Alfred Thayer Mahan's* The Influence of Sea Power upon History, Newport, RI: Diane Publishing (1991), pp. 67–80.

[98] J. März, *Landmächte und Seemächte*, Berlin: Zentral Verlag (1928), p. 35.

Europa was to uncover the elemental foundations of the contemporary European state system, and the present predicament of Germany. In so doing, he stressed the 'deeper, slower currents of national life and the barely changing geographical circumstances' that shaped history with 'unrelenting force'.[99] The substance of such geopolitical determinism lay in a profound (if, frankly, imprecise) interaction of drainage systems, natural mountain and desert boundaries, with the admixture of racial and cultural factors. Oswald Spengler too, of course, proposed a complicated account of the interaction of culture and geography in the determination of conflict and history.

At first glance, Schmitt's historical dynamic of land and sea might seem to have much in common with such geopolitically determinist accounts. But Schmitt's objectives are more refined and more subtle than a simple attempt to account for conflict along geopolitical lines.[100] Land and sea represent radically inconsistent modes of existence in relation to space rather than simply functionally distinct determinants of conflict. The problem of sea-power is not simply one of tactical assertion, but rather transforms the essence of political existence irreversibly. The abandonment of a terrestrial mode of political orientation changes everything, and the consequences are inestimably dangerous. And yet, as with the liberal exploitation of Hobbes' 'barely visible crack', Schmitt is appearing to suggest that the power of a maritime, universal mode of political (dis-) orientation is irresistible. Arguably, the starry-eyed appeal of Mahan to German geopolitical theorists of the inter-war period makes exactly this point.

Intriguingly, Schmitt and Vogel were both coming to the same conclusion – that, in Murphy's words, 'the nation-state as such, which [Vogel] said had arisen as a specific response to the conditions of European geography and the small continent's multiplicity of languages and ethnic-cultural groups, had exhausted its utility'.[101] But such a conclusion was less pregnant with danger for Vogel than for Schmitt. For Vogel, as for many ambitious geopoliticians in Germany, the challenge to achieve a spatial revolution was a challenge to be embraced, and an opportunity to break the shackles of Germany's geopolitical disadvantages. For Schmitt, however, such a move represented the challenge of a radically unstable, rootless and dangerously universal maritime mode of

---

[99] W. Vogel, *Das neue Europa, und seine historisch-geographischen Grundlagen*, Bonn: Schroeder (1925), p. v.

[100] Of course, any such acknowledgement of geographically determined lines of conflict would tend to contradict Schmitt's basic function on conflict as a purely political expression of sovereign will.

[101] Murphy, *The Heroic Earth*, p. 122.

existence that appeared to offer few prospects for order and containment. The dismantling of a Europe of states to be replaced by the confrontation of some spatially freewheeling counterpoise to Anglo-American maritime power was, frankly, a ghastly prospect. And yet that dismantling was, in Schmitt's analysis, an unavoidable fact of the present.

There are clear parallels between this understanding of geographic history, and Schmitt's account of the history of the sovereign state under conceptual challenge from liberalism. He depicts an ideal-conceptual notion of a static, ordered and comprehensive idea of the state. In the first instance, this is an idea derived from the theory of Thomas Hobbes and rooted in an anthropomorphic ideal of a decisionist sovereign. In the present case, it is a state that possesses a specifically terrestrial under-standing of the basis and limits of its spatial existence. In both instances, the static ideal is challenged by a progressively destabilising force that, in itself, offers no apparent hope for the creation of a new order. The sovereignty of the state is eroded by the political assertion of the individual subject. The terrestrial basis of the state is undermined by the emergence of a radically decontextualised assertion of bare maritime power. For Schmitt, these interrelated processes are, simply put, tragic.

Schmitt's critique of the *dialectic* or *dialogism* of land and sea is therefore part of his wider critique of the intellectual and historical processes of modernity. For him, the loss of a terrestrial base is of particular signifi-cance because of the sheer importance he places on it in the act of appropriation and the formulation of order. Territory is as close as we come to a foundation in Schmitt's thought, and the idea of trying to situate real politics without it seems absurd and fanciful. The spirit of the ocean might be detestable for all sorts of real and immediate reasons. But in its essence, this critique is exactly the same as Schmitt's critique of liberal individualism. It is a critique of the way that the intellectual currents of modernity have created a situation in which, to borrow a phrase from a quite different stable of thought, 'all that is solid melts into air'.[102] Or, in Schmitt's immediate context, into water. It is a part, then, of a more fundamental critique of the experience of time and the erosion of any sense of permanence in modernity. The task now, then, is to uncover this perspective on history a little more directly.

---

[102] K. Marx and F. Engels, *The Communist Manifesto* (trans. S. Moore), London: Penguin Classics (2002) p. 223.

5   Acceleration and restraint

I have a methodology that is peculiar to me: the phenomena that occur to me, so to speak, from things [*Stoff*] that I think about, and not from pre-existing criteria. One can call that phenomenological, but I myself prefer to avoid such general methodological questions. They tend to go on for ever.[1]

These intertwined stories of the dissolution of the state and the order of states are of inestimable importance in understanding Schmitt's personal intellectual and emotive response to the political world around him. They skewed his reading of contemporary phenomena, heightened his sense of the importance of the current age, and provoked in him a curiously energetic pessimism in contemplating the future. Unlike other epochal changes, Schmitt sees the twentieth century as dominated by the preordained collapse of the existing order, but without the evident advent of a new age. Any attempt to read Schmitt as a theorist of the present must, it would seem, weigh the effects of this intense spirit of *fin de siècle*.

Moreover, it would appear that any productive attempt to 'think with' Schmitt about normative order and the future of the political must share this fear of the end. The whole insistence on the logical priority and necessity of enmity feeds off such apprehension. Naturally, there may be many foundations for such a fear, and the basis of Schmitt's own concerns are hotly contested. It seems most likely, as argued in Chapter 3, that the language of Antichrist is more than mere metaphor, and represents a genuinely (if idiosyncratic) Christological historical framework. But to a very great extent, the historical frame that Schmitt produces would be equally relevant if the fear of dissolution were motivated by a commitment to purely human phenomena.[2] Schmitt's analysis of history is all about

---

[1] C. Schmitt, 'Gespräch über den Partisanen: Carl Schmitt und Joachim Schickel', in *Staat, Großraum, Nomos: Arbeiten aus den Jahren 1916–1969* (ed. G. Maschke), Berlin: Duncker and Humblot, pp. 619–42 (p. 621).

[2] In various places Schmitt addresses such motives as the maintenance of cultural difference and the maintenance of a *seriousness* to life.

how to mediate between the formlessness of total violence, and the formlessness that would ensue were there no violence whatsoever.

It is worth stressing, too, that Schmitt is clearly animated by the fear that both such dissolute states are entirely possible. In other words, he is a world away from the normative indifference of those who regard the system of sovereign states as here to stay. It would be foolish to seize on Schmitt's apparent assumption of the political as immutable evidence that he fits best as some bedfellow of international relations (IR) realists. Firstly, for Schmitt the state is nothing more than a temporary historical accident that will surely be swept away like every previous nomic order. But Schmitt's precise political concern is with the interrelationship of nomic orders and social institutions (the state, international law, cultures of rights) with the prior question of the political. Within orders, the concerns of realists certainly resonate with Schmitt. But ideas such as statecraft and the national interest take on a very different hue when they are related to this ultimate ratio of avoiding final dissolution.

As we have seen, Schmitt's depiction of the story of the modern state system follows a highly peculiar path. He uses fully formed theoretical accounts both of the state (as derived from Hobbes) and of international law (as derived from an idealised account of the achievement of Westphalia) as a hook on which to hang his historical narrative. Schmitt's history of modernity is more a *theoretical* history, and less a history of concrete events. Evidence that fails to fit Schmitt's account of the development of the modern state is largely ignored. In short, we are asked to accept these theoretical formulations as adequate synonyms for the concrete reality of these phenomena in their 'original' form. The story of the state and of international law is therefore one of deviation from original purity – a story of the loss of the vitality of that original moment of puncture.

The transmogrification of Hobbes' theory of the state into the concrete reality of the state, and the reading of international practice as synonymous with the professed standards of European international law, are the two key points of connection. But there are many other ways in which Schmitt excessively ties his own theoretical understanding together to historical reality in explaining progression away from these starting points. It is a point well made by Scheuerman: '… any attempt to deduce complex, real-life institutional trends from alleged contradictions of a particular intellectual system should meet with a healthy dose of skepticism. Far too often, Schmitt assumes that history accords with political and legal theory: the internal conceptual limits of liberal theory explain liberalism's real-life political ills.'[3]

---

[3] W. Scheuerman, *Liberal Democracy and the Social Acceleration of Time*, Baltimore: Johns Hopkins University Press (2004), pp. 119–20.

Although Scheuerman's precise concern is with the way that Schmitt reads the historical effect of liberalism, the point can be made more generally in relation to Schmitt's historical reasoning. He assumes that the intellectual foundations of the modern state have *the* decisive effect in how the state fares historically. Moreover, he extends this intellectual-foundational story to the international setting, and assumes that theoretically consistent pathologies are unfolding in world politics. Historical contingency appears to be something Schmitt can only account for at a revolutionary moment – i.e. in the foundation or destruction of a *Nomos*.

This manner of looking at the past immediately raises the question of *pace*. What precise events and processes increase the *rate* at which we move away from the original unities? Conversely, what is it that slows the processes of unravelling? By framing political actors so heavily in a predetermined logical setting, Schmitt is forced to measure their actions against the wider narrative of decline and dissolution to which he is now committed. In so far as we may talk about personified sovereigns, their world-historical status is referable to the extent to which they slow the logical disentanglement of sovereignty itself. Schmitt's method of historical reasoning elevates acceleration and restraint as important ways for evaluating real events against the wider historical framework. Change within the existing system can ultimately be read in terms of whether it hastens or restrains the logical disentanglement of the system as a whole.

This chapter aims to evaluate Schmitt's wider understanding of the relationship between (temporary) orders of the political, and the experience of time. How can these structuring principles of the political be reconciled to the survival of enmity as the basic human condition? How does acceleration in nomic orders affect Schmitt's underlying understanding of politics as immutable conflict? What is it that makes modern social acceleration of time so much more dangerous, in Schmitt's estimation, than previous shifts in social order? What is so special about the experience of time in late modernity when viewed from a Schmittian perspective? History, it is argued, is about far more for Schmitt than merely the concrete experience of agonal politics. The changing experience of time has done enormous damage to the sorts of foundations on which Schmitt roots his understanding of the political – territory, monopoly over truth, representative myths. Schmitt's fear, in other words, is that the collapse of the Eurocentric system of states might not be the starting point for a new order:

The most terrible transformation of the world lies in [the possibility of] a bewildering expansion of power in which things become certain, audible [*hörbar*] and clear [*vernehmbar*] that [nevertheless] surpass the capacity of our physical senses;

audible and therefore authoritative [*besitzbar*]. A new concept of property or, even more than this: the rule of functionality [*die Beherrschung von Funktionen*]; cuius regio, eius economia, now: cuius economia, eius regio. That is the new Nomos of the Earth; no more Nomos.[4]

Historical order and 'slow time'

At first glance, Schmitt's step from ideal theory into history appears to present a paradox or an internal contradiction. The immutable essence of the political is all about divisions and confrontations that are defined by the fact that they escape any normative order. Yet the survival of political dynamic over time relies upon structures of order that can be replicated. The concept of *Nomos* appears blind to the raw reality of the exceptional situation. As Alberto Moreiras puts it, 'Schmitt's position in *The Nomos of the Earth* seems to contradict his earlier position on the political successfully: the notion of a *Nomos* of the earth, of an order of the political, accomplishes, perhaps against Schmitt's own will, a deconstruction of his notion of the political'.[5] For Moreiras, this juxtaposition of the theoretical essence of the political and its historical containment in a *Nomos* leaves a glaring question that Schmitt refused to answer: 'Do we prefer to uphold the notion of a nomic order, or do we prefer to abide by a savage, anomic notion of the political? Is there a choice?'[6] It is, of course, a false question. Presumably, we would all (Schmitt included) choose to live in a stable normative order in which the possibility of 'real physical killing' is at its most contained. Schmitt does not contend that we should or do actively choose to live politically. His critics, to be sure, are quick to paint in him a celebration of violence, instability and perpetual aggression. But in fact, the political is hardly a matter of choice. It is an ever present possibility, the escape from which would amount to the end of history, the end of all truth, the end of belief, and the end of all seriousness. It is only here that Schmitt becomes a partisan in defence of the continuing possibility of Schmittian politics. What for some would amount to paradise on earth is, for Schmitt, the most ghastly prospect.

Schmitt does not offer a choice between anomic politics and the notion of a nomic order. The institutions of concrete political life contain political diversity in two ways. Firstly, Schmitt maintains, every system for the organisation and containment of politics has been predicated on a

[4] C. Schmitt, *Glossarium: Aufzeichnungen der Jahre 1947–1951*, Berlin: Duncker and Humblot (1991), 16 July 1948, p. 179

[5] A. Moreiras, 'A God without Sovereignty. Political *Jouissance*: The Passive Decision', *The New Centennial Review* 4:3 (2004), 71–108 (p. 82).

[6] *Ibid.*

hard-headed understanding that war and division is a normal and unavoidable part of life. The *complexio oppositorum* of medieval Europe, and the *jus publicum Europaeum* that succeeded it, merely remedied the worst dangers of the political, and refracted all political energy through a focussed lens. Schmitt not only maintains that anarchy and law are not mutually exclusive; his entire depiction of anomic politics mediated through institutions relies, it seems, on the basic contention that real law always derives from anarchical foundations.[7]

But secondly, whatever the social and political institutions that coalesce to create a *Nomos*, it is only ever a temporary arrangement. It therefore maintains political diversity temporally, in the fact of its own fragility. Every ordering of the political is a contingent act, and every concrete structure of order has no basis other than an inertia drawn from its foundational moment. Yet without principles of order *of some kind*, how can the political obtain traction in the concrete historical world? Or obversely, how can the dynamic of enmity encounter sufficient friction to avoid a slide into formless violence? The real meaning of Schmitt's famous contention that 'the concept of the state presupposes the concept of the political' comes to the fore once again.[8] How do we square the circle between these apparently timeless orders, and the truly timeless resistance of the political to any attempt permanently to impose order? How can the structures of order seem so strong, when their most basic attribute is mortality?

Put another way, Moreiras is correct to focus on the apparently irreconcilable tension between Schmitt's genuine commitment to the maintenance of the state system, and his belief in the immutability of violent politics. But he is wrong to expect or wish for a *logical* resolution of this tension. The tension is vital to the whole theory of politics as Schmitt presents it. Resolution of the tension would spell the end of history. Structures of the political cannot be so solid as to exclude the possibility

---

[7] What Schmitt demands, in other words, is an understanding of law that is not positivist. Although the link does not appear to have any direct basis, it is interesting to note how much Schmitt's understanding of the origins of habitual international law under conditions of anarchy has in common with the English School of IR. Schmitt could surely have subscribed to Martin Wight's view that international law arises out of the 'habitual intercourse of independent communities', even if he would have rejected the notion that the normative development of international law away from these origins might be desirable. M. Wight, 'Western Values in International Relations', in H. Butterfield and M. Wight (eds.), *Diplomatic Investigations: Essays in the Theory of International Relations*, London: George Allen and Unwin (1966), pp. 89–131 (p. 97). I am grateful to Doug Bulloch for sharing his insights on these points of interconnection.

[8] C. Schmitt, *The Concept of the Political* (trans. E. Kennedy), Cambridge, MA: MIT Press (1996), p. 19.

of their own demise. Yet at the same time, these structures must be *experienced* as permanent, or else politics will become wholly formless. Without the persistence of ideas such as state, international law, Christian princes, Roman Empire etc., the distinction between public and private cannot survive.

What we have in Schmitt, then, is a rather extreme juxtaposition of eternalist and presentist perspectives. There is no *necessary* contradiction in Schmitt's mind between the inescapability of violent politics, and the success of broadly normative orders that drive towards a containment of that violence. All of his deep theoretical analysis of the meaning of the political is aimed at distilling permanent rules to describe something essential about the human condition. On the other hand, Schmitt seeks to describe the various concrete phenomena through which man has created and experienced these timeless phenomena. Indeed, Schmitt's description of the universal Roman church as one such institution is apt, since at times Schmitt's attempts to describe this relationship resembles the theological account of the gap between transcendental Christian truth and the church as a human institution.[9] The concrete institutions of human life provide a barrier against the universal, and create a forum in which political existence does not have to engage directly with universal questions.

Principles of order therefore obtain an important but ultimately ambiguous place in Schmitt's theory. They must be ambiguous from a theoretical point of view, because they are not the products of reason, but products of historical events. But they are also ambiguous historically, because they possess the shadow of permanence, whilst remaining temporary. A principle of order only has the capacity to achieve order in so far as it is experienced as *the way* of ordering divisions. If the contours of an order are constantly and effectively challenged, then the order obviously fails to contain political dynamics, and is not, therefore, an order. It is essential that, from generation to generation, the institutions of order and authority are viewed as the natural order of things – as a given. Yet, if these institutions were, in fact, indestructible, this would preclude the

---

[9] In his diaries Schmitt remarks that:

The most important word [in the work] of Thomas Hobbes remains: Jesus is the Christ. The power of this sentence is that if he [Christ] appears on the edge of the intellectual construction, that means that he is also something external to the system of belief. This deportation [*Abschiebung*] is a characteristic of Christ that seems to be an analogous forerunner to Dostoevsky's Grand Inquisitor. Hobbes discussed and intellectually grounded the things that the Grand Inquisitor does: Christ's effect in the social and political spheres is rendered harmless; the anarchistic Christianity in which he remains in the background as an indispensable source of legitimacy. *Glossarium*, 23 May 1949, p. 243.

possibility of another, future point of rupture. As such, it would lead to historical stasis, and diminishing political returns within a reductive and *overly* stable order. Schmitt's orders seem to require an imperceptible but real form of dynamism.

Schmitt's study of the state and the system of international law confirms this impression of permanence. His European state is clearly the product of a convulsive historical accident. Of itself, the state could be described as a highly sophisticated way of securing the political community, providing a formidable machine for the maintenance of political authority, and a clear platform for the expression of enmity externally. His study of Hobbes enhances his own reading of the state in *The Concept of the Political* and *Political Theology*, emphasising its contingent nature as a response to concrete challenges. In the following centuries, the state dominates the exercise of politics to such an extent that organised human existence without the state becomes virtually unimaginable. Civil wars become a struggle *for* the attributes of sovereignty, and therefore uphold the nomic order. Indeed, it is precisely this impression of permanence that makes Schmitt's separation of the political from the state seem so radical. So great was the state's air of inevitability, most political theory had assumed it to be the originator of politics per se. At first inadvertently, Schmitt's study of the separation of concept of the state and the political necessarily involved a deeper study of the experience of time in the latter.

Motion is a central tension in Schmitt's study of the state. History must be dynamic. But there is an imperative to restrain that movement within a known normative order. It is of great importance to Schmitt whether history is fast or slow. As we have seen, he is far more comfortable thinking about the past in terms of moments of rupture. The ideal, for Schmitt, is a knife-edge interruption of the existing order – the revolutionary moment. It is a sense of social change that is somehow analogous to the earthquake. The tension between the existing order and the demands of the time grows unnoticed, until there is a sudden and drastic reformulation of the principles of order. This way of conceiving of change has the advantage for Schmitt that the establishment of order can be conceived as a moment of command and a product of political determination rather than as a flimsy product of impersonal social processes. Characteristically for Schmitt, it allows a view of the institutions of political life from the top down – from 'the realm of the powers'.[10]

Theoretically, the moment of rupture cannot be captured. The whole point is that it is a concrete, accidental point of departure. It does not have

---

[10] J. Taubes, *The Political Theology of Paul* (trans. D. Hollander), Stanford: Stanford University Press (2004), p. 51.

antecedents. And the potential for such revolutionary moments is vital for Schmitt's hopes for political renewal. But time *within* orders can be theorised historically according to its pace. Indeed, as Schmitt presents them, the primary historical purpose of political ordering principles appears to be to contain and restrain the dynamics of enmity within a manageable framework. Among states, contention and warfare become more limited affairs, and do not escalate towards absolute heights. Concerns remain partial, limited and specific. The existence of the order itself keeps absolute and universal questions at bay. For as long as enmity is contained in a system of mutuality, theological questions (that is, challenges as to meaning) are rendered harmless.

The immediate effect of an order of the political is therefore to allow a dynamic around questions of truth and authority that are real, but nevertheless possess a safe degree of irony. The system itself suggests a certain dynamic, and removes urges towards any final resolution. The system allows for productive and dynamic tension, without instigating a headlong rush towards logical (or theo-logical) resolution. This is true, of course, of the complex dynamics of medieval Europe. And, as we have noted previously, the imperative of slow time and the neutralisation of debates over absolute truth are a key part of Schmitt's recourse to Hobbes. What Schmitt seems to require, in other words, are complicated tensions in which concrete political concerns collide with truth claims in a dynamic but ultimately irreconcilable mêlée.

The only possibility of reconciliation – of a final resolution of the slow historical contretemps – is an interruption from the outside. An act of revelation, the foundation of a new order, or the coming of apocalypse. Slow time is therefore predicated on a latent understanding that the current order is not total. That it does not and cannot contain every historical possibility. As Ojakangas and Meier have both convincingly illustrated, it is this insistence on the removal of final historical possibilities from the imminent experience of order that leads Schmitt to his ultimate rejection of modern/progressive philosophies of history. Rationalist histories seek to resolve tensions on the basis of an assumption that historical outcomes can be determined rationally from within the existing order. For Schmitt, such an assumption incorrectly excludes the possibility that either unforeseen revolutionary events, or divine acts of revelation, will interrupt.[11]

---

[11] See M. Ojakangas, *A Philosophy of Concrete Life: Carl Schmitt and the Political Thought of Late Modernity*, Bern: Peter Lang (2006), pp. 205–11; and Meier *The Lesson of Carl Schmitt: Four Chapters on the Distinction between Philosophical Theology and Political Philosophy* (trans. M. Brainard), Chicago: University of Chicago Press (1998), p. 15. Ojakangas disputes Meier's assertion that, for Schmitt, this latent externality must ultimately be contained in a Christian idea of revelation. For Ojakangas, Schmitt rejects

Modern epochs

Schmitt's emphasis on time as delay is tied intimately to the figure of the Katechon. As we have explored previously, Schmitt uses this Pauline term rather broadly to describe the historical effect of certain kinds of political actors. Consciously or otherwise, there are forces or individuals in each age that have the effect of restraining the emergence of the Antichrist. Following the account given in 2 Thessalonians, Schmitt equates the realm of the Antichrist on earth to a hubristic period of peace in which all meaningful difference is eliminated. This is a period of total commensurability, in which it will no longer be possible to make meaningful distinctions on the basis of morality, aesthetics, religion, economics or any other set of criteria. Whether or not we wish to read this as a genuinely theological or merely allegorical position, it is the historical end point against which Schmitt gears his political thought as a whole.

Even before developing the specific historical critiques expressed in *Land und Meer* and *The Leviathan in the State Theory of Thomas Hobbes*, Schmitt developed a detailed and politically pregnant criticism of the modern experience of time as movement towards a neutral centre. There is something distinctive about the way that history is experienced through the prism of modernity that attempts to eliminate the complexities and tensions Schmitt regards as so important to the era of Christological time. The manifestations of this acceleration are extremely familiar from Schmitt's work, and broadly equate to all of the programmatic aspects of liberalism. The pursuit of peace, the reinstitution of laws of *jus ad bellum*, the marginalisation of religion, the creation of a positivist system of law and a generalised apolitical sentiment are all dangerous evidence that world politics is structurally oriented towards the pursuit of neutrality and the acceleration of social time.

Schmitt first gave detailed consideration to neutralisation as a historically problematic process as early as 1929 in a short essay entitled 'The Age of Neutralizations and Depoliticizations'.[12] As presentist as ever, Schmitt grapples with the historical process that has generated what he regards as the present malaise of European politics. 'Our present situation', Schmitt argues, 'can be understood only as the consequence of the last centuries of European development; it completes and transcends

Hegel because he rejects the historical force of events that lie outside our realm of knowledge. For Meier, Schmitt rejects Hegel because his philosophy of history denies the transcendence of God. Both agree, however, on the importance of Schmitt's reservation of an unknowable zone of historical indeterminacy.

[12] C. Schmitt, 'The Age of Neutralizations and Depoliticizations' (trans. M. Konzett and J. P. McCormick), *Telos* 96 (Summer 1993), 130–42.

specific European ideas and demonstrates in one enormous climax the core of modern European history.'[13] He sets out to trace 'the stages in which the European mind has altered over the last four centuries', suggesting that concrete human affairs are mediated by a particular central sphere of intellectual interpretation.[14] On a century-by-century basis, Schmitt argues that the previous 400 years had been shaped in turn by theological, metaphysical, humanitarian-moral and, finally, economic modes of mental existence. In the twentieth century, Schmitt argues, technology is supplanting economics as the 'central sphere' of 'intellectual life'.[15]

The power of these central intellectual spheres lies in their ability to provide an abstract point of convergence. Prefiguring the themes he developed in his study of Hobbes, Schmitt argues that the seventeenth-century turn from theology to metaphysics was motivated by the desire to find a zone of neutrality in which the violent disputes of theology would be avoided.[16] Hobbes' creation of a neutral category of total political authority was one manifestation of the metaphysical attempt to create neutral intellectual categories. 'Following the hopeless theological disputes and struggles of the sixteenth century, Europeans sought a neutral sphere in which there would be no conflict and they could reach common agreement through debates and exchange of opinion.'[17] The *motive* of avoiding theology 'because it was controversial' is the central point. There was a common enterprise 'to find minimum agreement and common premises allowing for the possibility of security, clarity, prudence and peace'. Metaphysics was the first attempt to posit a 'concept of truth' around which all interests could coalesce.[18]

Despite themselves, all attempts to create a neutral sphere have failed. In Schmitt's eyes, it is a misconceived effort, since it mistakenly posits the idea that a genuine, incontestable common truth can be established through the means of the central sphere. Whereas metaphysics began as an effort to establish a sphere of neutrality, the means of metaphysics soon became the basis of contesting claims, and the essence of new and more dramatic conflict. It is a process echoed by Schmitt's assertion in *The*

---

[13] Schmitt, 'Neutralizations', p. 131.   [14] *Ibid.*

[15] *Ibid.*, pp. 131–4. Schmitt had first developed his critique of the contemporary mythicisation of technology in 1916 in a commentary on Theodor Däubler's poem *Das Nordlicht*, in which he drew a link between liberalism, the myth of technology and the idea of the Antichrist.

[16] 'The transition from the theology of the sixteenth century to the metaphysics of the seventeenth century (which is not only metaphysically but also scientifically the greatest age of Europe – the heroic age of occidental rationalism) is as clear and distinct as any unique historical occurrence.' *Ibid.*, p. 132.

[17] *Ibid.*, p. 137.   [18] *Ibid.*

Concept of the Political that any substantive dispute (whether religious, moral, aesthetic, economic etc.) may become *political* if it provokes sufficiently deep divisions among groups of men. And as each mechanism for the pursuit of neutrality breaks down under the weight of its own hubris, it is replaced by another sphere that claims to possess the path to a common and neutral truth. Thus metaphysics was replaced by 'vulgarisation' of eighteenth-century moral philosophy, which was in turn replaced by Marxian economics.[19]

'The Age of Neutralizations and Depoliticizations' is an important early statement of Schmitt's critique of the blind modern pursuit of principles of neutrality. In large part, it is a critique of (what Schmitt holds to be) the erroneous idea that truth and knowledge claims can be settled in an apolitical direction. It possesses the same sort of ambivalence as Schmitt's political writing of the same period. On the one hand Schmitt despairs of the frequent modern beliefs that all truth is somehow immanent, and that all tension may be resolved intellectually.[20] Such belief in the universal truth of derivative claims provokes the sort of extremity, violence and disorder that, for Schmitt, always accompanies a loss of clear-headed acceptance of the political condition. The 'secret law' of the age of neutralisations is that 'the most terrible war is pursued in the name of peace, the most terrible oppression only in the name of freedom, the most terrible inhumanity only in the name of humanity'.[21] Yet, on the other hand, the fact that every sphere in the pursuit of this neutral centre rapidly breaks down is evidence of the futility of trying to posit a neutral anti-politics. The pursuit of a neutral core may be damaging, but it is ultimately delusional. As with most of Schmitt's work prior to 1933, the fear is not that neutralisation will succeed, but of the damage that will result from attempts to achieve it.

Indeed, in 1929 Schmitt is still at pains to point out that he is not arguing for some progression through various stages towards the achievement of neutrality. He 'speak[s] not of human culture as a whole, nor of the rhythm of world history' and maintains that 'the three successive stages of the changing central spheres are conceived neither as a continuous line of "progress" upwards nor the opposite'.[22] Indeed, 'The Age of Neutralizations' is rather optimistic about the potential for European renewal just as soon as Schmitt's analysis results in a general awareness of 'the pluralism of spiritual life' and recognition that 'the central sphere

[19] Schmitt, 'Neutralizations', p. 133.
[20] On Schmitt's reading of the modern shift from transcendent to immanent conceptions of metaphysics, see Ojakangas, *Concrete Life*, pp. 32–9.
[21] Schmitt, 'Neutralizations', p. 142.   [22] *Ibid.*, p. 132.

cannot be neutral ground'.[23] The idea that technology is achieving a neutral sphere results, he argues, from a confusion of the spirit of technicity with the fact of technology itself.[24] Technicity simply represents the same spirit of neutrality that has accompanied every other sphere. 'The spirit of technicity ... is still spirit ... It is perhaps something gruesome, but not itself technical and mechanical.'[25] And as such, technicity will fail in its drive towards a neutral centre.[26] In the final analysis, then, attempts to erect a mythology of technology as a neutral sphere are bound to fail.

The age of technology

If the spirit of technicity is just another false hope of neutrality, Schmitt nevertheless identifies certain apocalyptic dangers in the age of technology, each of which has very concrete political manifestations. From a very partial intellectual perspective, Schmitt is concerned that the spirit of technicity threatens the conceptual and intellectual primacy of Europe. Technicity is a product of the outside, turned against its European heritage. 'The Russians have taken the European nineteenth century at its word, understood its core ideas and drawn the ultimate conclusions from its cultural premises.'[27] In other words, although technicity is a false god like all the others, it is the first non-, or anti-European, epoch. As Duncan Kelly has argued generally of Schmitt in his writings prior to 1933, 'the threats [Schmitt] perceived from the Soviet Union were twofold: *first*, he feared the general Russian spirit of anti-authoritarianism, exemplified in both Dostoyevsky and Bakunin, and *second*, the Soviet Union's wholehearted embrace of technicity as ideology, represented to Schmitt its

---

[23] *Ibid.*, p. 142.

[24] See *ibid.*, pp. 140–1. Schmitt's argument here clearly prefigures his criticism in *The Leviathan in the State Theory of Thomas Hobbes: Meaning and Failure of a Political Symbol* (trans. G. Schwab), Westport, CT: Greenwood Press (1996), of the confusion between the concrete fact of the state as a machine, and the generalised and progressive notion of mechanisation as a rationally objective, neutralising phenomenon. See above, pp. 44–5.

[25] Schmitt, 'Neutralizations', p. 141.

[26] For more on Schmitt's ideas on the age of technicity see below, pp. 113–17. In drawing the gap between technology as a concrete fact of the modern age, and a Russo-centric 'spirit of technicity', Schmitt is clearly claiming back technology as a means at the disposal of political actors. This is not the same, however, as a valorisation or aestheticisation of technology for its own sake – a view misleadingly ascribed to Schmitt by several of his detractors. See for instance J. Herf, *Reactionary Modernism: Technology, Culture, and Politics in Weimar and the Third Reich*, Cambridge: Cambridge University Press (1986), pp. 118–20; and R. Wolin, 'Carl Schmitt: The Conservative Revolutionary Habitus and the Aesthetics of Horror', *Political Theory* 20:3 (1992), 424–47.

[27] Schmitt, 'Neutralizations', p. 131.

irrationality.[28] This early critique of Russia therefore prefigures much of Schmitt's more developed contemplation about the historical fate of the state. It emphasises the inadvertent significance of the present moment as the point at which nomic dissolution and intellectual neutralisation have reached their apotheosis. It heaps praise on the 'heroic age of occidental rationalism' and the achievements of Descartes, Hobbes, Spinoza and Grotius, whilst simultaneously tracing the unforeseen historical effect of their attempt to neutralise truth claims. And perhaps, above all, it displays an instinctive but theoretically undeveloped Eurocentrism. Schmitt mourns the end of a European intellectual and nomic order. He calls on Europeans to shake off 'the spell of cultural decline', and to renounce 'the security of the *status quo*' in a 'new political revolution'.[29] Yet the basis of this hope vested in Europe appears emotional rather than programmatic, since Schmitt recognises that there can be no return to the golden age of the sixteenth century, nor beyond to the order of the medieval Roman church. On the historical route out of the present, Schmitt concludes, 'every genuine rebirth seeking to return to some original principle, every genuine *ritornar al principio*, every return to pure, uncorrupted nature appears as cultural or social nothingness to the comfort and ease of the *status quo*. It grows silently and in darkness, and a historian or sociologist would recognise only nothingness in its initial phases.'[30] He refuses to conclude that the intellectual games of technology *actually* result in historical acceleration, despite their giving that appearance. Indeed, there is so much in the political manifestations of the modern age that tends towards the loss of quasi-foundations and the acceleration of time. Liberalism promotes an intensified and ironic individualism that refuses to engage with the concrete political order. Socialism embraces a deterministic idea of economics as the shared goal of humanity. As ideologies of life, both political models present a false ideal of historical convergence. The myth of mechanisation has 'turned the belief in miracles and an afterlife – a religion without intermediary stages – into a religion of technical miracles, human achievements and the domination of nature'.[31] All progress and all truth appear to be within the grasp of living men.

---

[28] D. Kelly, *The State of the Political: Conceptions of Politics and the State in the Thought of Max Weber, Carl Schmitt and Franz Neumann*, Oxford: Oxford University Press (2003), p. 212. Schmitt reads Dostoevsky's fable of the Grand Inquisitor from *The Brothers Karamazov* as a typically Russian expression of anti-authoritarianism. 'For [Dostoevsky's] basically anarchistic (and thereby, also, atheistic) instincts, every political power was something wicked and inhuman' (C. Schmitt, *Römischer Katholizismus und politische Form* (2nd edn), Cologne: Klett–Cotta (1925), p. 54).

[29] Schmitt, 'Neutralizations', pp. 140–1.   [30] *Ibid.*, p. 141.

[31] J. E. McCormick, 'Introduction to Schmitt's "The Age of Neutralizations and Depoliticisations"', *Telos* 96 (1993), 19–30 (p. 126).

Whereas the logical corollary of a belief in miracles and the divine was an impulse to obedience and the majesty of authority, technicity creates its own standards of legitimacy according to quantifiable outputs. The essence of the modern age, into which the European state has been sucked, is the remorseless elevation of rationality: 'As someone once said (rather crudely), in Kant's system God appears as a "parasite of ethics". Every word in his *Critique of Pure Reason* – critique, pure and reason – is polemically directed against dogma, metaphysics and ontology.'[32] But unlike the ages of metaphysics, moral philosophy, or even (to a lesser extent) economics, the primacy of technology threatens an inversion of questions of means and ends. Ironically for someone who would remain silent on the horrors of the Holocaust, Schmitt was acutely aware of the dangers that might result from conflation of moral fervour and technical means.[33] 'If humanitarian-moral progress is still expected by many today from the perfection of technology, it is because technology is magically linked to morality on the somewhat naïve assumption that the splendid array of contemporary technology will be used only as intended, i.e. sociologically, and that they themselves will control these frightful weapons and wield this monstrous power.'[34] The only politically certain thing about technology is that 'every strong politics will make use of it'.[35] Quite aside from its status as a source of myth, technology is historically significant for the way in which it alters the exercise of power. It opens up new possibilities in several directions, but the two that concerned Schmitt the most were changes in the capacity for violence, and changes to the meaning of space.

It might seem a rather prosaic fascination compared to a sociologically inspired critique of myth, but there is a case for saying that Schmitt's concern for the violent potential of modern weaponry trumped all his more abstract concerns. The fact that modern warfare increasingly involves the efficient slaughter of thousands, or potentially millions, is a

---

[32] Schmitt, 'Neutralizations', p. 133.

[33] Although many would regard it as perverse to cite Schmitt as a prescient critic of processes that resulted in the Holocaust, there are clear parallels between his analysis of the 'myth of technology' and sociological analyses of the Holocaust that look to a combination of rationality, myth and technology as a causal factor (see especially Z. Baumann, *Modernity and the Holocaust*, Cambridge: Polity Press (1991)). With their shared debt to Karl Löwith, it is striking the degree to which Schmitt's critique of technicity resonates with Jacques Ellul's sociological-anarchist analysis of modernity in *The Technological Society* (written 1964), thirty-five years later. Schmitt is clearly seized with the problematic that results from Ellul's observation that 'that which desacralizes a given reality, itself in turn becomes the new sacred reality'. See D. J. Fasching, *The Thought of Jacques Ellul: A Systematic Exposition* (New York: Edward Mellen Press (1981), p. 35, and J. Ellul, *The Technological Society*, London: Jonathan Cape (1965).

[34] Schmitt, 'Neutralizations', p. 139.   [35] *Ibid.*, p. 141.

very obvious challenge to a theorist whose avowed model of international law stems from a period of cavalry cabinet wars. Schmitt was well aware that the simple rejoinder to his nostalgia for the *jus publicum Europaeum* was to point out that eighteenth-century statesmen did not have access to missiles; machine guns; or chemical, biological and nuclear weapons. Of necessity, he considered the stability of the quasi-normative order of European interstate law as deriving from the (contingent) spatial order, rather than from a (deliberate) respect for the principle of *pacta sunt servanda*.[36] In part, Europe sustained a slow, contained, limited system of states and form of warfare because its leaders lacked the means to do anything else. Or, put another way, the fact that modern weaponry offers a whole new horizon of *victory* places the conscious restraint of statesmen into question with wholly unprecedented urgency.

It is not only the means of destruction, but also the territorial horizon that shift as a result of technological advance. The changes in spatial consciousness that Schmitt depicts in *Land und Meer* are intertwined with technological enablement. New ship design opens the oceans, aircraft open the skies, and telecommunications establish abstract new spatial connections. In contrast to previous attempts to find a neutral core through moral reasoning, technology does not come up against state boundaries, but rather lends itself to their transcendence. In this sense, it is technology as a concrete phenomenon rather than as myth that lends itself to historical acceleration. Technology destabilises the present nomic order not because it provides an avenue to the consensual elimination of divisions, but because it makes *these* divisions seem arcane and unworkable. In true Schmittian style, it is the concrete phenomenon that marks the most dramatic change.

The fact that late modernity provides such drastic means of annihilation does not, of itself, alter the basis of political calculus. Weapons alone are merely the expression of political calculus, and cannot be considered inherently dangerous. Writing in the 1960s, when the full potential of weapons of mass destruction had come to fruition, Schmitt was still able to write, somewhat optimistically, 'it is not in fact the means of destruction that annihilate, but men who kill other men by these means. The English philosopher Thomas Hobbes grasped the heart of this process in the seventeenth century already and formulated it in full precision, though at that time weapons were still relatively harmless.'[37] Instead, the advent

---

[36] See, for instance, C. Schmitt, *The Nomos of the Earth in the International Law of the* Jus Publicum Europaeum (trans. G. Ulmen), New York: Telos Press (2004), p. 148.

[37] C. Schmitt, *Theorie des Partisanen: Zwischenbemerkung zum Begriff des Politischen*, Berlin: Duncker and Humblot (1963), pp. 94–5.

of modern weaponry makes it more important than ever that the real essence of the political is fully recognised in its unromantic clarity. For Schmitt, if we continue the modern trend of pursuing some moral-rational fervour for homogeneity with the admixture of advanced weapons technology, it will not be long before the 'work of annihilation [*Vernichtungswerk*]' will begin.[38]

Schmitt is always torn between his critique of the abstractions wrought by the modern state form, and the undeniable success of the state form in solidifying agonal politics. It is almost as if the state has restrained time despite itself. And Schmitt cannot be anything other than ambivalent about the achievements of Westphalia. For all that the historical convergences of modernity are of concern, Schmitt never loses sight of the fact that the state marked a concrete historical barrier to a moment of total dissolution. Of all historical moments, Europe in the sixteenth and early seventeenth centuries marks the sum of all Schmitt's fears of apocalyptic violence. And whatever the substance of Schmitt's critique of the abstraction of the *Rechtstaat* and positivist international law, he remains in something of a performative contradiction. If the urge towards neutrality is a chimera, exactly what is it about the drive that we are supposed to fear? Is Schmitt simply arguing for an intellectual recognition of the reality of politics, rather than actually writing out of a fear of the end?

Schmitt cannot, for obvious reasons, accept the possibility that a spirit of technicity is succeeding in its neutralisation, but he nevertheless asserts the pregnancy of the present age. This is the moment in which he calls for a radical reassertion of the basic elements of political life, and an escape from the dangerous acceleration of rationality. Several commentators have argued that it is in this period, from 1929 to 1932, that Schmitt makes a decisive commitment in favour of fascist dictatorship as a vehicle for renewal.[39] And indeed, there are evident logical connections between his critique of modernity, and the hopes that he occasionally professed to see in Latin forms of fascism. Schmitt's entire historical orientation always called for some sort of radical and clear-headed break with the stifling philosophies of progress, humanity and neutralisation.

Schmitt's essay on 'Neutralizations and Depoliticizations' is an important, concise statement of the sort of historical mindset that would be further developed in *The Leviathan in the State Theory of Thomas Hobbes*. The task of the present age is to reassert the eternal and immutable

---

[38] *Ibid.*, p. 95.
[39] See for example J. E. McCormick, 'Dilemmas of Dictatorship: Carl Schmitt and Constitutional Emergency Powers', *The Canadian Journal of Law and Jurisprudence* 10:1 (1997), 163–87 (pp. 185–7); W. Scheuerman, *Social Acceleration*, pp. 121–2.

political truths from their obfuscation. But, as far as one can tell, this critique alone does not lead Schmitt to an abandonment of the state form. As the study of Hobbes shows, Schmitt reads the conflation of the state as a political structure with a neutralising historical dynamic as a potentially avoidable intellectual accident. Schmitt clings for an inordinately long time to a dissociation of the (recoverable) state form from the urge to historical acceleration. Indeed, the idea of post-state politics does not really seem to occur to him at this stage. Instead, Schmitt sought to distinguish the current conception of the state from previous ideas of feudal or absolutist states, thereby arguing for the possibility of a renewal of the state form.[40] Up to at least 1933, he still regards the framework of states as the principal barrier to acceleration – the principal locus, if not bearer, of restraint. In 1932, Schmitt had still seen the prime political task as the recovery of the essence of the state form – 'only a strong state can remove itself from non-state affairs'.[41] By the time he published his study of *Leviathan* and *Land und Meer* six years later, he regarded the stakes of political order as considerably higher.

World war and acceleration

In its backwards way, then, technology does have the accelerative effect that modernity always aspires to. It changes the territorial foundations of politics, it increases the means by which absolute warfare can be fought, and it raises the seriousness of political calculus to a new level. By 1938, Schmitt had squared the circle between his critique of the core anti-political tendencies of modernity, and the potential complicity of the state in this process of acceleration. The shadow of impending war presented a dangerous but emphatically decisive moment in determining the shape of political time to come. To a very large extent, Schmitt's eventual choice in favour of Nazism can be read as a decision in favour of a radical leap into the unknown as the only corrective against the forces of historical acceleration. A simple restoration of the Hobbesian foundations of the state was no longer credible. And as such, Schmitt finally accepted the collapse of the concrete link between the state and the political.

---

[40] See C. Schmitt, *Legality and Legitimacy* (trans. J. Seitzer), Durham, NC: Duke University Press (2004), pp. 3–14; 'Die Wendung zum totalen Staat', in *Positionen und Begriffe im Kampf mit Weimar–Genf–Versailles, 1923–1939*, Berlin: Duncker and Humblot (1994), pp. 146–58.

[41] C. Schmitt, 'Strong State and Strong Economy' (trans. R. Cristi), in R. Cristi, *Carl Schmitt and Authoritarian Liberalism*, Cardiff: University of Wales Press (1998), pp. 212–32 (p. 213).

In this respect, Schmitt was to read the Second World War as a battle to establish a new multipolar framework of world politics that could reset the clock, and allow for the re-emergence of agents of restraint. The parallel with the cataclysmic events of the seventeenth century is manifest in Schmitt's turn to Hobbes, and his tentative acceptance of parallels between his own search for new principles of order, and Hobbes' creation of a theory of the state. For the most part, Schmitt maintained a distance between his conventional analysis of current events, and his more abstract contemplation of the themes of theological time. He is frustratingly vague on how he understands delay and acceleration in their concrete manifestations. For this reason, a short essay that he wrote for the newspaper *Das Reich* on 19 April 1942 stands out in its significance.[42] In one short article, Schmitt both applies the logic of restraint and acceleration to the situation of world war, and emphasises the dangers he sees in the international setting.

Writing in 1942, Schmitt is quite clear that the Second World War is a *Raumordnungskrieg* – a war over spatial order.[43] In fact, he contends, not unreasonably, that there are actually two quite distinct wars subsisting side by side. On the one hand, there is a limited and rather conventional land war that started in Spain in 1936, and which had been won fairly decisively by Germany up to 1942. On the other hand, there is a more serious and more historically significant oceanic war that started with the Japanese attack on Pearl Harbor in December 1941. Schmitt observes that, contrary to the spell of Anglo-American omnipotence, 'the entry of the USA into the war was clearly not decisive, and so we must consider what the world historical and world political meaning of this is'.[44] Utilising the now familiar notion of a dynamic between land and sea, Schmitt holds out the hope that world war will solve this damaging relationship, and result in a new found clarity of political organisation, and restraint of political time. War has given the lie to the idea that America represents an irresistible trinity of oceanic spacelessness, liberal 'freedom', and terminal acceleration. Schmitt argues that the experience of war has emphasised the contradictions in America's position, and will

---

[42] C. Schmitt, 'Beschleuniger wider Willen, oder: Die Problematik der westlichen Hemisphäre', *Das Reich*, 19 April 1942. Collected at HStAD RW265 21149 and reproduced in *Staat, Großraum, Nomos*, pp. 431–40 (citations here are from *Staat, Großraum, Nomos*). The title translates as 'Hastener against His Will; or, The Problem with the Western Hemisphere'. *Das Reich* was a weekly Nazi party newspaper launched in 1940 as a very personal project by Joseph Goebbels, who frequently wrote leading articles. Intended as a 'quality publication' it is thought to have achieved a circulation of around one-and-a-half million by early 1944. See I. Kershaw, *The Hitler Myth: Image and Reality in the Third Reich*, Oxford: Oxford Paperbacks (2001), p. 244 n. 45.
[43] Schmitt, 'Beschleuniger', p. 433.   [44] *Ibid.*, p. 431.

force it to choose between a territorial and continental (and thereby inherently multipolar and 'political') orientation, or continue with its existing attempt to inherit the mantle of British oceanic universalism.[45]

Having already formulated the notion of large-space politics that we shall consider in the following chapter, Schmitt clearly hopes for an outcome to war in which America will choose to define 'the western hemisphere' as a concrete territorial space, rather than as an idea with universal application. But what is most significant in this essay is the link that he draws between territory, political responsibility and concern for acceleration. America is depicted as facing an urgent and real political choice between two ideas of its historical role. It is only by embracing one or the other that the United States can play its necessary role as a historical restrainer. If it pursues universalism with the same spirit as the British, America will produce new conflicts and new divisions, albeit of an unstable and violent nature. If it chooses decisively in favour of a limited continental identity, America will produce sharp new lines of division that will replace international politics with intercontinental politics. But instead, Schmitt sees America as overwhelmed by 'the same incompetence of decision [*Entscheidungsfähigkeit*] of a discursive politics that, for decades, has staggered between two extremes, and which squirms indecisively in the face of the present world-political emergency [*jetzt auch vor dem großen weltpolitischen Ernstfall zu lavieren sucht*]'.[46]

Counterintuitively, then, the essence of restraint is to act. And to a certain extent, delay will be achieved regardless of whether that action deludes itself with a universal end game. The pursuit of unity will generate divisions and violence, and will do so in new and unpredictable patterns. Preferable, to be sure, are the sorts of new division in which the legitimacy of difference is inherent to a system, and in which orders of the political emerge to restrain the worst extremes of violence. But the specific problem of the current age, in Schmitt's analysis, is the progressive desire to avoid animated and committed positions at all. 'Historians and historical philosophers', Schmitt argues, 'ought to examine and describe the differing figures and types of world historical hasteners [*Aufhalter*] and delayers

---

[45] Schmitt's describes the United States as 'dizzy' from the contradictions of its world political orientation. Picking up on an observation that has been repeated over several generations, Schmitt sees the United States as picking uncertainly between a series of binaries, most notably tradition–situation, isolation–intervention, neutrality–world war. ('Beschleuniger', pp. 433–5). Similar observations of the orientation of America to the world are too numerous to mention, but Henry Kissinger stands out: 'Torn between nostalgia for a pristine past, and yearning for a perfect future, American thought has oscillated between isolation and commitment.' H. Kissinger, *Diplomacy*, New York: Simon and Schuster (1994), p. 18.

[46] Schmitt, 'Beschleuniger', p. 435.

[*Verzögerer*].' Applying these figures to the contemporary world, Schmitt sees Roosevelt's 'absence of decision' as having thrown America into the 'maelstrom of history.' As a result, the United States is 'neither a great [historical] shaper/animator [*Beweger*], nor a great restrainer, but can only end up, against its will, as a hastener'.[47]

Schmitt's immediate target, quite obviously, is to launch a propagandist critique of the United States to an intellectual Nazi audience at a time of war. And in this, 'Beschleuniger' picks up on a Nazi ambivalence about the Anglo-Saxon world that has subsequently become a commonplace. Writing in 1942, a political accommodation between a Nazi-dominated Europe and its antipode in the Americas was apparently an acceptable position to be expressed in the Nazi press. Obviously, Schmitt could not have expressed the same hopes for Russia as a bearer of the political historical spirit. As evidence of Schmitt's genuine hopes for resolution of the 'crisis' then, this is not a reliable source. But it does prefigure a particular, katechontical attempt to discern the emerging patterns of world politics from the concrete events in front of him. Indeed, this strange convergence of concrete fact, conceptual formulation and historical fear perhaps means that Schmitt's own preferences are not the correct starting point. The right outcome, for Schmitt, is any outcome – anything that keeps the wheels of world history turning.

This, then, emerges as the sole yardstick for measuring the effectiveness of political leadership. The critique of Roosevelt emphasises the point that for Schmitt, evaluation of concrete politics lies not in virtue, in the maintenance of order, in the administration of law or any other tangible set of criteria. It lies in the fact of decision that acts as the bearer of historical restraint – the act of postponement. And since, in Schmitt's construct of history, God clearly moves in mysterious ways, the locus of the decision, and the distinction between authentic and false decisions, cannot be discerned rationally. On this diagnosis, the only options appear to be acceptance of our fate as being subject to the political, and reconciliation to the fact that political authority will always be arbitrary by definition – its only source is the fact of its genesis.

What is the responsibility of political actors on this account? What will it mean to act as a delayer rather than a hastener? As with all of Schmitt's work, the only sure conclusion is that 'only the actual participants can correctly recognise, understand, and judge the concrete situation'.[48] Sometimes delay will entail preserving the nomic order, sustaining a context and living within a historical centre. At other times, among

---

[47] *Ibid.*, p. 436.   [48] Schmitt, *The Concept of the Political*, p. 27.

which Schmitt includes the present, delay can only be served by rupture and plotting a new path. But the wider context in this critique appears to be that modernity ring-fences any attempts to achieve the latter. It reduces and rationalises rapture within its own intellectual frame. It has removed every mystique. It has closed the space available for an ironic mediation between the particular and the universal. The ambiguity of Schmitt's notion of restraint – the fact that it can be pursued through particular and universal mindsets, through attack and defence, through globalism and localism – points to a conclusion that Schmitt's commitment to order and his belief in the Katechon are not reconcilable rationally. As Žižek has argued, Schmitt gets caught between the principle of order and the actuality of order in its concrete content. He is committed to the latter, but as a theorist his entire career hangs on the formulation of the concrete through conceptual tools.[49]

From within the horizon of a moralised modern politics, Schmitt seems to ask for a surfeit of irony on the one hand, and an unimaginable degree of mental regimentation on the other. In the age of nuclear weapons, it seems essential that political leaders – those actors or forces who insert themselves into the void, and take the political decision – should experience their political drives with an ironic twist. To be sure, they will be nationalists or socialists or whatever, but their moral commitments must never be sufficiently serious to make wars of annihilation a reality. Late modernity drastically reduces the room for miscalculation. On the other hand, as Schmitt's critique of Hobbes makes clear, the people should subscribe wholly to the authority of the political decision, without question and circumspection. To allow another private sphere would, it would seem, invite a repeat of the moralising irony that has hollowed out politics from the inside. If the invitation to recognise the essence of the political is to be more than merely a critique – an explanatory and retrospective framework – then it seems that Schmitt must untangle this Gordian knot of his own making.

Hastener despite himself?

As with so much of Schmitt's commentary on the present age, this statement on the world-historical failings of the United States invites much derision. The observation of American military limitations is clearly

---

[49] See S. Žižek, *The Ticklish Subject: The Absent Centre of Political Ontology*, London: Verso (1999), p. 114. Žižek argues that a 'paradox thus lies in the fact that the only way to oppose legal normative formalism is to revert to decisionist formalism – there is no way of escaping formalism within the horizon of modernity'.

premature, and the assertion of American indecisiveness appears undermined by the very subject matter of the piece – the USA's entry into the war. Nevertheless, Schmitt's critique does give a clearer picture of how we are supposed to understand the crisis of the present. And above all, this is a crisis of modernity. Schmitt is treading the line between his commitment to a politics that is somehow 'better' in its concrete manifestations, and the impossibility of formulating rules, norms or concepts to determine either what 'better' might mean, or how it might be achieved. It is a vulnerable position, and Schmitt's search for a new basis of order ultimately led to an erroneous faith in Nazism as a concrete answer to an unknowable problem. In the end, the only exit from the horizon of modernity will be a point of rupture with no antecedent, no historical continuity and no *logos*. It is a position that seems inevitably to invite miscalculation from those, such as Schmitt, who hope for it.[50]

Schmitt may have struggled to reconcile his modern mind to the critique of modernity, but by situating modernity as an historical event – a story of epochs with a clear point of departure – he opens the door to a new age with new mindsets. Schmitt's pupil, confidant and acolyte, Reinhard Koselleck, presents a better summation of this reading of modernity than Schmitt was ever to distil.[51] Nevertheless, it expresses something of Schmitt's perspective on the present age:

The crisis caused by the morality's proceeding against history will be a permanent crisis as long as history is alienated in terms of its philosophy.

That crisis and the philosophy of history are mutually dependent and entwined – that ultimately one must indeed go so far as to call them identical – this must, when our enquiry has reached its goal, have become visible at several points in the eighteenth century. Its Utopianism arose from an interrelation to politics that

---

[50] As Scheuerman points out, in Schmitt's account of law under Nazism,

> [n]o evidence is produced to support the implausible assumption in Schmitt's argument that Hitler necessarily possesses the awesome cognitive capacities required by the enormous tasks of contemporary economic and social regulation: Schmitt simply appears to assume this. The fact that National Socialism is no longer 'past oriented' suffices to render Hitler a 'better legislator' than any ever known to liberal democracy. (Scheuerman, *Social Acceleration*, p. 122)

[51] On Koselleck's relationship with Schmitt, see J.-W. Müller, *A Dangerous Mind: Carl Schmitt in Post-War European Thought*, New Haven: Yale University Press (2003), pp. 104–13. Müller suggests that Koselleck's *Critique and Crisis: Enlightenment and the Pathogenesis of Modern Society*, Oxford: Berg (1988), 112–21 '[comes] closest to being a direct elaboration of Schmitt's 1938 *Leviathan*' (p. 106). Many of Schmitt's insights were developed more productively after the war by a group including Koselleck, Hanno Kesting and Werner Sombart than by Schmitt himself. As Habermas observed, it was through figures such as Koselleck 'that we know what Carl Schmitt thinks nowadays' (J. Habermas, 'Verrufener Fortschritt – verkanntes Jahrhundert: zur Kritik der Geschichtsphilosophie', *Merkur* 14 (1960), 112–21.

was caused by history, but which was then solidified by a philosophy of history. The critical crossfire not only grounded up topical politics; politics itself, as a constant task of human existence, dissolved in the same process into Utopian constructs of the future. The political edifice of the Absolutist State and the unfolding of Utopianism reveal one complex occurrence around which the political crisis of our time begins.[52]

As a critical perspective on the obfuscations and self-delusions of modernity, the Schmitt–Koselleck story of the state, society and international order is nothing if not profound and stimulating. Many who have shared the same hostility to an all-encompassing modernity have chosen the intellectual sphere in which to launch a response or to attempt a corrective. Koselleck himself – 'a significantly subtler thinker than … Schmitt'[53] – chose to develop and refine the analysis of social acceleration and the experience of time in a critical direction.[54] Stephen Toulmin concludes his own critique of modernity with a call to reformulate a 'humanised modernity' that distinguishes between the rational and the reasonable, that deploys a practical philosophy, and that 'recover[s] the idea of rationality that was current before Descartes'.[55] It is also a critical perspective on modernity that lends itself to the intellectual formulation of radical anti-modernisms – a critique that could prompt the sort of anti-foundationalism that would surely mark the end of the political as Schmitt understood it.

But, for Schmitt, the temptation to provide a response from within the horizon of the concrete was too great. Having diagnosed the crisis of late modernity with such force, and with the use of such elegant political and historical concepts, Schmitt faced the problem of the future – how to conceive of, shape, interpret and identify the contours of the coming age. And it is a task that Schmitt set about with zeal from the moment that the collapse of the hollow edifice of the state seemed evident to him. For Schmitt, the preferable outcome is a new territorial order in which, as with the *jus publicum Europaeum*, units inherently accept difference, and live according to the maxim *cuis region, eius religio*. The alternative would be a radically unstable fight for ideals, politics disentwined from territory, escalating violence and the absence of order. Schmitt was to dedicate

---

[52] Koselleck, *Critique and Crisis*, p. 12. There are striking points of convergence between Koselleck's (and, by extension, Schmitt's) account of modern historicity, and Stephen Toulmin's critique in *Cosmopolis: The Hidden Agenda of Modernity*, Chicago: University of Chicago Press (1990). Toulmin represents an alternative vision of how to apply this diagnosis to future politics.

[53] Müller, *A Dangerous Mind*, p. 106.

[54] His work *Futures Past: On the Semantics of Historical Time* (trans. K. Tribe), New York: Columbia University Press (2004) concludes simply with a call to realign the experience of past and present.

[55] Toulmin, *Cosmopolis*, pp. 200–1, Chapter 5 *passim*.

the remainder of his career to the search for principles through which order might be recovered.

The remaining chapters will consider Schmitt's two principal attempts to provide a conceptual response to the challenge he diagnosed, and which we have explored in the previous three chapters. Ultimately the difficulties inherent in his own position would reduce the impact of these attempts to little more than an extension of his critique. Schmitt's *Begriffsmagie* would never attain the same sparkle in shaping the future as it did depicting the past. But in the course of considering his attempt to provide a *conceptual* commitment to the future, we should also bear in mind Schmitt's one, irrefutable, concrete decision on the matter – his decision to believe in Nazism as Katechon. It is a decision that shows the risks involved with Schmitt's politics of rupture, and which suggests that it might have been Schmitt, and not Roosevelt, who acted as a hastener against his will.

6   *Großraum*

... according to Schmitt, the only politics is international politics.[1]

If one is to identify one pre-eminent theme in Schmitt's entire effort as a political theorist it would undoubtedly be to uncover the specifically political failings of liberalism (both internally and externally), and to trace the consequences of those failings. Schmitt consistently piques interest as the 'foremost critic' of liberalism. He is frequently taken as a 'challenge' in the renewal and repair of democratic forms of governance, and in the remedying of liberalism's most evident failings. Such a characterisation is by no means unfair. Schmitt was constantly preoccupied with the dangers, as he saw them, of liberal abstraction, legal formalism, *potestas indirecta* and the multiple *Ent-Entungen* of modern 'politics'. In this account, Schmitt occupies a double negative position that mirrors the liberal 'de-deings' he attacks – he is anti-anti-politics.[2]

So far this work has argued for a deeper understanding of the historical-theoretical aspects of that critique. Both in his detailed account of the origins of the liberal 'problem' and in his ideas of the irrepressible tide of liberal historicism, Schmitt displayed a complex pessimism about the prospects of the modern state and, hence, the prospect of politics in form (or, at least, in the form that we have known). The infusion of liberalism into the state is written as part tragedy, part farce, and sways between dismayed fatalism and bitter criticism of those who have blindly accelerated the process. By the time Schmitt acknowledges that the process of dissolution is complete, what remains is the gaping problem of how to restore, re-create or create a new political order capable of restraining

---

[1] S. Holmes, *The Anatomy of Antiliberalism*, Cambridge, MA: Harvard University Press (1994), p. 41.

[2] *Ent-Entungen* is a phrase coined by Schmitt as a collective term for all of the processes of dissolution encouraged by liberalism (e.g. depoliticisation, detheologisation, dehistoricalisation etc.). As Marcus Brainard points out, the most accurate rendering of *Ent-Entungen* would be 'de-deings' (although he chooses the less absurd 'un-doings'). See H. Meier, *The Lesson of Carl Schmitt: Four Chapters on the Distinction between Political Theology and Political Philosophy* (trans. M. Brainard), Chicago: University of Chicago Press (1995), TN1, p. 175.

terminal formlessness. The remainder of this work examines Schmitt's response to this self-diagnosed challenge.

Given the range of analytical tools at his disposal, and his urgent prescription of the need for novel political categories, it is initially surprising that Schmitt's response to this challenge is so apparently limited. If Schmitt intended his critique of both the legal-positivist state and normative international law to prove devastating, it seems inevitable that he should have been moved to consider positive alternative strategies. However, although during the 1930s 'these negative criticisms give way to the, as it were, positive vision of an international order that Schmitt offers', the content of that positive vision is somewhat sparse.[3] Against the *Begriffsmagie* on display in Schmitt's reflective and analytical works, the hollowness of his efforts at political innovation are all the more remarkable. This section seeks to outline these limitations, and to explore possible relationships between Schmitt's understanding of the past, and his imagination of the future.

In this chapter we shall consider the concept of *Großraumordnung* (an order predicated on large spaces) as the most detailed and most heavily conceptualised of Schmitt's attempts to theorise beyond the state towards a renewed political future. This is a novel category with its origins in international law, and it reached its most comprehensive expression in Schmitt's 1938 treatise 'Völkerrechtliche Großraumordnung mit Interventionsverbot für raumfremde Mächte'.[4] Following exegesis of the concept and its relationship to Schmitt's other work, we will go on to examine the complicated and tentative distinctions that Schmitt draws between a novel *Großraum* and the Westphalian state. International lawyers in the 1930s were themselves concerned with the question of how exactly Schmitt's concept was distinct from simply a territorially expanded state, and this line of critique remains relevant to the present concerns. Given the failure Schmitt identifies in the relationship of *Staatliche* political authority and the individual (the 'barely visible crack') it is clear that any novel concept would have to be conceptually highly distinct from the discredited state. It is unclear whether Schmitt achieves the necessary degree of novelty in the *Großraum* concept.

---

[3] A. Carty, 'Carl Schmitt's Critique of Liberal International Legal Order between 1933 and 1945', *Leiden Journal of International Law* 14 (2001), 25–76 (p. 34).

[4] This somewhat clunky title is perhaps best rendered as 'International Law of Large Spaces with a Prohibition on Intervention by External Powers'. The fourth edition of the treatise (1941) is reproduced in the collection edited by G. Maschke: C. Schmitt, *Staat, Großraum, Nomos: Arbeiten aus den Jahren 1916–1969*, Berlin: Duncker and Humblot (1995), pp. 269–371. Later page references in the chapter refer to this edition.

Finally, this chapter will conclude with a brief examination of the reception of Schmitt's idea of *Großraumordnung* in subsequent and divergent political theory. In many respects, the idea of a politics of large spaces has maintained a self-evident appeal right through to the turn of the century. The very modern challenges that Schmitt once felt necessitated a new, wider spatial horizon for politics have themselves accelerated (especially modern communications and weapons of mass destruction). Moreover, Schmitt's problematic reflections on the need for a common 'political idea' (*politische Idee*) that permeates a greater political community have appeared to resonate with those, such as Huntingdon, who feel that culture will come to define the lines of enmity between larger-sized political units.[5] In the context of the foregoing discussion, this section will conclude by arguing that any attempt to redeploy the *Großraum* concept in a modern setting must take into consideration the complicated political problems to which it was initially addressed. That some may find potential value in an idea of reconfigured and enlarged quasi-states should not blind us to the comparative failure of the *Großraum* idea to address the consequences of the Schmittian historical acceleration.

Schmitt's path into international law

Schmitt's idea of *Großraum* began life as a series of theses in international law.[6] Although this may seem unremarkable given his profession, it is significant to note that his initial response to the apotheosis of international disorder in the 1930s came in the form of academic legal studies rather than the emphatic theoretical style of his earlier political works. In so far as the idea of *Großraum* was an attempt to solve the problems those earlier works and the contemporaneous study of Hobbes identified, Schmitt resorted to the solid foundations of legal theory to structure his solution.

Prior to the late 1930s, Schmitt's academic career witnessed only limited critical work in international law. These occasional forays focussed on the flaws of the Versailles–Weimar legal system, the hypocrisy of the victorious powers in the First World War and the need to restore the

---

[5] See Schmitt, 'Völkerrechtliche Großraumordnung', pp. 295–6.
[6] 'International Law' is a highly problematic rendering of the far more flexible and multi-valent German word *Völkerrecht*, which defies direct translation. One possible rendering would be 'law of peoples', but this proves misleading since the latter term has gained a specific meaning in Anglo-American international jurisprudence and political philosophy. It is perhaps most obviously defined in the negative – i.e. as that law that exists outside the domestic legislative and juridical competence of a state (although such a definition is itself self-evidently problematic).

anti-normative foundations of the old *jus publicum Europaeum*. As such, it was a legal counterpoint to Schmitt's political condemnation of the post-1919 international order. In 'Die Rheinlande als Objekt internationaler Politik,' and 'Völkerrechtliche Probleme des Rheingebiets' (published in 1925 and 1928 respectively), his concern had been to criticise the legal and political indeterminacy created by the tenuous status of the Rhineland, and the unsustainable attempt to make it subject to international law.[7] Although these studies cohere with Schmitt's parallel career as a political theorist, his academic reputation was firmly based in his work on constitutional law.

In 1933 Schmitt held a full professorship in law at the University of Bonn, and already stood out as a prominent constitutional lawyer. Indeed, constitutional law had predominated in Schmitt's scholarly career to that point. In 1928 he had published his *Verfassungslehre* to considerable acclaim, and had pursued his technical critique of the failings of the Weimar constitution alongside his more polemical critique of the tandem failings of liberalism.[8] His career as a constitutional theorist reached the height of its notoriety with his advocacy of the use of emergency powers under Article 48 of the Weimer constitution, and his subsequent legal justification of the Nazi ascent to, and consolidation of, power.[9]

Schmitt's initial response to the ascent of Nazism was thus as a constitutional lawyer. Whatever his emotional inclinations may have been, Nazism did represent a certain realisation of the constitutional principles espoused in the *Verfassungslehre*, and the ancient ideal of Roman constitutional law that Schmitt had earlier outlined in *Die Diktatur*. In other words, Nazism appeared to hold out the promise of closing the formalist-liberal gap between political authority and the law. A certain excitement at this prospect is evident in Schmitt's reflections on the new constitutional circumstances of Nazi Germany in 1933 and 1934.[10] Schmitt celebrated the ongoing attack on legal positivism, and looked forward to a new era of legal indeterminacy in Germany, in which the exercise of

---

[7] Both essays are reproduced in C. Schmitt, *Positionen und Begriffe im Kampf mit Weimar–Genf–Versailles, 1923–1939*, Berlin: Duncker and Humblot (1994), pp. 29–37 ('Die Rheinlande'), pp. 111–23 ('Völkerrechtliche Probleme').

[8] Jan–Werner Müller describes the *Verfassungslehre* as 'a brilliant conservative effort in deconstructing and containing mass democracy'. J.-W. Müller, *A Dangerous Mind: Carl Schmitt in Post-War European Thought*, New Haven: Yale University Press (2003), p. 31.

[9] See Chapter 2 above.

[10] See especially C. Schmitt, *Staat, Bewegung, Volk: Dreigliederung der politischen Einheit*, Hamburg: HAVA (1933); and *Über die drei Arten des rechtswissenschaftliche Denkens*, Hamburg: HAVA (1934).

direct and responsible power would replace the formless abuses of liberal *potestas indirecta*.[11]

At the same time, Schmitt immediately recognised the linkage between these new constitutional opportunities, and ancillary opportunities to challenge the international legal status quo. National Socialism had fed, of course, on a generalised sense of discontent with the Versailles settlement, and it presented itself as an internationally revisionist regime. In *Nationalsozialismus und Völkerrecht* (1934), Schmitt revisited his critique of the post-1919 international legal order, but this time his critique was infused with the evident hope that the new political order in Germany would translate to a new international legal order.[12] He appeared to believe that the creation of a new concrete political order in Germany would finally destroy the legal abstractions of the League of Nations. At this point, however, Schmitt's thoughts still lay with some act of *re-creation* of some pre-1914 *Grundrechte* as the likely replacement. In 1933 and 1934, he continued to focus most of his energy on working out the constitutional implications of National Socialist Germany.

Following these energetic opening chapters, however, the prospects of Schmitt developing a sustained position as a constitutional theorist of Nazi Germany quickly diminished. The very notion of Nazi constitutional law contained a hint of oxymoron, and it quickly became evident that substantial academic intrusion into questions of the structure of the state and its authority were neither desired nor welcomed. From 1934 onwards, opportunities to make a meaningful contribution as a constitutional lawyer were increasingly foreclosed. In common with all the other leading legal academics in Germany, Schmitt inevitably faced a dilemma – quiescence or silence.[13]

Events interceded to make Schmitt's position as a constitutional theorist increasingly untenable. Following the Röhm putsch, Schmitt effectively endorsed Hitler's untrammelled authority as Führer in his (now infamous) article 'Der Führer schützt das Recht' ('The Führer Protects the Law').[14] Schmitt's constitutional contributions became

---

[11] For more on Schmitt's reaction to National Socialism as a constitutional lawyer, see Ellen Kennedy, *Constitutional Failure: Carl Schmitt in Weimar*, Princeton: Princeton University Press (2005), Chapter 1.

[12] C. Schmitt, 'Nationalsozialismus und Völkerrecht', in *Frieden oder Pazifismus?: Arbeiten zum Völkerrecht und zur internationalen Politik 1924–1978* (ed. G. Maschke), Berlin: Duncker and Humblot (2005), pp. 391–421; see also Carty, 'Carl Schmitt's Critique', pp. 31–4.

[13] Detlev Vagts gives a superb account of the response of German academic lawyers to the ascent of Nazism in 'International Law in the Third Reich', *The American Journal of International Law* 84:3 (1990), 661–704.

[14] C. Schmitt, 'Der Führer schützt das Recht', *Deutschen Juristenzeitung* 39:15 (1934), 945–50.

increasingly dominated by the self-protective imperatives of the period, and such constitutional theory as he continued to produce developed an integrally anti-Semitic tone.[15] This apparent slide into sycophancy reached its low point with Schmitt's organisation of a conference in 1936 aimed at uncovering and eliminating those Jewish influences that supposedly contaminated German jurisprudence.[16]

Despite such attempts to build racialist credentials with the regime, Schmitt's position as a constitutional lawyer was nevertheless compromised by his status as a latecomer to Nazism. As Bendersky illustrates, suspicion remained within the Nazi hierarchy that this volte-face was bald opportunism, and not to be trusted.[17] Partly because of these limitations to the practice of constitutional law, and the frustrations of academic life in Nazi Germany, Schmitt turned his attention to broader questions in international law. Certainly this shift was the most realistic way for Schmitt to maintain a productive role within the academic hierarchy. Indeed, as documents uncovered by Maschke prove, at least one agent of the SS *Sicherheitsdienst* felt that this shift was little more than opportunistic manoeuvring: '[Having realised] his total exclusion from shaping internal National Socialist law, he is now searching for a new field in order to avoid his comprehensive marginalisation.'[18] Practical considerations aside, however, it does seem that Schmitt was moved by a genuine desire to examine *how* the radically new Nazi regime might transform the structures of international law. With the internal constitutional arrangements now thrown into a 'properly political' vortex of decision and authority, it perhaps seemed safest and most productive for Schmitt to turn his attention to the proper realm of politics – the international sphere. The development of a theory of large spaces as a successor to the *jus publicum Europaeum* constitutes his fully formed attempt to conceive of how the ascent of Nazism might radically alter the basis of world politics, and reproduce a solidly rooted, anti-internationalist arena for conflict.

This cannot be read, of course, as specifically a response to the realisation of a changing *Nomos*. Schmitt only realised a fully formed concept of *Nomoi* after the idea of *Großraum* in international law had been and gone. However, even without this terminology, it is evident that the basic ingredients of this historical realisation fell into place during the 1930s.

---

[15] Schmitt's anti-Semitism and his relationship to Nazi policies are considered in more detail in Chapter 3, pp. 54–59.

[16] For more on this conference, see G. Balakrishnan, *The Enemy: An Intellectual Portrait of Carl Schmitt*, London: Verso (2000), pp. 205–7.

[17] J. Bendersky, *Carl Schmitt: Theorist for the Reich*, Princeton: Princeton University Press (1983), pp. 248–9.

[18] See G. Maschke, *Der Tod Carl Schmitts*, Vienna: Karolinger (1987), p. 352.

The essays in *Positionen und Begriffe*, published as an edited collection in 1940, clearly addressed themselves to the unsustainability of liberal internationalism. In his constitutional theory, Schmitt was concerned with reversing the long-term consequences of liberal formalism, and recovering direct political authority. Ellen Kennedy is correct in her conclusion that 'Schmitt thought of the Third Reich as a new state, and his work in the first year of Hitler's regime locates it as a revolutionary break with its predecessor.'[19] At some point between 1933 and the publication of 'Völkerrechtliche Großraumordnung' in 1938, Schmitt appears to have reached a deeper conclusion that the Third Reich heralded a more fundamental break than a mere 'new state', and instead held out the opportunity radically to reshape the foundations of international order.

During 1937 Schmitt was preoccupied to a great extent with his deeper study of Hobbes, and reflection on the historical trajectory of the state. The completion of his study of *Leviathan* in 1938 illustrates Schmitt's understanding of the destiny of the modern state. His thinking at this stage is intensely historical, and he addresses himself to a far broader canvas than ever before. Whereas his initial response to National Socialism had been precise and technical, he had by now developed the grandiose, *epochal* mode of expression that would characterise much of his international work. All of Schmitt's work of this period is possessed of a *fin de siècle* tone that transcends the immediate circumstances of Germany between 1937 and 1938. We can probably say with some certainty, therefore, that it was in this eighteen-month period that Schmitt finally concluded the state of Hobbes and Bodin to be beyond resuscitation. If renewal and restoration were no longer credible solutions, the key political imperative became innovation and the discovery of novel categories. The theory of large spaces was therefore Schmitt's initial attempt to adopt a predictive stance, and to grasp for future principles of global order.

'Völkerrechtliche Großraumordnung'

By his own admission, Schmitt had struggled to escape a critical mindset, and to address himself to the positive search for new ordering principles. Rather than attempting to innovate from first principles, Schmitt suggests that he was instead trying to identify the quasi-organic birth pangs of a new order. Such an anticipatory approach is consistent with the conservatism we have witnessed in the previous chapters but, more prosaically, was

---

[19] Kennedy, *Constitutional Failure*, p. 20.

probably a sensible strategy for a theorist under pressure in a Germany where the contours of future foreign policy had not yet become clear. According to Detlev Vagts, 'confusion was occasioned by the sheer difficulty of knowing what sort of international law National Socialism really implied or needed'.[20] It took time for Schmitt to summon the confidence to comment on the possible parameters of a new international law under Nazism:

> When, in autumn 1937, I completed my study *The Turn towards a Discriminatory Concept of War* as a research piece for the Academy of German Law, the political conditions [for this new international law] were not yet clear … The natural response to that piece would be to pose the question, what would I propose to take the place of the old order of states … Today, I can give the answer.[21]

His answer is that 'the new ordering principle of the new international law is our concept of the *Reich*'.[22] Schmitt clearly has in mind here the particular and immediate circumstances in Germany that, according to this view, have made possible an alternative vision of international order: 'The thought of a German *Reich* as the architect and builder of a new international law would previously have been a utopian dream, and the content of the international law it creates would have remained an empty dream. But today a powerful German *Reich* has arisen.'[23] Ignoring, in so far as one can, the evidently unsettling self-identification Schmitt makes here with bellicose German foreign policy, the broader point remains that he is identifying the rise of the Third Reich with his long-diagnosed need for a particularist, territorial, anti-liberal counterpoise to the dangerous ascent of liberal universalism.

The basic outlines of the *Großraum* concept can be summed up in one paragraph. A predominant power (the *Reich*) exists within a larger territorial space (the *Großraum*), in which it essentially acts as hegemon. This larger space is a geopolitical category, but should also be characterised by sufficient cultural homogeneity to allow the 'political idea' of the leading *Reich* to radiate and to unify. The *Reich* itself is charged both with ideological definition, and with asserting the power to decide on the external orientation of the *Großraum* as a whole: 'A *Reich* in this sense is the leading and forceful power whose political idea radiates [*ausstrahlt*] throughout

---

[20] Vagts, 'International Law', p. 686.
[21] Schmitt, 'Völkerrechtliche Großraumordnung', p. 306. The core legal-theoretical argument remained constant between the first and fourth editions of 'Völkerrechtliche Großraumordnung'. However, the latter is somewhat more extensive in its argumentation. It also takes a broader and more generalised perspective, focussing less specifically on Central and Eastern Europe, and laying a heavier emphasis on the idea of *Großraum* as a new and transformative category for international law as a whole.
[22] *Ibid.*   [23] *Ibid.*

the entire *Großraum*, and which fundamentally prevents the intervention of foreign powers in the *Großraum*.'[24] Although Schmitt intends the idea of *Großraum* as a novel and transformative category in international law, he regards the Monroe Doctrine as a 'precedent for an international legal principle of large spaces'.[25] As Schmitt reads it, the Monroe Doctrine of 1823 was the first instance of a quasi-legal great space with a prohibition on intervention by foreign powers.[26] The United States, as the pre-eminent power (or *Reich*), asserted the right to prevent intervention by external powers in the American continent. It thereby asserted some form of pan-American political homogeneity that nevertheless fell short of direct annexation or imperialism. The American continent constituted a defined territorial-political space that was nevertheless distinct from its predominant power. And beyond its obvious territorial integrity, Schmitt argues that there existed some form of cultural homogeneity in the Americas that made the dominance and leadership of the United States acceptable and effective.[27]

As Schmitt interpreted it, the Monroe Doctrine contained two novelties of the highest relevance to the new international circumstances. Firstly, the United States reserved for itself the power to interpret the basis of the doctrine under concrete circumstances. Schmitt had previously posited this kind of international legal indeterminacy as a contrast to the dominant positivism. In 1932 Schmitt had written in praise of US legal decisionism in the context of its 1903 treaty with Cuba – a treaty that gave the USA power to ensure non-intervention in Cuba.[28] In contrast to the kind of treaty-formalism in the ascendancy after 1919, Schmitt saw such arrangements as allowing for the true exercise of direct political power. He firmly approved of Hughes' definition of the US's relationship to the Monroe Doctrine: 'When asked in 1923 to characterise the essential content of the Monroe Doctrine, Secretary of State Hughes responded with a classic example of pure decisionism [*Dezisionismus*]: the meaning of the Monroe

---

[24] *Ibid.*, pp. 295–6.   [25] *Ibid.*, p. 277.

[26] In the late 1930s the Monroe Doctrine became a popular analogy used by German leaders in defence of their proposed foreign policy. Ribbentrop cited the Doctrine in March 1939 as a precedent for the partition of Poland, and Hitler himself deployed the analogy in a speech to the Reichstag in April 1939. Schmitt was apparently warned not to claim authorship of the idea so as to avoid offending the Führer's dignity. (See Balakrishnan, *The Enemy*, p. 236; Bendersky, *Carl Schmitt*, pp. 258–9). The accuracy of Schmitt's understanding of the actual basis of the Monroe Doctrine need not detain us here, but suffice to say that most American legal historians would probably challenge his interpretation (see Vagts, 'International Law', p. 689).

[27] See Schmitt, 'Völkerrechtliche Großraumordnung', pp. 277–85.

[28] See C. Schmitt, 'Völkerrechtliche Formen des Modernen Imperialismus', in *Positionen und Begriffe*, pp. 184–203.

Doctrine could only be "defined, interpreted and sanctioned" by the United States alone.'[29] There was no pretence of rule-based behaviour in the Monroe Doctrine. The USA would make the decision to act in the concrete instance.

The second distinct feature of the Monroe Doctrine lay in its understanding of space. In contrast to the European state-form, Schmitt regarded it as the first concept of international law that directly acknowledged the existence of a planetary space.[30] As such, it was capable of placing the actual territory of the American *Großraum* within the context of the planetary space it inhabited. Schmitt's earlier writings on international law displayed profound irritation with the growing tendency to create indeterminate territorial categories (protectorates, international territories, economic zones etc.), whose prime definition lay in some universal idea rather than a geographic reality. By contrast, the Monroe Doctrine implicated a precise and particular territorial space.

This, Schmitt argues, is a distinct contrast to the incapacity of European powers to reconcile their ideas of territory to their new realisation of the vastness of the planet. In particular, he regards the British Empire as representing the precise opposite of *Großraum*. The British response to the global space, Schmitt argues, had been to de-territorialise and universalise, detaching the abstract idea of power from any concrete orientation. To illustrate this contrast, Schmitt points to the British creation of an indeterminate territorial status for the Suez Canal, and the classification of the canal in reference to British 'interests' rather than its physical status.[31] As such, the Monroe Doctrine (as originally conceived)[32] represents a modestly successful attempt to reconcile order and orientation, within the context of the new planetary spatial environment.

Despite its prominence, the Monroe Doctrine is intended merely as a starting point for a more theoretical working-out of legal principle. The intention is not simply to lift the Monroe Doctrine as a model, and to impose it elsewhere. Schmitt argues that his intention in referring to this precedent is to 'clarify an international legal principle of large spaces, and to make this applicable to all *Lebensräume* and other historical

---

[29] Schmitt, 'Völkerrechtliche Großraumordnung', p. 281.
[30] *Ibid.*, p. 282.   [31] *Ibid.*, p. 287.
[32] Schmitt goes on to describe how the United States had subsequently mortgaged the territorial basis of the Monroe Doctrine, and fallen into the same universalist trap as the British. Unsurprisingly, Schmitt particularly targets President Wilson for his attempt 'to transform a concrete, territorially defined notion of order into a universal "world" idea, and thereby to turn the core international legal principle of non-intervention in large spaces ... into a pan-interventionist world ideology'. *Ibid.*, p. 285.

situations'.[33] Schmitt's objectives are both theoretical and practical – 'to clear the way for a fruitful and auspicious change in both theory and practice'.[34] Inevitably this meant that his principal concern lay with the effective marriage of his theoretical *Großraum* with the concrete circumstances of Germany on the eve of its expansionist phase.

In the immediate context, Schmitt envisioned a European *Großraum* in which Germany would stand as the pre-eminent power – the *Reich*. In the aftermath of the *Anschluß* and Germany's annexation of the Sudetenland, the push towards German domination of Central Europe must have seemed assured. Through both its material power, and the force of its 'political idea' (*politische Idee*), the *Reich* would act to ensure that no external power could intervene within the determined *Großraum*. In other words, 'the guiding principle of the present international law [is] the fundamental exclusion of powers from outside the territorial area'.[35] This prohibition on intervention by external powers in the *Großraum*, coupled to the predominance of the leading power within the *Großraum*, appears designed to rationalise and clarify the real substance of international relations. In the European context, international relations would be subdivided into two categories. Firstly, the relations between the powers within the *Großraum* would consist essentially of technical arrangements for coexistence and the maintenance of German primacy.[36] Secondly, as the *Reich*, Germany itself would retain all power to define the external relations of the *Großraum*, and to ensure the non-intervention of external powers.

In some respects, this promotion of a European territorial answer to Germany's predicament was familiar from Weimar debates on the restoration and rehabilitation of German power in the face of American and Russian intrusion. Walther Vogel, for instance, had concluded in 1925 that Germany would only restore its international credibility by transcending the limits of the traditional nation state, and standing instead at the forefront of some kind of federal Europe.[37] The idea of Germany at the centre of a legally reconstituted European space was by no means a novelty when Schmitt was developing his *Großraum* theory. However, he did give a novel and unusual juridical account of how the legal architecture of this new transnational unit might operate.

---

[33] *Ibid.*, p. 278.   [34] *Ibid.*, p. 314.   [35] *Ibid.*, p. 295.
[36] In the event, of course, Germany adopted a complicated nomenclature and systems of control within occupied Europe. Among those territories attacked early on, certain among them were annexed, and a *Generalgouvernement* was established in Poland, whilst Bohemia and Moravia became protectorates. Most later conquests were treated as bare occupations. See Vagts, 'International Law', p. 697.
[37] W. Vogel, *Das Neue Europa, und seine historisch-geographischen Grundlagen*, Bonn: Schroeder (1925), pp. 416–22.

Schmitt actually talks of four kinds of relationship mediated by his new system of international law. Firstly, relations between different *Großräume*. Secondly, relations between *Reiche*. Thirdly, relations between the various *völkisch* groups within a *Großraum*. And finally, relations between *völkisch* groups across the boundaries of a *Großraum*.[38] However, these categories clearly break down into an internal–external divide. If one defining characteristic of the *Reich* is its capacity to define the 'foreign policy' of the *Großraum* as a whole, then one can presume that the external orientation of that *Großraum* will cohere with the external orientation of the *Reich*. Relations among groups inside the space are clearly an important issue, but now seem removed from the subject matter of specifically *international* or *external* politics. Finally, as noted by Peter Stirk, given that the various nations within the *Großraum* were 'subject to the prohibition of intervention by powers alien to the *Großraum*', it is doubtful how significant their relations to *völkisch* groups in other *Großräume* could possibly be'.[39] Certainly Schmitt makes no effort to suggest what the content of such relations might be.

If the *Großraum* concept replicates an internal–external divide with such clarity, how is this distinct from simply an enlarged and technically more efficient state? Schmitt is at pains to argue that 'the *Reich* is not simply an enlarged state, in the same way that a *Großraum* is not simply an expanded *Kleinraum*'.[40] After all, his self-declared objective is to look beyond the failed concepts of inter-state law, and to uncover radically new principles for a new age. In arguing for the novelty of his categories, he turns broadly to two areas of argumentation that we shall consider in turn. Firstly, he looks to the human community that inhabits the *Großraum*, and that forms a reception community for the political idea. Secondly, he argues that the *Großraum* concept radically reconstitutes our understanding of political space, providing an escape route from the corrupted spatial ideas of inter-state international law. The transformative capacity of the *Großraum* concept lies in the coherence of these two arguments.

The 'political idea'

Whereas the only glue holding together Schmitt's Westphalian state was the act of decision and a naked typology of power, he is here moved to make reference to the necessity of a 'political idea' that somehow

---

[38] Schmitt, 'Völkerrechtliche Großraumordnung', p. 305.
[39] P. Stirk, 'Schmitt's "Völkerrechtliche Großraumordnung"', *History of Political Thought* 20:2 (1999), 357–74 (p. 370).
[40] Schmitt, 'Völkerrechtliche Großraumordnung', p. 309.

originates in the *Reich* and imparts energy and unity into the *Großraum*. At first glance this appears to mark a departure from his pure decisionist definition of politics per se. However, this cultural or intellectual role ascribed to the *Reich* is placed alongside its more familiar power-political role in guaranteeing non-intervention by external powers. Schmitt does not create a hierarchy between these two roles of the *Reich*, and offers little clarification on the mechanics of its 'radiation' through the *Großraum*. In some respects, we are returned to David Pan's dilemma (outlined in Chapter 3) of the gap between the act of decision, and the existence of an environment in which that decision takes root – a reception community. Schmitt recognises that the coherence and stability of the *Großraum* concept relies on a certain concrete, pre-existent homogeneity – a *völkisch* environment in which some special, unique, particular and anti-universal mode of being can make sense – but he offers no theoretical insight into the content of that homogeneity.[41]

Both in theory and in practice, the content of this 'political idea' remains elusive. Perhaps Schmitt is caught in a gap between a desire to provide immediate legal and intellectual categories for Nazi Germany, and a desire to produce a generalised and replicable theory of the new international order. For Diemut Majer, who regarded Schmitt as a highly culpable shaper of Nazi foreign policy, the 'political idea' that Schmitt hopes to see radiated through Central and Eastern Europe is simply Nazi racial and *völkisch* doctrine.[42] Such a view is supported by the explicit exclusion of the Jews from any place within this *völkisch* international system,[43] and by the language Schmitt uses to describe the specific 'political idea' of the new German *Reich*:

... respect for peoples as unique in form and origin, a way of life defined by blood and soil, radiation into Central and Eastern Europe, and the removal of interference by external [*raumfremd*] and foreign [*unvölkisch*] powers. The actions of the Führer have provided our concept of the *Reich* with political reality, historical truth and a great future in international law.[44]

According to Majer's interpretation, the 'political idea' amounts to nothing more than Nazi ideology, and its 'radiation' is nothing more than imposition by force.

---

[41] The only effort Schmitt makes to clarify this vagueness is definitively to exclude Jews from any possibility of a place as participants in the present European *Großraum*. See *ibid*., pp. 294–5.

[42] D. Majer, *Nationalsozialismus im Lichte der juristischen Zeitgeschichte*, Baden-Baden: Nomos Verlagsgesellschaft (2002).

[43] See above, p. 58.

[44] Schmitt, 'Völkerrechtliche Großraumordnung', p. 306.

Certainly it was necessary for Schmitt's notion of the 'political idea' to resonate with concrete political circumstances. Stirk suggests, somewhat more prosaically than Majer, that the 'political idea' was an elusive and largely unsuccessful attempt to distinguish Nazi expansionism from naked annexation:

[Schmitt's] difficulty lay in the need to reconcile German hegemony with something short of direct annexation and radical Germanization. [He] needed a cohesive force to endow the *Großraum* with some unity and identity ... It is this need which the political idea, as formulated in 'The Monroe Doctrine as the Precedent of the *Großraum* Principle in International Law' sought to fill.[45]

According to Stirk, therefore, the notion of the political idea was Schmitt's somewhat feeble attempt to ground German dominance in something deeper and legally more substantial than mere aggression. Stirk suggests that Schmitt was grappling with the question of 'how to generate sufficient political homogeneity to be able to dispense with the cruder forms of occupation and repression'.[46] As such, the vagueness of the concept derives from the difficulty of the problem it was intended to solve.

Certainly Stirk is right to argue that Schmitt is engaged in an exercise of political distinction, and an attempt to provide a justification for German expansion that avoids bare imperialism. But Schmitt does so in a way that speaks to the wider distinction between particularism and universalism. Schmitt intends *Reich* and *Großraum* to represent qualitatively new concepts of international order: 'Reich, Imperium and Empire are not the same ... Whereas "Imperium" often promotes a sense of a universal world order and humanity ... our German Reich [is] in its essence a non-universal legal order.'[47] Whilst Stirk and Majer are both quite right to stress the need to take into account Schmitt's objectives in legitimating and theorising Nazi expansion, it does not necessarily follow that the concept of the 'political idea' was only intended to make sense in that context.

Although Schmitt believed that new principles of international law were unfolding first and foremost in Germany, he had nevertheless expressed a belief that his *Großraum* theory should be 'applicable to all *Lebensräume* and other historical situations'.[48] If he simply wished to assert the political predominance of Nazi ideology, and the hope that it would provide the socio-political glue to hold together a new European space, why did he choose to express himself in such legally generalised language? If the Americas under the Monroe Doctrine had been a quasi-*Großraum*, and

---

[45] Stirk, 'Schmitt's "Völkerrechtliche Großraumordnung"', p. 372   [46] *Ibid.*, p. 373
[47] Schmitt, 'Völkerrechtliche Großraumordnung', p. 296.   [48] *Ibid.*, p. 278.

the emergence of other *Großräume* was both likely and necessary, then surely the notion of the 'political idea' had to exist as a distinct conceptual category. It had to be possible for there to be a unique and particular idea that would provide homogeneity to the Americas, to south Asia, or wherever else a large space might emerge.

What appears to be at stake here is not the content of the particular 'political idea' at hand, but the very possibility of a 'political idea' as the highest reference point for a political community. The concept of a 'political idea' is definitively anti-universal. Schmitt's definition of the German political idea is synonymous with his general, particularist critique of the post-1919 order. The uniqueness of peoples, the orientating effect of blood and soil, the concept of *Volk* as Schmitt deploys it – all of these are simply extensions of the general critique. They represent modes of being and concrete ordering principles that are essential to the maintenance of 'the political'. In this sense, the 'political idea' represents the possibility of the concrete – the possibility of an idea that, in its content, is incapable of replication and universalisation. The German political idea is made of its own content, could not have emerged elsewhere, could not be generalised, and will never adhere to a positivist and universal doctrine. In other words, it marks a pluralist stance against a universal world.

Perhaps it is this that explains Schmitt's vagueness on the content of the 'political idea'. One can no more predict the content of a specific political idea than one could predict theological revelation. Schmitt's fervent hope is that Germany's new political circumstances will ensure a continuing, unique political vision. The dangers of conceptual overreach are only too well evidenced, in Schmitt's view, by the slide of the Monroe Doctrine into universalism. The political idea must remain defensive and aggressive, rooted in the particular combination of order and orientation of its concrete circumstances.

Far from being a novel and sinister political category, the 'political idea' appears to be the flip-side of Schmitt's dominant critique of liberalism and universalism. If the 'political idea' amounts to little more than the fact of particularism, it is difficult to see what the concept really adds to his existing critique. His stated purpose is to discover new principles to stop 'the non-state [*unstaatlichen*] and non-national [*unvölkischen*] of a universal world law [*Weltrecht*]'.[49] But the concept of the 'political idea' seems woefully inadequate to the task. Indeed, if read in this way, it even appears as a rather simplistic adjunct to Schmitt's critical argument – we need to resist universalism; we shall do so by means of powerful political units that

---

[49] *Ibid.*, p. 305.

are committed to non-universalism. This is hardly the conceptual leap forward that Schmitt claims to be able to give.

Furthermore, it is unclear why the notion of the 'political idea' and its 'radiation' in a large space is qualitatively distinct from the state-form that Schmitt regards as obsolete. It is clear that states, as Schmitt understood them, were possessed of a political idea in the sense of a specific orientation, an understanding of their own peculiarity and their successful functioning in a pluriverse. This imperative to posses a political idea is therefore little more than an amplification of Schmitt's existing theory of the state – the philosophical bolstering of the core component of sovereignty, and a definitive barrier to the assertion of liberal universalism. Certainly the 'political idea' is never expressed in such terms as an essential component of a coherent state in Schmitt's earlier work. The language is new. But if the content of 'political idea' turns out to be little more than the potential for uniqueness, what has he really added? This is simply an underdeveloped and incomplete answer to the question of what cultural or intellectual content is given, in practical terms, to the political community that is bound by the political decision.

A new definition of space

If the 'political idea' fails sufficiently to distinguish a *Großraum* from a traditional state, then the key political criterion of the *Großraum* must lie instead in its specific understanding of space. Clearly the *Großraum* is intended as a spatial category. Schmitt is critical of the increasing failure of the state to represent a concrete spatial reality. During the colonial period, he argues, states created a whole myriad of intermediate and indeterminate spatial categories such as 'spheres of influence' (*Interressensphären*) that were expressly designed to break the link between political power and territorial orientation.[50] He contrasts the American *Großraum* with the British empire, criticising the latter for its refusal to acknowledge its own territorial specificity, and its constant attempts to generalise and universalise its political precepts in a non-territorial direction.[51] Schmitt saves special contempt for Disraeli's flippant notion that New Delhi would be a more appropriate British capital city that London.[52] This appears to represent *par excellence* that process of deterritorialisation that has so dogged the international system, and that has contributed so drastically to the modern crisis of the state.

---

[50] See especially *ibid.*, pp. 271–5.   [51] *Ibid.*, pp. 286–91.
[52] C. Schmitt, *Land und Meer*, Stuttgart: Klett–Cotta (1954), p. 38.

Alongside the wilful tendency of governments to obfuscate concepts of territory, Schmitt also acknowledges the impact of modern technology in altering the realistic horizons of spatial organisation. New technologies of communication make the sovereignty of small spaces seem increasingly tenuous, and suggest that a new coherent spatial organisation would have to embrace a larger sense of territory – literally a *Großraum*.[53] Both in its stress on the territorial basis of political orientation (as a *Raum*), and in its acknowledgement of the need to re-create a new order with a more realistic sense of political territory (as a *Großraum*), Schmitt established the question of territoriality as the central category of the *Großraum* concept. At first glance, he is seeking to define a new, politically charged understanding of space that can serve as the basis of a new order:

Space, per se, is clearly not a concrete order. But equally clearly, every concrete order and community has a specific content in terms of place [*Ort*] and space [*Raum*]. In this sense, one can say that every legal establishment [*Rechtseinrichtung*] – every institution – has a concept of space internal to itself, and thereby brings with it its own internal substance and its own internal boundaries.[54]

On the one hand, the idea of space that underlies the *Großraum* concept is relatively straightforward and prosaic. Tied to the immediate instance in Germany and Europe, and with the Monroe Doctrine as the key precedent, we appear to be talking about essentially continental spaces. The prime spatial category would appear to be the *Großraum* as a whole, since it is this new, wider concept of space that is presented as novel and necessary 'in overcoming the monopoly of the empty state-area concept [*Staatsgebietbegriffs*]'.[55] This being the case, one must assume that the *Reich* itself is a second-tier spatial characterisation. Firstly, Schmitt presents the *Reich* as important in an intellectual-historical rather than a spatial sense. The *Reich* gives moral content and material power to the (qualitatively distinct) larger territorial space. As such, it is not presented as a spatial category in its essence.[56] Secondly, if 'Germany' and the 'United States' are the principal precedents for a new spatial politics, it is hard to see how Schmitt could infuse his argument with an urgent new categorisation of territory. He is at pains to argue that the *Großraum*

[53] Schmitt, 'Völkerrechtliche Großraumordnung', p. 304.
[54] *Ibid.*, p. 319.   [55] *Ibid.*, p. 320.
[56] Schmitt nevertheless appears to think of the *Reich* and the separate component 'peoples' within a *Großraum* in territorial as well as cultural-ethnic-social terms. One presumes that the *Reich* would continue to be a territorially defined space that could be depicted on a map. The key distinction is that boundaries between these units are now conceived as internal boundaries, and hence subordinate to the primary spatial category of *Großraum*. Schmitt offers little clarification of the importance of territorial distinctions within the *Großraum*.

is something qualitatively distinct from an enlarged state, yet Germany and the United States as '*Reiche*' would appear to possess exactly that quality.

Beyond the fact of largeness, what is new in this theory of political space? Schmitt is clear that we are experiencing a revolution of spatial consciousness analogous to that which purportedly occurred in the sixteenth century:

> The true modernity of our age lies in the fact that the spatial-revolutionary alter-ation of the medieval world perspective (that started in the sixteenth century and came to full scientific fruition in the seventeenth century) offers us an opportunity better to understand the alteration of spatial perspective [*Raumbildes*] and spatial imagination [*Raumvorstellung*] occurring today.[57]

This current change in spatial sense is presented as the most significant change in human consciousness in 400 years, fundamentally impacting all aspects of human life. What remains unclear is whether Schmitt is theorising a new spatial category that coheres with this changing under-standing of space, or is merely commentating on the inevitability of new spatial categories and the *need* to uncover them. By the standards Schmitt sets for himself – to outline a 'new ordering principle of the new inter-national law' – and from the concrete content of the theory he presents, one would assume that he has achieved the former.[58] In fact, it is by no means clear that Schmitt achieves the clarity necessary to claim a radically new political understanding of space.

The *Großraum*, it is argued, is not simply 'an expanded *Kleinraum*'.[59] As such, the defining point of departure cannot be size. The largeness of the new political space is descriptive rather than definitional in any foundational sense. 'Large' and 'small' would anyway make sense only in a relative and specific sense as the spatial contrast between the European and American instances serves to illustrate. It seems strange that Schmitt retreats so decisively from scale as at least one defining point of his new concept of space. Given this retreat, it is curious that he persisted with *Großraum* as the label for this concept, given the inevitable connotations of largeness.[60] *Groß* is, of course, a somewhat multivalent word that cannot be rendered simply as 'large'. It also connotes greatness, and is akin to the

---

[57] Schmitt, 'Völkerrechtliche Großraumordnung', p. 314.
[58] For Schmitt's bold claims for the importance of the *Großraum* concept in offering a radical alternative to the state system, see *ibid.*, p. 306.
[59] *Ibid.*, p. 309.
[60] The word *Großraum* is in common usage in Germany to refer to the greater geographic hinterland or region attached to a city, such as 'Großraum Hamburg' or 'Großraum Frankfurt'.

original geographic use of the word 'great' in the sense of 'Great Britain'. As Schmitt puts it, 'as with many other contexts (such as "great" power, "great" king, "great" revolution), the word [*Groß*] implies a qualitative level'.[61] When attached to -*raum*, however, the spatial attributes of the word are clearly emphasised.

Again, Schmitt is perhaps caught between a desire to present a specific justification of German expansion in the European space and a more profound reflection on the political category of space in a post-Westphalian environment. Whatever the reasons, he steers clear of tightly defining these new spatial foundations he claims to have uncovered. Having given a fairly clear impression of the precise spatial characteristics of the unfolding European *Großraum*, Schmitt suddenly denies that these attributes are characteristic of the *Großraum* concept per se. As with the specific content of the 'political idea', the specific content of this 'new' and 'revolutionary' spatiality remains tantalisingly elusive. Rather than following through on his discussion of the precise territorial failings of the state under conditions of modernity, Schmitt turns instead to a somewhat sophistic meditation on the *meaning* of space.

Schmitt claims that his idea of *Großraum* has a transformative capacity:

> *Großraum* is therefore not a relatively larger space in relation to a relatively smaller space – not an expanded *Kleinraum*. Clearly the pathetic mathematical-physical-natural-scientific neutrality of the existing idea of space must be overcome ... The inclusion of the word *Gross* should and can *alter the conceptual playing field* [*Begriffsfeld*]. That is of decisive significance both for the law and for the development of state and international legal knowledge, because all verbal (and as such, all juristic) ideas influence the conceptual field, interacting and growing with their conceptual neighbours.[62]

Rather than representing the achievement of a new and reproductive concept of space, Schmitt turns his attention to the role of the *Großraum* as 'a bridge from the old to the new concepts of space'.[63] As with the 'political idea' we explored above, his most profound claim about his 'new' understanding of space is in its capacity to sharpen a critique of the existing order: 'The change to the conceptual terrain achieved by the opposition of the word *Großraum* to the word *Raum* would lie above all in causing the latter to lose its previous mathematical-natural-scientific-neutral connotations.'[64] Schmitt wants to sharpen his critique of the previous, discredited spatial order for lacking the depth and intensity of specifically territorial content necessary to avoid the slide into formlessness. The state was a territorial unit, but Schmitt criticises the *Raumtheorie*

---

[61] Schmitt, 'Völkerrechtliche Großraumordnung', p. 315.
[62] *Ibid.* Emphasis in the original.   [63] *Ibid.*, p. 315.   [64] *Ibid.*, p. 316.

of this space as having rendered 'an empty two-dimensional space'.[65] He stresses the need to avoid a situation in which the spatial foundation of a particular political order is conceived as nothing more 'than a specified area for a people organised by law', as, he argues, has occurred with the spatial foundations of the state system.[66] Schmitt repeats his familiar critique of depoliticisation and universalisation, but this time emphasises the links between these processes and the erosion of spatial consciousness. The trends are depicted as symbiotic, and Schmitt returns to his theme of the links between liberalism, scientific rationality, and the incompatibility of Judaism with a spatial understanding rooted in the earth.[67] This is a specifically spatial addition to Schmitt's wider critique of modern positivism.

This novel *Großraum* category is therefore intended to criticise the 'flat' conceptions of space that have dominated hitherto, and which tend towards a loss of the fundamental link of order and orientation. But Schmitt fails to convey an adequate sense of what a 'deep' conception of space might consist of. Is a concept of *Großraum* intended as a process or as a destination? Exactly how would an international order based on a system of *Großräume* avoid positivist and 'flat' conceptions of space that purportedly plagued the state system? What is the link between the imperative for breadth that Schmitt explicitly accepts (i.e. the need for larger spaces adequately to contain political authority under modern conditions), and the more abstract notion of spatial depth and integrity that he is attempting to develop?

Schmitt's answer to these obvious criticisms comes in the form of a disconcerting and provocative formulation – he envisages a new concept of space in terms of a space for activity or achievement (*Leistungsraum*).[68]

The spatial is generated only in and on (subjective) physical reality [*Gegenstände*], and spatiotemporal [*Raumzeitlich*] orders are no longer mere clerical entries [*Eintragungen*] in a previously empty space, but instead correspond far more closely to a real situation, an actual event. Only now has the idea of an empty dimension [*Tiefendimension*] and a basic formal spatial category finally been overcome. Space has become a space for accomplishment [*Leistungsraum*].[69]

Quite what one is to make of this categorisation is unclear, and is perhaps deliberately left unclear. Certainly one can identify with Schmitt's association of space with the particular, and the need to implicate space as part of the barrier against universalism and formlessness. One can likewise recognise the linkage of space to particular human activity, so that space is tied to the concrete reality of people rather than the triumph of abstract ideals.

---

[65] *Ibid.*   [66] *Ibid.*   [67] See *ibid.*, pp. 316–18.   [68] *Ibid.*, p. 319.   [69] *Ibid.*

Once again however, it is unclear what the 'novel' category of *Großraum* adds to the basic critique of positivism. What is new about this concept that wouldn't likewise be achieved by a radical reassertion of the territoriality and particularism of the state? Schmitt goes to great pains to say that a *Großraum* is not simply a larger *Kleinraum*. He claims that the difference lies in the capacity of the former to re-emphasise the particularity of space. But couldn't this be achieved equally via a *fundamental* recovery of the state (i.e. the recovery of the state with its essential territorial consciousness)? If what is at stake is the discovery of new concepts to address the problems of the current age, why does Schmitt end up lowering his ambitions to merely presenting a transformational category? With its sense of territoriality, as with the category of 'political idea', the *Großraum* concept appears to break down in the space between critique and innovation, and ends up achieving little in either direction.

Why should the conjunction of *Gross* and -*raum* have the transformative conceptual effect that Schmitt claims in contrast to other approaches? Consider his concluding claim for the relevance and importance of the *Großraum* concept:

The idea of *Großraum* is therefore of service in overcoming the monopoly of the empty state-area concept [*Staatsgebietsbegriffs*] and prepares us to experience the international system of the *Reich* as the decisive concept of our legal thought. Through this a renewal of legal ideas becomes possible, recapturing the old and eternal unity of order and orientation, [which in turn] makes possible the return of meaning to the word 'peace', and restores the character of unique being [*den Charakter eines artbestimmenden Wesenmerkmals*] to the word 'home'.[70]

The final line above represents, in truth, the sole significant message conveyed by the concept of *Großraum*. Schmitt is concerned that the modern organisation of states has lost the capacity to sustain and protect the character of unique being. Positivism is accelerating history towards an unrooted, unpolitical, ungrounded universalism from which there can be no return. But how can one really go about 'theorising' a return to the particular? The achievement of that specific, concrete grounding of politics in a unique idea, the unique cultural content of the *Volk* and the unique territorial orientation of that people is not the stuff of theory but rather the stuff of concrete achievement – it is a *Dasein* that cannot be prescribed by political theory. As with the fact of political existence in the state, one assumes that, by definition, the fact of the political existence of the *Großraum* can never be normatively justified (or at least, can only

---

[70] *Ibid.*, p. 320.

receive such justification from within, on its own terms). One is reminded of the famous passage from *The Concept of the Political*:

There exists no rational purpose, no norm no matter how true, no program no matter how exemplary, no social ideal no matter how beautiful, no legitimacy nor legality which could justify men in killing each other for this reason. If such physical destruction of human life is not motivated by an existential threat to one's own way of life, then it cannot be justified.[71]

The *Großraum* concept represents an attempt simply to affirm the possibility of content to 'a way of life' and to stress its spatial characteristics.

If Schmitt realised the impossibility of grounding a new concept of concrete, particular order in theory, does this mean that his claim to have uncovered the principles of a new geopolitical legal order were essentially fraudulent? Certainly, beyond a cursory appraisal of the concrete situation in Nazi Europe, Schmitt does not, in fact, offer any such principles or vision of a future order. The idea of *Großraum* is almost totally without substance beyond its status as a critique of the status quo. Whilst certainly of interest in its assertion of the need for a new basis for political uniqueness, the conclusions it reaches are inadequate. Why is a continental form of politics better as an assertion of a thorough and anti-universal appreciation of territory? Why can't the state-form be revived as genuinely particular? What distinguished the 'political idea' of a *Großraum* from the bare sense of existential collectivity that defined the political community in *The Concept of the Political*? Schmitt wholly fails to address these foundational questions, and offers no thorough justification of his position.

Behind the *Blut und Boden* language of the *Großraum* concept, it does represent Schmitt's cold analytical attempt to think seriously about how Nazism might fulfil his pet concern – the creation of a plural, territorial order to replace the collapsed order of nation states. From the outset Schmitt's prime point of reference in this work is his longstanding critique of current international law – from the initial definition of international law as a *jus gentium* – a law of peoples – and the familiar critique of the way that this law has witnessed the elevation of the individual subject on the one hand, and a slide into treaty-positivism (*Vertragspositivismus*) on the other.[72] Schmitt rehearses his criticisms of the destructive and abusive role of the League of Nations in using positivist international law, adding an additional critique of the idea of collective and regional security.[73] The

---

[71] C. Schmitt, *The Concept of the Political* (trans. G. Schwab), Chicago: University Press of Chicago (1996), p. 49.
[72] Schmitt, 'Völkerrechtliche Großraumordnung', pp. 270–5.   [73] *Ibid.*, p. 275.

specific challenge for Germany at that precise historical moment was therefore to stand as a barrier against these abstractions and indeterminate categories.

The suspicion must be that the tension between Schmitt's two objectives in presenting and promoting the *Großraum* concept was too great. On the one hand, publishing between 1938 and 1941, Schmitt wished to write explicitly about the novel geopolitical conditions in German-dominated Europe. He sought to defend and contextualise Nazi aggression, to rationalise the ascendant politics in terms of his existing political theory (perhaps as much for the sake of his own peace of mind as for any higher motive) and to think positively about a new global order. And yet there was a clear dissonance between Schmitt's conservative hopes of particularism, a territorially defined way of life and anti-universalism on the one hand, and the realities of Nazi foreign policy on the other. The result is a vague, under-theorised and tentative elaboration of a new order that never really moves beyond a critical mindset. It certainly fails to live up to Schmitt's bold claim to have uncovered radically new spatial and political foundations of a new geopolitical order – purportedly the most radical spatial transformation in 400 years.

The *Großraum* after 1945

The vision of Europe presented in 'Völkerrechtliche Großraumordnung' was clearly unsustainable following Germany's defeat. Schmitt must surely have realised even earlier than this that his hope for a restrained and pluriversal geopolitical order of large spaces did not cohere with the reality of Nazi foreign policy. His increasing isolation in the circle of Nazi international legal theorists reflected in part his failure to capture the essence of the age, and adequately to analyse the real basis of Nazi ambition.[74] With the power of hindsight, it may appear that Schmitt's ambitions were delusional. Certainly, as his conversations with Nicolaus Sombart illustrate, he was seriously disillusioned with Germany's own slide into expansion and the crypto-universalism of its racial ideology: 'Hitler's historical task: overcoming the Versailles diktat through land war. But now we conduct a war of racial annihilation in the East and a worldwide sea war in the West.'[75] Far from recapturing particularity, territoriality and a specific German way of life, Schmitt saw Germany as having been sucked into the kind of global conflict of ideas he so feared. With the invasion of Russia and, especially, the entry of the United States

---

[74] See Vagts, 'International Law', *passim*.
[75] N. Sombart, *Jugend in Berlin*, Munich: Carl Hanser (1984), p. 266.

as a combatant in the European theatre, the prospects for *Großraum* politics appeared doomed.

In one sense, perhaps, the immediate foreclosure of prospects for a German-European *Großraum* resolved the dilemma between theory and practice we identified above. No longer preoccupied by the specific political prospects of Nazi Germany, Schmitt was freed to develop his ongoing critique of treaty-positivism and the universal assault on the state without the need to tie his critique to hopes for the future. From 1943 onwards, he could develop his idea of *Nomos* in a purely theoretical direction, and indefinitely postpone the question of what comes next – a question he had already posed for himself in 1938 with the publication of *Die Wendung zum diskriminierenden Kriegsbegriff*.[76] Certainly *Nomos* represents a far weightier and far more authentic obituary for the European state than the critique in Schmitt's shorter and more agitated works of 1936–40. Nevertheless, it is equally clear that the essence of his pessimism for the prospects of the state, and the imperative to realise new principles of order, were already in place in the mid-to-late 1930s.[77] Schmitt's initial response had been to search for answers. After 1945, perhaps chastened and directionless, he appears to have largely given up the hunt for new categories.

Certainly, Schmitt was forced to reappraise his ideas of *Großraum*. After all, with the simultaneous triumph of the United States and Soviet Russia, the field appeared to have been cleared for a test of rival universalisms rather than the re-creation of the particular, the unique and the partial. With the defeat of Germany and Japan, the exhaustion of Europe and the pre-eminence of the external powers, the prospects for *Großraum* politics appeared dim. Certainly there was no immediate evidence of an emergent new power to counteract the bipolar political system. In contrast to his troubled optimism of the 1930s, Schmitt fell back into a reflective and ambivalent viewpoint about the coming order.

Despite the intercession of events, Schmitt nevertheless held on to the theoretical idea of *Großraum* politics as a potential future answer to the problem of sustaining genuine plural politics at a global level.

---

[76] C. Schmitt, *Die Wendung zum diskriminierenden Kriegsbegriff*, Berlin: Duncker and Humblot (1938).

[77] I would therefore disagree with Jean-François Kervégan when he argues that 'there is a remarkable contrast between texts written before or after the Second World War (or National Socialism) – so much so that they can be gathered into two completely independent groups'. (J.-F. Kervégan, 'Carl Schmitt and "World Unity"', in C. Mouffe (ed.), *The Challenge of Carl Schmitt*, London: Verso (1999), pp. 54–74 (p. 55). Such a strict separation pays too much attention to the tonality of Schmitt's writing, and fails to appreciate the lines of progression and the sustained interest in certain core political phenomena.

In the concluding chapter of *The Nomos of the Earth*, he held out the prospect of three potential conclusions to the unsustainable and unsatisfactory confrontation of the superpowers. Firstly, one of the superpowers could 'win' – a 'last round' or 'final step' in the march towards world unity, with unknowable and, it is supposed, terrible consequences. Secondly, there could be some amplification of current divisions, expanding into new technological and spatial dimensions. Whilst maintaining political plurality, such a solution would presumably maintain the dangers and instability of the current situation. And finally – Schmitt's clear preference – 'a combination of several independent *Großräume* or blocs could constitute a balance, and thereby could precipitate a new order of the earth'.[78]

The prospect of a new order based on radically distinct 'large spaces' continues to be dangled as the best possible exit from the current malaise. However remote, fanciful and difficult to envisage, Schmitt refuses to abandon an idea that was initially conceived as a rationalisation and theoretical rooting of the precise international circumstances of the 1930s. It remains as an understated, unknown and undertheorised possibility, and as the only true 'new *Nomos*'.

It would be as well if the global perspectives of these three possibilities were to become generally known. Most of those considering this frightful problem would rush blindly towards a single sovereign of the world. That idea certainly has a primitive simplicity, but it must not be permitted to displace the other possibilities. The second possibility, continuation of the former hegemonic balance structure, has the greatest chance of accepted custom and tradition on its side. The third possibility, an equilibrium of several independent *Großräume*, is rational, if the *Großräume* are differentiated meaningfully and are homogenous internally.[79]

This final sentence encapsulates in brief the essence of Schmitt's *Großraum* concept: large units, few in number, that possess a uniqueness – a discernible, particular content unto themselves. After all the chaos and closure of world war, Schmitt nevertheless clings to the hope that large-space politics might offer a way out of the political impasse.

Writing in 1952, Schmitt continued to express the belief that both communist and liberal aspirations for world unity would be foiled by the emergence of a new, more complex pluriverse with new large spaces intruding on the East–West dualism.[80] This, Schmitt suggests, remains a more likely outcome to the unsatisfactory status quo than the achievement

---

[78] C. Schmitt, *The Nomos of the Earth in the International Law of the* Jus Publicum Europaeum (trans. G. Ulmen), New York: Telos Press (2004), p. 355.
[79] *Ibid.*
[80] C. Schmitt, 'Die Einheit der Welt', in *Staat, Großraum, Nomos*, pp. 496–512 (*passim*).

of world unity. He continues to contrast his plural vision of particular, unique large spaces to the aspirational universalism and, specifically, erroneous beliefs in a progressive philosophy of history: '[H]istory remains stronger than any philosophy of history, and therefore I do not take the current dualism of the world to be a preparatory step on the path to world unity, but take it instead to be a step on the path to a new plurality [*Vielheit*].'[81] He returns to his theme of this coming new plurality in 1962, expressing confidence that 'it appears that we will live through the present (difficult) times, and that the dualist-bipolar world system will be overcome by a pluralist-multipolar structure'.[82] Indeed, Schmitt now argues that the period following German defeat represents a decisive turning-away from the dangers of world unity. In 1943, he suggests, the Allied powers possessed a strong vision of world unity and perpetual peace. They were committed to such universal-pacific ideals as the United Nations, and appeared to believe that Hitler represented a last barrier to the achievement of their historical project. In truth, Schmitt argues, this 'first phase' was 'nothing more than a prelude. As early as 1947, just two years after the end of the Second World War, the Cold War entered its second phase.'[83] The world took a step back from unity and peace, and entered a phase of bipolar confrontation that could still serve as preparation for a new era of multipolar, regional systems of large spaces.

Even now, Schmitt is annoyingly elusive about the contours and content of this future system of *Großräume*. But it is equally clear that the substance of his wartime study remains the basis of his thinking:

The spatial pluralism that is emerging today is, in reality, a plurality of *Großräume*. But '*Großraum*' means something that must be strongly distinguished from an old sense of space that has simply been broadened. When we think of space, we first and foremost imagine a two-dimensional space. The state (in the sense of international law) is primarily a bordered territory within which the national legal regime, the national government and national courts hold sway. Also, our traditional ideas on war and battle bind us to a flat [*flachhaften*] mode of thought. We think of war as a series of battles that take place and are decided on a battlefield. This is a baroque idea – that war resembles theatre. Against this perception, we must remember that ... only one tenth of real revolutionary war is visible. The greater part of this conflict does not take place in comparable spaces and open battlefields, but in the multidimensional space of the Cold War.[84]

This marks a re-emphasis of the original technical-spatial concerns that appeared to necessitate an expansion of the territorial basis of politics.

---

[81] *Ibid.*, p. 505.
[82] C. Schmitt, 'Die Ordnung der Welt nach dem zweiten Weltkrieg', in *Staat, Grosβraum, Nomos*, pp. 592–618 (p. 602).
[83] *Ibid.*, p. 601.   [84] *Ibid.*, p. 603.

Continental spaces appear to possess the necessary scale to contain multidimensional space, and to allow for real political control over all the various spatial levels at which modern politics will operate. Schmitt hints once again at his concern for airpower and modern weaponry, and the difficulty of grounding the political control of these facets of power in a spatial reality. Once again, he presents the politics of large spaces, vaguely conceived, as the outcome.

Subsequent readers of Schmitt have often called on this image of continental, anti-universal politics as a programmatic basis for opposing the duopoly of the superpowers or, subsequently, the monopoly of the United States. In 'Die Ordnung der Welt', Schmitt suggests that the global anti-colonial movement might give rise to new, powerful political agglomerations in Africa and Asia that resemble the sort of *Großraum* able to re-create plural politics.[85] And, of course, Europe remains as the prototypical and most fervently hoped-for *Großraum*. The very vagueness of Schmitt's ideal of continental politics has allowed an astonishingly broad range of theorists to superimpose their own continental-political aspirations onto the architecture of *Großraum* politics.[86] In so far as such approaches simply aspire to the possibility of particularity and difference on a continental basis, they *do* cohere with the essence of Schmitt's theory. Although largely unacknowledged, it is at least possible that some subsequent advocates of European political and legal unity have been influenced to some degree by Schmitt's construct.[87]

As we have seen, the idea of *Großraum* amounts to little more than the *de facto* existence of spaces that are 'differentiated meaningfully and are homogeneous internally'.[88]

---

[85] See *ibid.*, pp. 596–7. Kervégan argues that 'with remarkable acuteness, Schmitt observes that from the mid 1950s onwards the political emergence of the "Third World" was called on to alter the equilibrium of the blocs significantly, even to the extent that one or other of these blocs attempts to lean on it'. Kervégan, 'Carl Schmitt and "World Unity"', p. 70.

[86] The great irony, of course, is that many of those who have engaged with Schmitt's idea of *Großraum* in fact harbour the hope that a politically unified Europe might act as the bearer of emancipatory ideals; see especially C. Mouffe, 'Schmitt's Vision of a Multipolar World Order', *The South Atlantic Quarterly* 104:2 (Spring 2005), 245–51. Kojève was one of the earliest such 'universalists' to engage critically with Schmitt's ideas on *Großraum*, and indeed proposed his own schema of large-space politics as a transitional stage towards world unity. See A. Kojève, 'L'Empire latin', *La regle du jeu* 1:1 (1990), 89–123.

[87] For arguments to this effect, see J. Laughland, *The Tainted Source: The Undemocratic Origins of the European Idea*, London: Little and Brown (1997); and C. Joerges and N. S. Ghaleigh (eds.), *Darker Legacies of Law in Europe: The Shadow of National Socialism and Fascism over Europe and Its Legal Traditions*, Oxford: Hart (2003).

[88] Schmitt, *Nomos*, p. 355.

Großraum as latent possibility

Despite all the evidence to the contrary, Schmitt does not finally abandon his belief that *Großraum* politics might represent the future of agonism. But beyond an ill-defined sense of the changing spatial possibilities of politics, and the sharp critique of the failings and collapse of the nation state, what is unique, distinctive and new about Schmitt's idea of *Großraum*? Schmitt *hopes* that large-space politics will develop, and considers it the most likely solution to the present malaise. He offers mild suggestions about how and where such politics might emerge, with regional blocks based in the 'Third World' and in Europe. And in the idea of the *Reich* within the wider *Großraum*, we have some sense of how the transition might be achieved between the governmental remnants of the Westphalian system and the assertion of a new regional politics.[89] We know that such spaces must enjoy homogeneity and some moral-cultural content unto themselves. But why should this be the only realistic option on offer in the concluding remarks to *The Nomos of the Earth*?

As the earlier discussion indicated, the *Großraum* is essentially a critical and transformative category. It is conceived as a radical indictment of the failure of the state system to maintain, on the one hand, its sense of territoriality, and, on the other, its capacity to enshrine and protect a particular and unique conception of a way of life. In the immediate instance, it represented an attempt to think legally and internationally about the rise of Nazism in Europe. It clearly orientated itself towards the emergent contours of Nazi foreign policy. It celebrates the anti-universal particularism of the German *Reich*, and looks forward to a new and complicated form of German domination in Central and Eastern Europe. It claims to see the lie in continued ideas of formal equality between states, and, with the concrete situation in Germany as its starting point, predicts a new form of order that is more relevant to changed circumstances. As such, it is a curiously tepid response to reality, and certainly fell a long way short of the sorts of *Lebensraum* theses that came to resonate more clearly with actual German foreign policy. It seems clear that Schmitt's lens of international legal organisation was radically at odds with the real tenets of German foreign policy.

Beyond the concrete situation that Schmitt so misjudged, the concept does seek to represent a replicable and generalised vision of how global politics might be redeemed. After 1945, Schmitt keeps the idea on a form

---

[89] That core states would expand and dominate, translating the remnants of their governmental/political power into a capacity to bind and protect the larger political space as a whole.

of perpetual life-support, maintaining it as a moribund but potent possibility for the future. Without evidence of its emergence, without a foundational argument for its desirability and with a rather sophist reflection on the changed meaning of space, Schmitt relies on *hope* and unaccountable *suggestion* to maintain the idea of *Großraum*. It clearly lacks programmatic value, or the potential to provide real architecture for the design and creation of new political forms. Just as Schmitt claims to have observed the emergence of a new order somewhere in late 1937, the *Großraum* idea is maintained as an invitation to wait and observe the Damascene emergence of a new political form along preordained, continental lines.

In the final analysis, a *Großraum* is definitively the opposite of that which it is intended to critique. It is non-universal (but as the examples of the Monroe Doctrine and Nazi expansion illustrate, in practice it may not continue to adhere to its anti-universal foundations). It represents a concrete particularity (although, as Schmitt remarks, a *Großraum* requires difference and homogeneity in order to exist, which suggests that the *Großraum* itself is derivative rather than generative of such difference). It represents a spatial reality against non-spatial politics (although Schmitt is unable to pin down the relationship between the two-dimensional space of continents with the radically new spatial imperatives that have apparently rendered the two-dimensional spaces of states insufficient).

In 1938, Schmitt's claim to have discovered in the *Großraum* the answer to the future order of the planet fails to convince. *Großräume* continue to look suspiciously like large states, and Schmitt fails to make his case about the uniqueness of their spatial sense. There is little attempt to refine and clarify the political essence of the *Großraum* beyond a mere extension of the public *auctoritas* depicted in *The Concept of the Political*. We are given scant information on the methods of authority and domination that might exist between the *Reich* and other political units. Beyond the fact that the *Großraum* clearly represents a concentration of power – a bolstering of the *de facto* power to decide – Schmitt does not really consider why this more complex and more *penetrable* political arrangement should be a better guard against the individualist claims of liberalism that he considered so corrosive. In its wartime formulation, the *Großraum* appears an undertheorised and somewhat ill-fitting translation of the political attributes of the classical European state onto an apparently emerging reality. After 1945, it is clearly unsustainable in its original form.

Whether or not 'large spaces' were to remain the key to a future order of the political (and Schmitt apparently never lost hope that this could be the case), the limits of the *Großraum* theory suggested a need to reconsider the locus of politics more radically. Having tried and failed to pour the old political wine of state sovereignty into the (not dissimilar) new bottle of *Großraum* power, Schmitt was eventually to realise the need to clarify further the very essence of politics. With little left to lose in the apparently dismal malaise of post-war political stalemate, Schmitt slowly developed a more authentic interest in the historical reality of politics outside the state structure. Faced with the absence of the state, he slowly realised that the typology of the political that he sought to apply in the *Großraum* relied on certain unnecessary assumptions derived from the historical reality of the state. To extend our metaphor, there was potential to distil the concept of the political still further to provide a clearer, purer and stronger classification that truly separated the concept of the political from the concept of the state. In a final and dangerous attempt to find a new theoretical path away from world unity, deterritorialisation and eschata, Schmitt turned to the history of the partisan as a way of achieving this redefinition.

7   Partisan

After 1945, Schmitt was, to borrow A. C. Goodson's apt phrase, an 'historically disappointed man'.[1] His political, moral and intellectual gamble in favour of Nazism had collapsed around him. The dream of a European *Großraum* under German stewardship had been rendered absurd. Far from 'restraining' the onward march of individualism and nihilism, Nazism had given way to a political setting that seemed to confirm Schmitt's worst fears. Domestically, it is an understatement to suggest that 'the "restorationist" Bonn Constitution must now have seemed to [Schmitt] decisively inferior to the Weimar Constitution'.[2] The Federal Republic's new constitutional arrangements and their legal management from Karlsruhe marked the total ascendancy of legal positivism and liberal indeterminacy. Internationally, the only corrective to 'Atlanticism' was the even more moralistic and annihilatory spectre of revolutionary Communism. A divided Germany appeared to represent in microcosm the very consequences that Schmitt had sought to prevent – the collapse of the European state, the privileging of morality above politics, and the elevation of the enemy from a mere existential other to a mortal foe.

In this extreme setting, much of Schmitt's response was embittered, maudlin and reactionary. Schmitt was interred awaiting possible indictment at Nuremberg, spending nearly two years in American custody. His letters and essays written in prison (many collected and published in 1950 under the title *Ex captivitate salus*) are unapologetic for his association with the Nazis, and express regret for their defeat.[3] He remained convinced that his diagnosis of the malaise of Weimar in particular, and the state of world politics in general, necessitated some radical attempt at restoration.

---

[1] A. C. Goodson, 'About Schmitt: Partisans and Theory', *The New Centennial Review* 4:3 (2004) 1–7 (p. 1).
[2] G. Balakrishnan, *The Enemy: An Intellectual Portrait of Carl Schmitt*, London: Verso (2000), p. 258.
[3] C. Schmitt, *Ex captivitate salus*, Cologne: Greven Verlag (1950).

His regret was for the contingent failures that undermined the project rather than the criminality or moral failings of the enterprise: regret for Hitler's own self-defeating instincts, for the ongoing failings of the Prussian elite to make a decision in favour of reaction, for the Staufenberg plot.[4] Regret, in short, for the collapse of his own world-historical ambitions for Nazism. By abstracting out into the world-historical context, Schmitt justifies his decision in favour of Nazism as both a legitimate attempt at renewal, and a historical necessity.

In the later 1940s, Schmitt flits between an intensely personal reflection on the meaning of these events for himself, and a coldly juridical reflection on the treatment of Germany at the hands of the Allies. On the one hand, given his well established aversion to Romantic introspection, the publication of *Ex captivitate salus* is a surprisingly personal and exposed account of Schmitt as a broken man. Yet at the same time, he still busied himself with providing a critique of the post-war political setting using the same critical categories he had developed previously. Nuremberg, in this account, offered up the same kind of moralising and persecuting 'justice' as Versailles, only with fewer prospects for political renewal.[5] He never realistically acknowledges the unique horror of Nazi crimes.[6]

---

[4] The attempt to assassinate Hitler appears to have had a peculiarly intense effect on Schmitt, not least because of the central involvement of his close friend Johannes Popitz, with whom he had been staying shortly before the plot. Schmitt had no knowledge of the plot, and the experience put into conflict his sympathies as a friend and his political-intellectual decision in favour of Nazism. He later describes his 'beloved Popitz' as possessing 'something of the humanist holiness of Thomas More'. C. Schmitt, *Glossarium: Aufzeichnungen der Jahre 1947–1951*, Berlin: Duncker and Humblot (1991), pp. 51, 55–6.

[5] Schmitt prepared a pre-emptive defence for his friend, the businessman Friedrich Flick, who was tried at Nuremberg on a charge of assisting a war of aggression. Schmitt here acknowledges that certain crimes of Nazism were outside the juridical freedoms of international law, but nevertheless argues that Nuremberg was essentially all about the crime of aggression and, as such, a violation of the basic principles of state sovereignty and *justus hostis*. See C. Schmitt, *Das internationalrechtliche Verbrechen des Angriffskrieges und der Grundsatz* Nullum crimen, nulla poena sine lege, Berlin: Duncker and Humblot (1994). For an examination of Schmitt's wider legal and personal response to his implication at Nuremberg, see C. Schmitt, *Antworten in Nürnberg* (ed. H. Quaritsch), Berlin: Duncker and Humblot (2000).

[6] Schmitt's retrospective position on Nazism and his complicity in it are beyond the scope of this work. His response is perhaps the more troubling in that he acknowledged the crimes of Nazism without apparently according them any particular moral opprobrium. Schmitt wrote to Ernst Jünger in 1948 that Hitler had been 'a criminal, but neither the last nor the greatest (since the world-historical spirit chooses other means for the greatest crimes)'. Letter of 20 July 1948 in H. Kiesel (ed.), *Ernst Jünge–Carl Schmitt Briefe, 1930–1983*, Stuttgart: Klett–Cotta (1999), p. 228. For a good overview of the immediate post-war years and Schmitt's ambivalent reflections on Nazism, see 'Masks and Mirrors', in J.-W. Müller, *A Dangerous Mind: Carl Schmitt in Post-War European Thought*, New Haven: Yale University Press (2003), pp. 51–62.

Throughout the 1950s, Schmitt was a background figure. Removed from public life, he started his strange second career as an underground mentor to intellectual adventurers of both Left and Right, and as a source of productive controversy in the legal and political debates of the Federal Republic. As Müller's superb study amply illustrates, Schmitt became an active and influential participant in debates on contemporary Germany from behind the veil of his own internal exile.[7] In large part, Schmitt's work during the 1950s was more nostalgic, more reactionary and more conventionally conservative than previously. Joseph de Maistre and Donoso Cortes became key figures of interest. And his reflections were also more personal and (even) more self-aggrandising. Increasingly, Schmitt himself became an object of study – a sort of anthropomorphic representation of the fate of an authentic conservative intellectual in the twentieth century. This merging of personal and political reflection is well captured in *Ex captivitate salus*:

By recognising [the Other] as my enemy I recognise that he can put me into question. And who can really put me into question? Only I myself. Or my brother ... Adam and Eve had two sons, Cain and Abel. Thus begins the history of mankind ... That is the dialectical tension which keeps world history moving and *world history has not yet come to an end*.[8]

Notwithstanding his pessimism and contempt for the political status quo, Schmitt nevertheless avoided the conclusion that either the political or a new order had become impossible.

In spite of his dire wartime predictions, the pessimism of *The Nomos of the Earth* and the lack of any evidence of emergent new orders, Schmitt could not accept the conclusion that world history had come to an end. Too many of the old questions that had motivated the search for a new *Nomos* of the earth remained. Can something akin to political authority exist without the modern state? Is a new ordering principle possible? Are there emergent new ways to achieve the unity of order and orientation? Whatever the inadequacies of its foundations, the longer the Cold War persisted, the greater the hope that it represented a changing of the seasons rather than a final step. As we saw in the previous chapter, Schmitt made periodic attempts to adapt and apply his ideas on *Großraum* to a post-war setting. But too much had changed for him to answer such questions with the simple abstractions of his theory of state that lay at the heart of the *Großraum* theory. Increasingly towards the end of his career, he was drawn back towards a deeper reframing of his core conceptual language

---

[7] Müller, *A Dangerous Mind*.
[8] Schmitt, *Ex captivitate salus*, pp. 89–90 (my emphasis).

as a way out of his self-imposed theoretical cul-de-sac.[9] His study of the phenomenon of partisan warfare is perhaps the most significant such attempt to think anew through Schmitt's whole edifice of political categories and their status as historically conditioned concepts.

Alongside his *Großraumtheorie*, the 'Partisan' represents Schmitt's second attempt to generate a way of thinking conceptually about politics after or outside the European state. But rather than attempting to build a new edifice of political order, his concern here is to strip away his political categories to discover a more basic understanding of the political, and how it might survive outside the state form. It is both an historical depiction, and an attempt to distil a new concept to remedy the current situation. Developed from a pair of lectures given in Pamplona and Zaragoza early in 1962, the *Theorie des Partisanen* is an historical-theoretical meditation on politically motivated violence outside the state, and the changing political meaning of such partisanship.[10]

Schmitt presents us with a snapshot history of the partisan from his origins in Spanish and Tyrolean resistance against Napoleon, right up to (anti-)colonial partisan warfare in Indochina and Algeria. As such, we are considering a relatively narrow time frame from 1800 to the present in which (despite the success of the Congress of Vienna as 'one of the most astonishing restorations in all world history') the classical state-form had come under terminal pressure.[11] This historical account is used to construct a theoretical ideal-type partisan, and to suggest the ways in which the fate of this idealised partisan has fared in tandem with the fate of the state. Such partisan activity, Schmitt argues, is a precise symptom of the growing weaknesses of the European state, and the increasing incapacity of the *jus publicum Europaeum* to contain politics and warfare. In certain respects, therefore, *Theory of the Partisan* is offering a shadow narrative

---

[9] Alongside the oblique reappraisal of the concept of the political in *Theorie des Partisanen: Zwischenbemerkung zum Begriff des Politischen*, Berlin: Duncker and Humblot (1963), in later years Schmitt also published a consciously direct reappraisal of the theme of political theology in *Politische Theologie II: Die Legende der Erledigung jeder politischen Theologie*, Berlin: Duncker and Humblot (1970).

[10] Schmitt, *Theorie des Partisanen*. Two preliminary English translations of this work have appeared within journal studies of Schmitt. See C. Schmitt, 'The Theory of the Partisan: A Commentary/Remark on the Concept of the Political' (trans. A. C. Goodson), *The New Centennial Review* 4:3 (2004), 1–78; and 'Theory of the Partisan' (trans. G. Ulmen), *Telos* 127 (Spring 2004), 11–78. Both translations have already succeeded in opening Schmitt's work to a wider audience. However, since they are somewhat provisional in nature, I have used them only as an aid, relying on my own translation. Telos Press have subsequently produced a monograph translation which, as with their *Nomos of the Earth*, will doubtless become the standard English-language resource. See C. Schmitt, *Theory of the Partisan* (trans. G. Ulmen), New York: Telos Press (2007).

[11] Schmitt, *Theorie des Partisanen*, p. 16.

to the grand narrative of the state Schmitt presents in *The Nomos of the Earth*. It is a conceptual study of the underbelly of European history since Napoleon.

Both in tone and substance, it is hard to conceive of an approach more in contrast with the stolid, programmatic conceptual language of *Großraum*. After the hubris and certainty of his geopolitics, Schmitt's approach here is tentative, contemplative and non-committal. The partisan is not presented as the direct 'answer' to the current malaise, but rather as a conceptual device enabling us better to understand our current politics and how we have arrived here. We are invited to take an interest in the partisan because he represents a radically different way of determining and articulating enmity and, as such, gives rise to differing political possibilities. Moreover, as a defensive figure, the partisan might open the possibility of new avenues to the restriction and limitation of enmity – that is to say, the partisan *might* be a source of order. In its own way, *Theory of the Partisan* is an attempt to think through the end of the *jus publicum Europaeum*, and to look outside the state for a solution. We must assess it on those terms.

This chapter seeks to analyse the extent to which the notion of the partisan offers a political corrective on Schmitt's own terms. Does it bolster the state system, or hasten its departure? Can it provide the ingredients for a new order, or is the partisan a twilight figure – the last, insignificant representative of radical particularism? The argument shall proceed along four broad avenues. Firstly, the theory of the partisan must be considered on its own terms as a re-evaluation of the basic political categories that Schmitt developed in the 1920s and 1930s. How does he use the partisan as a means of clarifying his political starting point and, from the perspective of 1962, what is to be achieved by means of such a reappraisal?

Next we shall consider the substance of the partisan concept itself, and the method Schmitt deploys. Once again, we are presented with a story of conceptual fragility, and the imminent danger of regression along a pre-ordained path. Schmitt depicts the path via which the defensive, natural, particular partisan is so easily subsumed by total, unlimited, ideological concerns. We will consider Schmitt's purpose in delineating an ideal-type partisan, and the form of historical argumentation he deploys to highlight the fragility of the partisan concept. Thirdly, we shall consider the three precise points of vulnerability in the concept that Schmitt highlights. These centre on the tendency to re-create the partisan as a philosophical category, the impact of technological change on partisan warfare, and the exposure of the partisan to the increasingly globalised mechanics of world politics. All three phenomena, Schmitt argues, exert a pressure on the partisan, transforming him from a particular-defensive into a universal-spaceless figure. We shall examine the extent to which 'authentic' partisanship is able to resist these pressures, and the prospects Schmitt envisages for partisans of the future. That is to say, despite the historical vulnerability that Schmitt outlines, should we nevertheless think of the partisan as a significant locus of politics in the future?

Inevitably, perhaps, much contemporary scholarship on Schmitt's partisan focuses on the possibility that this work is helpful in illuminating the contours of the post-9/11 world. In its examination of the relationship between the regular and the irregular, and his distinction of 'real' defensive enmity from 'absolute' revolutionary enmity, *Theory of the Partisan* is Schmitt's one work that appears to speak most directly to the circumstances of our contemporary politics. His language of political and anti-political violence and of imperialism and anti-colonialism is a source of appeal to a wide range of theorists. Naturally, such attempts to apply Schmitt's categories to a radically new situation entail dangers of simplification and obfuscation. Yet, in many respects, these attempts to adapt and apply Schmitt's categories are a useful retrospective test on whether the partisan succeeds on Schmitt's own terms – that is to say, whether or not the idea of the partisan represents a useful reframing of the concept of the political. Schmitt's own conclusions on the value of thinking in terms of partisanship are somewhat equivocal. By presenting the contrast between authentic partisans and global revolutionaries, he already prefigures a core ambiguity in how to frame violence outside the state. The question that remains for us is whether or not the partisan transcends the limits of the European state, and how it speaks to an ongoing, problematic interplay of politics and order.

The four criteria of partisanship

Schmitt starts his account in Spain in 1808. This marks a new point of departure in his account, because of the intense contrast between the extraordinary *regularity* of Napoleon's troops, and the *irregularity* of the Spanish partisans. The partisan as a distinct conceptual category relies on this status as 'irregular'. And since 'the distinction between regular and irregular depends on the degree of regularity', it is only with the advent of the modern, mobilised armies of the French Revolution that the distinct concept of the partisan emerges.[12] A similar intensity of contrast is to be seen in Austria, where Tyrolean partisans likewise emerged in response to

---

[12] *Ibid.*, p. 10.

Napoleon. Schmitt presents these two settings as instances of spontaneous, defensive, particular, irregular and autochthonous responses to a
foreign invasion. As we shall explore below, they become the basis of an
idealised and naturalised ideal-type of partisan. They are the locus of a
quasi-political determination in the absence of a credible state, and so
offer the only basis for expressing enmity. 'The salient point of the Spanish
partisan's situation in 1808 was that he took the risk of fighting on his
home soil [*Heimatboden*], while his own king and the royal family had not
yet decided who the real enemy was.'[13]

From the example of this resistance to Napoleon, Schmitt draws a
typology to describe this form of autochthonous partisanship. Firstly, by
definition, such partisans are irregular. They come into being in the face of
an external regular force, and as a consequence of there being no source of
regularity upon which they can rely politically. Schmitt goes to great
lengths to distinguish between the authentic, irregular partisan, and
light troops who may display certain characteristics of the partisan, but
whose identity and orientation derives from the regular authority of the
state. It is no accident, therefore, that the *locus classicus* of the partisan
fighter is colonial and civil war – the two arenas that most precisely denote
the absence of political regularity on one side of the conflict. Where states
succeed in dominating the political horizon, the partisan is an insignificant
figure.[14] The role of the partisan depends on a highly contingent situation
in which there is both a stark and firmly defined 'regular', and an external
space in which the 'irregular' is counterpoised to it.

The second feature (or 'touchstone') that Schmitt identifies is the
partisan's intense political commitment. On the one hand, this distinguishes him from the mere criminal 'whose motives aim at private enrich-
ment'.[15] This criterion works in tandem with the designation of the
partisan as irregular. The two criteria define the partisan in two directions.
He is distinguished from regular light troops by virtue of his definitional
irregularity. He is distinguished from the criminal or thief by virtue of his
intense political commitment. As such, he can be considered as an in-
between category. 'The Partisan personifies a radicalised enmity', but this
enmity is radical in the sense that it is determined outside the structures of
the state, rather than in the sense that it is apolitical or anti-political.[16]
Despite his profound individuality and the lack of structure that attends to
his methods of fighting, the partisan is nevertheless a group figure. He is
committed to political goals that transcend his own individuality.

---

[13] *Ibid.*, p. 14.   [14] *Ibid.*, p. 17.   [15] *Ibid.*, p. 21.
[16] E. Horn, '*Waldgänger*, Traitor, Partisan: Figures of Political Irregularity in West German
Postwar Thought', *The New Centennial Review* 4:3 (2004) 125–43 (p. 128).

Having situated the partisan as a political actor on a spectrum stretching from the absolute state to radical individualism (the criminal) Schmitt illustrates the partisan's disposition by means of two further criteria. Firstly, the partisan is telluric. He is 'a specifically terrestrial type of active fighter' who is tied to a locale.[17] He is a creature of the land, tied to the valleys, mountains and homesteads of his *own* environment. This intimacy with the land is, of course, the classic source of the partisan's tactical strength. But more than this, his autochthonous relationship with the land serves to define him categorically. In his original and ideal formulation, in Spain and the Tyrol from 1808 to 1813, the partisan occupies an 'essentially defensive situation'.[18] He fights *pro aris et focis* – for the altars and the hearths.[19] That is to say, in defence of his home, his people and his culture against the perceived enemy. This telluric situating of the partisan is an essential component in grounding his perspective on enmity, and Schmitt uses it as a hallmark distinction between the classic defensive partisan and other irregular fighters who pursue abstract objectives detached from territorial space.[20]

The fourth feature distinguishing Schmitt's partisan is his mobility. The partisan does not stand and fight, but rather moves seamlessly within the population. In *Theorie des Partisanen* this element of speed is somewhat simply rendered as an aspect of the partisan's military status. 'Agility, speed, and the sudden change of surprise attack and retreat' are elements of the tactical and functional circumstances of irregularity.[21] The reader is intended to recognise a clear tension between the partisan's tellurism, and the imperatives of mobility. Subsequently, however, Schmitt sought better to clarify his meaning of mobility as the interplay of the partisan's irregularity and his intimate connection to the land. In this sense, Schmitt associates 'mobility' with 'unpredictability'. Drawing on Maoist language of partisanship, he casts mobility in terms of an absence of any *Standort* – a situation that allows the partisan to move 'like a fish through water'.[22]

These, then, are Schmitt's conceptual foundations. Four criteria, or 'touchstones', that are intended to describe both historically real partisans, and an ideal type in theory. Irregularity, political commitment, tellurism

---

[17] Schmitt, *Theorie des Partisanen*, p. 27.   [18] *Ibid.*, p. 26.   [19] *Ibid.*, p. 77.

[20] As Goodson puts it, the use of the telluric category is of importance in illustrating that '[authentic] politics is visceral, a matter of the local hero who fights *pro aris et focis* because usage, custom and habit are the real substance of the political'. A. C. Goodson, '*Pro aris et focis*: Schmitt's Partisans in Münkler's Theory of War', *The New Centennial Review* 4:3 (2004), 145–59 (p. 157).

[21] Schmitt, *Theorie des Partisanen*, p. 11.

[22] C. Schmitt, 'Gespräch über den Partisanen Carl Schmitt und Joachim Schickel', in *Staat, Großraum, Nomos: Arbeiten aus den Jahren 1916–1969* (ed. G. Maschke), Berlin: Duncker and Humblot (1996), pp. 619–42 (p. 625).

and mobility – these four interpenetrating ideas represent a political disposition that Schmitt clearly wishes to cast as authentic and admirable. This is
not the state politics and strictly public enmity of *The Concept of the Political*.
It is a form of enmity that represents the limits and failings of the *jus
publicum Europaeum*. But despite this, the partisans of 1808 represent
politics in the raw – a final corrective to the anti-political ambitions of
Napoleon. In the first instance, therefore, Schmitt's study stands in support
of his contention that the political is immutable. In the face of Napoleonic
universalism and the failure of states to make the necessary declaration of
enmity, some form of enmity declaration emerged. Mangled and inchoate,
and lacking the refined features of classic sovereignty, this decision against
Napoleon nevertheless constituted a judgement that 'the adversary intends
to negate his opponent's way of life and therefore must be repulsed or
fought in order to preserve one's own form of existence'.[23]

Schmitt's concern in the remainder of the book is to consider how well
the phenomenon of partisanship fares throughout the remaining twilight
years of the *jus publicum Europaeum*.[24] Schmitt is seeking to discover
whether a 'theory of the partisan' as resistance to universalism can be
distilled from the concrete experience of individual partisans in certain
places. The prospects for such a distillation are essential to Schmitt's
hopes of plotting a fresh conceptual barrier to nihilism. Much of
Schmitt's technique here is familiar from his previous works. The way in
which he embeds his concepts into a carefully selected historical narrative
evokes *Land und Meer* and *The Nomos of the Earth*. His eventual conclusion
that the phenomenon of partisanship might be prejudiced by its very
conceptual origins is reminiscent of his critique of Hobbes and the fragility
of the modern state.

The notion of the partisan differs from the other conceptual innovations
we have studied in one important respect, however. As Eva Horn points
out, the theory of the partisan is anthropomorphic. It involves the 'translation of an abstract "question" or human situation into a human figure'.[25] In a clear departure from his high political narratives of states,
systems and grand theoreticians, Schmitt illustrates his theory by depicting the outsider individual.[26] The isolated figure of the partisan presents

---

[23] C. Schmitt, *The Concept of the Political*, p. 27.
[24] Schmitt himself accepts the description of his method as 'phenomenological', but 'prefer[s]
to avoid such general methodological questions' as 'they tend to go on and on without end'.
Schmitt, 'Gespräch über den Partisanen', p. 621.
[25] Horn, '*Waldgänger*', pp. 126–7.
[26] Horn illuminates the parallels between Schmitt's use of the partisan to denote a position in
contrast to the modern crisis, and the way in which Ernst Jünger constructs a figure 'of
radical dissent and autonomy whom he calls the *Waldgänger*'. *Ibid.*, p. 127.

something of a paradox. Although quintessentially modern (a by-product, in a sense, of the modern state), the partisan cuts a simple, almost primordial figure. By hanging his insights on this figure, Schmitt appears to signal his own intention to present a theoretical perspective that is prior to, and outside, the assumptions of state and sovereignty. He represents a radical disjuncture with order, and a figure of conceptual danger. Through the figure of the partisan, Schmitt suggestively raises the question of the Last Man, placing the isolated fighter in the context of radical and accelerating political dissolution. In contrast to all his earlier theory of political order, Schmitt is turning the tables, and writing a study that aspires to engage with the outside, rather than axiomatically seeking to defend the existing order. In many respects, *Theory of the Partisan* is one of Schmitt's humblest works.

Theorie des Partisanen and *The Concept of the Political*

Schmitt presents the theory of the partisan as a *Zwischenbemerkung zum Begriff des Politischen*. A phrase that defies accurate translation into English, it might be rendered as a 'parenthetical comment upon', or 'a digression on the subject of', the concept of the political. Goodson leaves interpretation of the subtitle open, choosing to translate it as 'A Commentary/Remark on the Concept of the Political'.[27] As Schmitt himself puts it, the choice of subtitle:

is explained by the specific date of the publication [1963]. The publishers are making the text of my essay of 1932 [*The Concept of the Political*] accessible again at this time. In recent years several corollaries to this theme have emerged. The present treatment of the subject is not one of these, but a free-standing work which – though only in a sketchy way – issues unavoidably in the problem of the distinction between friend and enemy.[28]

In itself, this is a sketchy and vague explanation of the linkage between the works. Schmitt is unwilling to frame his work on the partisan explicitly as a reference to the question of the political as an autonomous category, and invites his readers to draw their own conclusions about this relationship.

As Slomp helpfully points out, we can learn much about Schmitt's intentions by studying his preface to the 1963 edition of *The Concept of the Political* published in tandem with *Theorie des Partisanen*. Schmitt reflects on three flaws in his 1932 work. Firstly, that its self-consciously lean and punchy style is perhaps too abstract and reductive (although

---

[27] Schmitt, 'Theory of the Partisan' (trans. Goodson).
[28] Schmitt, *Theorie des Partisanen*, p. 7.

essential, of course, to its polemical effect). Secondly, and vitally, that the work reduces enmity to two simple types (the concrete enemy and the foe), whereas in reality a threefold distinction of 'conventional, real, and absolute' enemies is more helpful. Finally, he reflects on the limits of systemic conceptions of politics, and the need to turn instead to new, less conceptual methods of theorising the political.[29] Whatever the precise points of intersection between the two works, Slomp correctly points out that these three criticisms are key influences in *Theorie des Partisanen*.

In Chapter 2 of this work, we considered the two central contentions of Schmitt's pre-war theory of the political, each pithily encapsulated in the opening lines of his two most famous works. First, 'sovereign is he who decides on the exception'.[30] Second, 'the concept of the state presupposes the concept of the political'.[31] These are the explosive contentions that give *The Concept of the Political* its extravagant conceptual force. Yet very quickly, Schmitt's theory of the political as an autonomous category becomes concerned with the precise distinction of two quite *particular* kinds of enmity that only make sense if we assume the state-form. On the one hand we have the limited, public, just *hostis*. This is distinguished by the universal, private *inimicus* that cannot be framed by any reference to justice. As we noted, Schmitt has seamlessly imposed categories of the state onto his supposedly autonomous category of the political. The declaration of the enemy may be an autonomous moment, but it is only a political, sovereign act if it gives a certain kind of grounding to that enmity. It is a *state-like* determination. It must possess the ring of *public* authority, and reproduce this authority in the way it grounds that decision. As such, for all practical purposes, it was always difficult to conceive of Schmitt's concept of the political prior to and apart from the concept of the state.

By targeting its enquiry at enmity outside of the state, the *Theorie des Partisanen* clearly represents an attempt to penetrate and untangle this gloss. It is an attempt to clarify the declaration of enmity as a real, concrete, imaginable and autonomous act. The study is therefore *about* the possibility of real politics outside the state and, I would contend, is motivated by the search for new principles that can situate the political without the state. It therefore involves an 'elucidation and elaboration of the claim' that the state has lost its monopoly on the political.[32] The same

---

[29] See G. Slomp, 'The Theory of the Partisan: Carl Schmitt's Neglected Legacy', *History of Political Thought* 26:3 (2005), 502–19 (p. 502).

[30] C. Schmitt, *Political Theology* (trans. G. Schwab), Cambridge, MA: MIT Press (2005), p. 5.

[31] C. Schmitt, *The Concept of the Political* (trans. G. Schwab), Chicago: University of Chicago Press (1996), p. 19.

[32] Slomp, 'The Theory of the Partisan', p. 503.

claim, that is, that Schmitt makes in *The Nomos of the Earth* and elsewhere. But more than this, it is an attempt to find a way out of the nostalgic, epitaphic language of *Nomos*, and to think productively about the problem of the political and order in an age *apart from* the state.

Ever since the mid 1930s, Schmitt had been enormously preoccupied with the collapsing political competence of the state. At various stages this prompted determined defence, aggressive reaction and mournful resignation. Yet the constant feature was Schmitt's unstinting emotional and conceptual attachment to the European state-form as the highest organisational achievement of politics. *Theory of the Partisan* appears, on the surface, to mark Schmitt's attempt to reconcile himself to the historical process of dissolution. But it does so in trying to rethink the very essence of the political that Schmitt has distilled, and to rescue this kernel from the wider context of the state. The obvious starting point, therefore, is to consider concrete evidence of the divergence between the state-form, and the decisionist basis of the political.

Schmitt considers in depth two instances in which the state fails to make a determination of enmity. One we have considered already in the Spanish instance. The failure of the Spanish king to recognise Spain's true enemy created a zone of indeterminacy that was solved by the autochthonous expression of that enmity by the partisans. The other example derives from the same period, but is very different. Schmitt considers the case of General York as one of several members of the Prussian military elite (Clausewitz among them) who took commissions in the Russian army in 1812 and 1813. Although not a partisan in the terms Schmitt gives, York illustrates the central importance of 'decisionist exactness' in situating the political.[33] Schmitt considers York's letter to the Prussian king, and its explanation for his desertion. 'What gives York's letter its proper, tragic, and rebellious meaning,' Schmitt contends, 'is that he – in all his devotion to the king – reserves judgment of who the "real enemy" is'.[34] In both instances, the failure of the *state* to make the necessary political decision against Napoleon creates an arena of indeterminacy in which groups or individuals seek to impose their own decision.

Schmitt sees Europe between 1808 and 1812 as a unique historical moment. The types of determination made by autochthonous partisans,

---

[33] Schmitt, *Theorie des Partisanen*, p. 88. Schmitt is particularly struck by the fact that, of all people, a Prussian general could find himself subject to the same decisionist impulses as the partisan. There can hardly be a greater counterpoise to the shabby irregularity of the partisan than the high political regularity of the Prussian state. Schmitt concedes that after 1813 'the notion that a Prussian general could become a partisan would have become grotesque and absurd even as a heuristic device'. *Ibid.*, p. 90.

[34] *Ibid.*

and the questions that troubled Prussian generals, were symptoms of the weakness of the old, conventional methods of determining enmity through the state apparatus.[35] Before the 1790s, to be sure, the contained, idealised game structures of the Westphalian order had fulfilled this task well. This conventional monopoly of the political by states was sustainable for as long as 'their domestic as well as their inter-state concepts of regularity and irregularity, legality and illegality, [were] in alignment or at least structurally homogeneous to some extent'.[36] After the Congress of Vienna, such homogeneity would once again allow a structural ordering of conventional enmity. But the failure of these classical European states to develop a coherent sense of enmity towards Napoleon's total, escalatory hostility exposed the gap that had developed between the calcified orientations of state governments, and the concrete political imperatives of statehood. In this context, Schmitt draws the distinction between the formalised structures of enmity under the *jus publicum Europaeum*, and the 'real' enmity expressed by partisans.

Slomp discusses this distinction at length, stressing the link between 'the emergence of real enmity' and 'the weakening of the state'.[37] My reading is slightly different, in that I do not agree with Slomp that 'whereas the conventional enemy is described as a challenge to the state from outside, Schmitt defines the real enemy as a challenge to the state from within'.[38] The language of inside–outside threatens to distract from the fact that the determination of 'real' enmity is an existential declaration of the group at precisely the point that the mechanics of conventional enmity fails to deliver. The declaration of 'real' enmity is always a response to the perceived vulnerability of the conventional mechanics of decision. It is a response to the dangers of obsolescence that Schmitt had noted in 1932 when he remarked:

For as long as a people exists in the political sphere, this people must, even if only in the most extreme case – and whether this point has been reached has to be decided by it – determine by itself the distinction of friend and enemy. Therein resides the essence of its political existence. When it no longer possesses the capacity or the will to make this distinction, it ceases to exist politically.[39]

Civil war, in this context, involves the dispute over who best protects and promotes this capacity to make a decision. It is a conceptual dispute that nevertheless looks to the outside, and to the maintenance of the group.

[35] I follow Slomp in using the term 'conventional' to describe the traditional, pre-1789 forms of state-determined enmity to which Schmitt refers as his default position. See Slomp, 'The Theory of the Partisan', pp. 508–10.
[36] Schmitt, *Theorie des Partisanen*, p. 41.   [37] Slomp, 'The Theory of the Partisan', p. 510.
[38] *Ibid.*   [39] Schmitt, *The Concept of the Political*, p. 49.

The declaration of real enmity, although authentically political, is problematic precisely because it takes place out of context. Classical states possessed their own grammar of enmity according to which everyone knew where they stood. In some respects, the conventional arrangements of the *jus publicum Europaeum* are simply the outlines of this grammar. Both practically and conceptually, 'conventional' declarations of enmity benefit from the web of quasi-legal 'conventions' in which they took place. The partisan, by contrast, makes his declaration of 'real' enmity anew each time, throwing himself into an interaction with his enemy, the contours and consequences of which cannot be predetermined. As such, the declaration of 'real' enmity entails distinct complexities that do not attach to conventional enmity.

The partisan falls outside any pre-existing structure of international law. The partisan does not expect to benefit from the codified limitations and restrictions to warfare that exist in inter-state war, nor does he grant such benefits to his enemy. He is irregular, after all, and the very fact of his irregularity places him outside these conventions – he is outside the system. 'A partisan would act [in resisting an occupation] neither really legally nor illegally, but on his own account and in a *risky* way.'[40] If caught, the partisan will be dispatched as a spy. 'He risks not only his life, like every regular combatant. He knows, and accepts, that the enemy places him outside law, statute, and honour.'[41] In turn, he exposes the regular soldier to an indeterminate threat. He will seek to attack the soldier by any means, in any place, and at any time. The only limitation on this form of conflict is the partisan's defensive disposition and the fact that his objectives are political.

Both 'real' enmity and more traditional forms of *staatlich* enmity contrast with the third category Schmitt presents – 'absolute' enmity. This disposition is a familiar, default position throughout Schmitt's oeuvre. It is the sum of his fears. Here, Schmitt sums up the ingredients of absolute enmity in language immediately recognisable from *The Concept of the Political* or *The Nomos of the Earth*:

[The danger of absolute enmity] consists in the inevitability of moral compulsion. Men who turn [nuclear weapons] against others consider themselves compelled to annihilate their victims as objects in a moral sense. They have to consider the other side as totally criminal and inhuman – totally worthless. The logic of value and its obverse, worthlessness, unfolds its annihilating consequence, compelling increasingly new, deeper discrimination, criminalisation and devaluation to the point that it annihilates all that unworthy of life.[42]

---

[40] Schmitt, *Theorie des Partisanen*, p. 33 (Schmitt's emphasis).
[41] *Ibid.*, p. 35.   [42] *Ibid.*, p. 95.

In other words, in both cause and effect, 'absolute enmity' corresponds more or less exactly with the category of 'foe' in *The Concept of the Political*. It results from the elevation of moral compulsion above political recognition. And it results in the kind of limitless annihilation and disorder depicted in *Die Wendung zum diskriminierenden Kriegsbegriff* (only now with the dangerous admixture of nuclear weapons).[43]

Whatever the precise circumstances in which it is expressed, 'absolute' enmity is a symptom of the breakdown of political restraint. It is both a categorical disposition, and a symptom of failings within pre-existing orders of the political. Within *Theorie des Partisanen*, we can distinguish at least three historical settings in which Schmitt located this form of absolute and dangerous enmity. The first two concern absolute enmity that manifests itself as a perversion of the structures of the state. Napoleon, of course, represents the first outlet of absolute enmity in modern times. His enemy was not the concrete opponent of the *jus publicum Europaeum*, but an abstracted and limitless enemy. Lenin's Russia likewise represents the replacement of concrete political logic with aggressive ideology. Both are instances of total enmity in tandem with the machinery of governance and outward *staatlich* features. Indeed, the 'regularity of the state and of the military in Napoleonic France receive a new and exact determinateness'.[44] Schmitt has already had much to say about the shift from conventional to absolute enmity within the context of the state system.[45] The main point of interest here, then, is the parallel process by which 'real' enmity is replaced by 'absolute' enmity, and the 'partisan' becomes his antipode, the 'global revolutionary'.

The vulnerability of the partisan – three points of weakness

Just as Schmitt is concerned with the internal flaws that allowed the state to dissolve into an inauthentic shadow of itself, so too is he concerned to illuminate the aspects of partisanship that tend to undermine its very essence. He is concerned to illustrate the conceptual incompatibility between the autochthonous partisan who fights defensively, and the rootless irregular fighter whose enmity knows no limits. From the perspective of the 1960s, Schmitt's readers would have been expected to make a very strong association between 'partisan' and Communism. From Indochina to Latin America, partisan warfare seemed intimately connected with the

---

[43] C. Schmitt, *Die Wendung zum diskriminierenden Kriegsbegriff*, Berlin: Duncker and Humblot (1938).
[44] Schmitt, *Theorie des Partisanen*, p. 11.   [45] See Chapters 3 and 4.

spread of global Communism. The connection is self-evident too for Schmitt. But rather than seeking to explain the appeal of partisanship as a revolutionary tactic, he instead seeks to trace ideological politics and partisanship as intertwined concepts in a feedback relationship. We can isolate three points of vulnerability in his ideal-type concept of the partisan that both stimulate the turn to 'absolute' enmity, and in turn expose the remaining authentic partisan to the dynamics of 'absolute' enmity. We shall consider them in turn.

Philosophical abstraction

The ideal-type partisan is a concrete figure. Schmitt considers the Spanish partisans against Napoleon to have fought instinctively, from first princi-ples. There was no pre-existing method, no handbook on how to be a partisan, and, presumably, no particular self-awareness of themselves as a *type* of combatant. They simply acted. As with most historical examples Schmitt uses to exemplify his position, this contention is undoubtedly open to question in terms of its historical accuracy.[46] Nevertheless, Schmitt is keen to discriminate between the partisan as a concrete figure in a particular time and place, and what we might term 'partisanism' – or put another way, 'modern theories of the partisan'.[47] He contends that the elaboration of ideas of the partisan as a philosophical figure has a serious effect on the survival of the partisan in its natural form.

Schmitt situates this philosophical seroconversion of the idea of the partisan in Hegel's Berlin. He suggests that between 1808 and 1813, 'a spark flew north from Spain' and found fuel in the philosophical debates surrounding the question of German resistance to Napoleon.[48] This spark 'did not kindle the same flame that gave the Spanish Guerrilla War its world-historical significance. But it started something whose continuance today in the second half of the twentieth century changed the face of the earth and its inhabitants. It produced a *theory* [Schmitt's emphasis] of war and of enmity that culminates in the theory of the partisan.' Rather than acting as partisans out of the sort of moral compulsion felt by the Spanish and the Tyroleans, these Berlin philosophers instead attempted to en-capsulate the partisan as a world-historical figure – as a philosophical category.[49]

---

[46] As with the Monroe Doctrine as an idealised theoretical depiction of the *Großraum*, or Hobbes' *Leviathan* as an idealised depiction of the early modern state.
[47] Schmitt, *Theorie des Partisanen*, p. 17.   [48] *Ibid.*, p. 14.
[49] Schmitt apparently fails to see the irony in his criticism of this excessive attempt to categorise and conceptualise autonomous political phenomena.

Schmitt sees the Prussian *Landsturm* Edict of April 1813 as the key document in this philosophical transformation – as 'a sort of Magna Carta of partisanship'.[50] A bid to stimulate widespread resistance to Napoleon, this edict is significant because of its attempt to justify partisan behaviour on the basis of state authority. The essence of this shift is so important that we must quote Schmitt at length on the effect he attributes to this decisive step:

It is a special legitimisation, namely, one that proceeds from a spirit and a philosophy that were current in the Prussian capital Berlin at that time. The Spanish Guerrilla War against Napoleon, the Tyrolean uprising of 1809, and the Russian Partisan War of 1812 were elemental, autochthonic movements of a pious Catholic or Orthodox people whose religious traditions were untouched by the philosophical spirit of revolutionary France; they were *underdeveloped* ... By contrast, the Berlin of 1808–1813 was characterised by an intellectual atmosphere on intimate terms with the French Enlightenment: so intimate as to be equal if not superior to it.[51]

He lists an impressive group of thinkers apparently engaged with the question of the partisan at this time. Fichte, Scharnhorst, Gneisenau and von Kleist ('*the* writer of national resistance to the foreign conqueror'[52]) are all cited. But without doubt, the pre-eminent figure in this depiction of the partisan as a philosophical figure is Clausewitz who, in Werner Hahlweg's words, saw guerrilla warfare as 'pre-eminently a political matter in the highest sense of the word'.[53] In his recognition of the interpenetration of politics and warfare, in his sense of warfare as a reflection of political foundations, and his attachment to the tenets of German idealism of the state, Schmitt reads Clausewitz as the original theorist of the partisan and a 'hitherto unacknowledged figure of the world historical spirit'.[54]

As elsewhere in Schmitt's work, Clausewitz operates here, to use Slomp's phrase, as 'a two-way link between practice and theory'.[55] He is a military man who understands the mechanics of enmity in the raw. But he is also a man of letters who can draw linkages between high politics and warfare. In his recognition of the primacy of political orientation, he is always a sympathetic figure in Schmitt's work. But his fateful, inadvertent step, Schmitt claims, was in sowing the seeds for a theory of the partisan that would break away from the moorings of its concrete political situation. Although Clausewitz was concerned with the specific question of

---

[50] Schmitt, *Theorie des Partisanen*, p. 47.   [51] *Ibid.*, p. 48 (Schmitt's emphasis).
[52] *Ibid.*, p. 15.   [53] See *ibid.*, p. 49.   [54] *Ibid.*, p. 51.
[55] Slomp, 'The Theory of the Partisan', p. 513.

German resistance to Napoleon,[56] he posited the partisan as an actor whose recognition of the political imperative and whose sense of enmity were potentially deeper and of greater world-historical significance than that of the state. He granted the partisan a world-historical role, and granted legitimacy to his status as a *Figur*, in the philosophical sense.[57]

This elision from the concrete to the philosophical takes place, in the German instance, around the question of nationalism. Fichte, von Kleist and Clausewitz are all engaged with the national question as a political and philosophical problem. Schmitt himself always had surprisingly little to say directly on the question of nationalism, and once again here he sets the question of the relationship between nationalism and enmity in a wider context. Nationalism, according to this understanding, is just one of a number of factors that may either support or undermine sovereignty, and that may sustain or undermine existing international orders. As with any economic, religious or cultural distinction, the division of 'nations' is only politically pregnant in terms of the intensity of association and separation that it denotes. In terms of *The Concept of the Political*, the 'nation' would always be subordinate to decision and to the sovereign as a political category. The sovereign decision might be shaped by the pre-existing parameters of the nation, to be sure, but might equally create the nation by its own force.[58]

For Schmitt, in other words, the nation is not a foundational concept. But he recognises that for Fichte and Clausewitz the nation is exactly this – it is a world-historical ideal. The purer the understanding of the nation, the more that the nation itself might be an expression of partisan hostility – that is to say, rather than inter-state warfare, European states increasingly fought, in Hegel's phrase, as 'the nation armed'.[59] The study of the partisan is therefore part of Schmitt's wider recognition that 'the twentieth century has witnessed the strengthening of bonds between individuals in groups and parties'.[60] Partisans are literally, in Clausewitz's phrase, *Partei-gänger* – adherents of a party, and advocates of a 'partisan' position.

Although Schmitt never makes the point particularly explicit, he is clearly suggesting that the collision of an idea of the partisan with a certain philosophy of the state has resulted in a dangerous mixture of the façade of

---

[56] Schmitt considers Clausewitz's concern with the specific question of irregular resistance to Napoleon at far greater length in his short essay 'Clausewitz als politischer Denker: Bemerkungen und Hinweise', *Der Staat* 6:4 (1967), 479–502.

[57] For a deeper reading of Schmitt's understanding of Clausewitz as a philosophical thinker see R. Gasché, 'The Partisan and the Philosopher', *The New Centennial Review* 4:3 (2004), 1–7.

[58] For a discussion of this wider point, see Chapter 2

[59] Schmitt, *Theorie des Partisanen*, p. 61.   [60] Slomp, 'The Theory of the Partisan', p. 507.

states with the mechanics of partisan enmity. The Prussian state itself came close to an 'Acherontic' moment in which enmity in its real sense was almost expressed blindly outside 'the secure framework of the state order and regular war.[61] But since then, Schmitt suggests, states have increasingly become organised parties, geared around a unstable derivation of enmity from philosophies of nationalism, socialism or perhaps some other comprehensive ideology. One must assume that this is one way of explaining the violence of the First World War, which Schmitt has elsewhere described in terms of the collapse of a legal system of *justus hostis*.

In Clausewitz's own time, the ramifications of this transformation of the partisan into a philosophical category remained unclear. Clausewitz 'still thought all too much in the classical categories' of the state and international law to recognise the radical potential of a theory of partisanship.[62] The Congress of Vienna temporarily removed the vacuum in which real enmity develops. Nevertheless, Schmitt contends, the existence of a philosophical understanding of the partisan as possessing a radically alternative concept of enmity outside the state system was ripe for expansion – it now possessed a world-historical logic of its own that was to be exploited to its apogee by Lenin:

What Lenin learned from Clausewitz, and he learned it well, was not just the famous formula of war as a continuation of politics. It involved the larger recognition that in the age of revolution the distinction between friend and enemy is the primary distinction, decisive for war as for politics. Only revolutionary war is true war for Lenin, because it derives from absolute enmity. Everything else is a conventional game.[63]

By exposing the gap between conventional and real enmity, and bestowing a certain philosophical honour on the latter, the theory of the partisan generates a persistent pressure on the existing order. Partisanship becomes an ideal – the act of opposition and of uncovering a new intensity of enmity becomes part of a political programme that evolves rapidly into a logic of pure hostility and total enmity. Lenin himself, Schmitt points out, exploited a perceived distinction between war (*Woina*) and play (*Igra*). The unanticipated effect of Clausewitz's theory of the partisan was to discredit the validity of limited and contained forms of enmity, and to encourage the push towards total hostility.

Increasingly, therefore, the philosophy of the partisan would overtake the possibility of the partisan as a concrete figure. Whereas the partisans of Spain and the Tyrol were essentially reactionary, and saw themselves as a

---

[61] Schmitt, *Theorie des Partisanen*, p. 46.   [62] *Ibid.*, p. 51.   [63] *Ibid.*, pp. 55–6.

last defence of the old forms of enmity, partisans of the future would increasingly be caught up in the logic of their own apartness. Schmitt's argument here is surprisingly resonant with his logic of the 'barely visible crack' in the Hobbesian state. What emerges as an authentic solution to a problem of the political is increasingly calcified within its own logic. As a concept, it develops a direction of travel that it hard to resist, and that creates its own feedback relationship.

This criticism of the partisan as a philosophical category must surely be read as part of Schmitt's wider sense of the dangers of *philosophy* as a way of situating and theorising the political, as highlighted by Meier. It is a criticism that speaks (albeit somewhat subtly) to Schmitt's distinction between philosophical and theological modes of grounding politics. Schmitt is careful to distinguish the ideal-type partisans of 1808–13 in terms of their traditional, authoritative religious motivations derived from the Catholic or Orthodox traditions. Surely this is no coincidence. He is keen to highlight the vast gulf between the philosophical French and Germans, and their religiously conservative opponents. As ever, for Schmitt, the philosophers deride the simplicity of their opponents. With wry amusement, he quotes Napoleon deriding the Spanish as 'a treacherous, superstitious people misled by 300,000 monks, who could hardly be compared with the diligent, hardworking, and reasonable Germans'.[64]

If my understanding is correct, Schmitt's purpose is certainly not to conflate partisanship with a slide to revolutionary total enmity. A partisan can just as well be a conservative, religious, particular, tellurian defender of the old order. A partisan who fulfils the four criteria of the ideal-type will inevitably be of this kind – a partisan of the concrete instance. In the terms we have explored above, the determination of his enmity has a revelatory aspect. He sees his enemy as a revealed truth rather than a philosophically mediated other. But the emergence of a theory of the partisan creates its own logic, and encourages a philosophical response to the failings of the conventional order of enmity. In part, I agree with Horn that Schmitt is seeking 'a criterion serving to distinguish the good partisan from the bad'.[65] The question that persists, however, is whether these 'good partisans' can credibly escape the advancing philosophical dominance of partisanship.

Tellurism and technology

The partisan's connection to a locality is essential to the ideal-type. Schmitt chooses the term 'telluric' quite deliberately to emphasise the

---

[64] *Ibid.*, p. 48.   [65] Horn, '*Waldgänger*', p. 142.

intimacy and particularity of this connection. It is a term of art that emphasises the contours of the land and the colours of the soil. It positions the partisan in his environment in the sense of a life lived in a unique and beloved three-dimensional space. It is a Romantic evocation of an intensely political sense of *territorial* belonging. This is territory not in the more abstract sense of state territory, with its corollary of conventional enmity. Instead, it is territory in a concrete sense, as a home.[66]

We have already explored the importance of tellurism in Schmitt's ideal-type. This connection to the land is a vital source of the partisan's particular conception of enmity. He defends his home. The notion of 'home' gives rise to his particular sense of group identity, and preordains the distinction of the enemy. The defence of his home is a political commitment par excellence – the assertion of his own particularity against a *foreign* enemy. And the motivation of defence – his telluric orientation – results in a fundamentally defensive expression of enmity. The partisan's cause is identical to his identity in a territorial place.

In 1808, the Spanish partisan was a simple, agrarian figure. He fought with spades and pitchforks against the occupying army.[67] Despite this 'pre-industrial agrarian primitiveness', he is more than a match for the regular French troops. With the tactical advantages of his irregularity, and his knowledge of the land, the partisan could strike quickly and retreat. Conflict was always conducted face to face. As such, French access to cannon, rifles and other industrial weaponry might have been an advantage in terms of the efficiency of killing, but it did not alter the dimensional parameters of the conflict. Partisans and regular troops continued to engage one another in a precise territorial context, and it remained more than possible for the partisan to inflict casualties.

Schmitt was acutely aware that this Romantic picture of the plucky partisan fighting with little more than his bare hands had become increasingly anachronistic. 'The old-style partisan whom the Prussian *Landsturmedikt* of 1813 wanted to force to take up the pitchfork would cut a comical figure today. The modern partisan fights with machine guns, hand grenades, plastic bombs, and soon perhaps with tactical atomic weapons. He is motorised and wired to a communications network with secret transmitters and radar.'[68] With the rapid development of modern

---

[66] This intimacy with the land is also the factor that has always given the partisan or *guerrilla* his distinct tactical advantage. He knows the land. He knows every foxhole, cave and riverbank – facts that feed in to his mobility and unpredictability.

[67] Schmitt notes the particular recommendations of the Prussian *Landsturm* that partisans should fight with 'axes, pitchforks, scythes and shotguns'. Schmitt, *Theorie des Partisanen*, p. 47.

[68] *Ibid.*, p. 79.

weaponry, the partisan is forced to modify his arsenal of weapons. He must develop or obtain more sophisticated methods of violence.

Although Schmitt is not particularly explicit here, it seems that he attributes two consequences to this change. Firstly, this imperative for increased sophistication contributes to a broader process by which the partisan's understanding of territorial space changes. In a reflection of the themes from *Land und Meer*, Schmitt points out that 'every technical improvement produces new spaces and unforeseeable modifications in traditional spatial structures. This holds true … for our old earthly living spaces, work spaces, ritual spaces and spaces to move'.[69] We need hardly spell out how access to the modern technology of weaponry might alter the autochthonous partisan's understanding of spatial possibilities.

In many respects, his avoidance of the battlefield and the set theatres of war positions the partisan ahead of the curve. He has already added 'another, darker dimension, a dimension of depth' to warfare.[70] But at the same time, modern weaponry and communications open new horizons for the partisan that are at odds with his telluric orientation. What does it mean for the partisan's tellurism that he can now escalate conflict outside his own domain? Surely it is *tactically* expedient for him to attack the enemy at his points of vulnerability, wherever they may be. The advance in technology encourages the partisan to use more abstract means to achieve his concrete goals. And while this might not place his *telluric* nature into question per se, it undoubtedly creates greater indeterminacy in the his orientation. The point Schmitt appears to be making is that the technologies of modern warfare make it that much easier for the irregular fighter to lose sight of his original, spatial, concrete goals. As Schmitt puts it, '[the partisan's] mobility is so enhanced by motorisation that he runs the risk of total dislocation'.[71]

The technology of warfare also raises a second area of vulnerability in the original concept of the partisan. The ideal-type agrarian partisan fought with pitchforks because these were the only means at his disposal. In so far as such means were adequate, the partisan could, in practical terms, remain a more or less autonomous figure. But in an age of advanced weaponry, how is a partisan supposed to source machine-guns and grenades, to say nothing of artillery, vehicles and telecommunications. The industrial and manufacturing complexes that such means require are wholly at odds with the partisan's telluric invisibility. They are the products of regularity – of organised societies and functioning states. In sourcing such weapons, therefore, the partisan is drawn out of his unique

---

[69] *Ibid.*, p. 71.   [70] *Ibid.*, p. 72.   [71] *Ibid.*, p. 27.

environment, and exposed to complicated arrangements and relationships with the outside world.

The interessierte Dritte

This exposure to the international political context involves far more, however, than simply the technological aspect. It also poses deeper questions about how the partisan can situate and sustain his expression of enmity. It is not enough simply to decide on the enemy in an isolated political context and to react spontaneously to the fact of an outside power. The reality of a multipolar international context places demands on the partisan to give further content to his *position*. Outside powers try to situate him, and manipulate him to their own ends.

Drawing on Rolf Schroers' phrase, Schmitt describes such external powers that engage the partisan as the *interessierte Dritte* – the interested third party.[72] The partisan cannot resist the appeal of relations with this third party, for reasons that Schmitt explains at length.

> The *intessierte Dritte* is not some banal figure like the proverbially laughing third party. It belongs rather, and essentially, to the situation of the partisan, and thus also to his theory. The powerful third party delivers not only weapons and munitions, money, material assistance and medicines of every description, he offers also the sort of political recognition of which the irregularly fighting partisan is in need, in order to avoid falling like the thief and the pirate into the unpolitical, which means here the criminal sphere.[73]

This is a hugely significant realisation. What it amounts to is an acceptance that the kind of recognition that comes through a decision on the 'real' enemy is, by itself, never enough. The partisan does not gain the necessary political self-recognition – sufficient *thymos* if you will – from the concrete fact of his enmity towards a specific enemy. The act of decision itself is not enough to anchor the political identity of the group. Schmitt underscores the point for emphasis: 'In the longer view of things the irregular must legitimise itself through the regular, and for this only two possibilities stand open: recognition by an existing regular, or establishment of a new regularity by its own force. This is a tough alternative.'[74] This is a profound admission of the limits of partisanship and, in turn, highlights the

---

[72] Schmitt was strongly influenced by Schroers' book *Der Partisan: Ein Beitrag zur politischen Anthropologie*, Berlin: Kiepenhauer and Witsch (1961). For an explanation of this reception see Horn, '*Waldgänger*' pp. 138–40. Schmitt's library testifies to the depth of his engagement with Schroers. See D. van Laak and I. Villinger, *Nachlaß Carl Schmitt: Verzeichnis des Bestandes im Nordrhein-Westfälisches Hauptstaatsarchiv*, Siegburg: Republica-Verlag (1993), p. 659.

[73] Schmitt, *Theorie des Partisanen*, p. 78.   [74] *Ibid*.

limits of the raw political decision depicted in *The Concept of the Political*. The fact of enmity in the concrete situation ends up being of little significance unless it can obtain regularity. This regularity might be achieved by recognition from outside, or the force of its own drive towards a new meaning of regularity. The fundamental point is that the coherence of the partisan as an ongoing political category relies on its own demise. It must collapse into regularity.

As a definitively 'irregular' figure, the partisan is always dependent on his relationship to 'regularity' of some kind. It is a relational category, and 'the distinction between regular and irregular depends on the degree of regularity' that pertains outside the partisan's real enmity.[75] In other words, Schmitt reads the partisan as an important and illuminating reflection on the state of regular, conventional politics, but is sceptical of the possibility of any flourishing new order based on some hybrid of 'irregular' real enmity and conventional structures. Beyond its historical depiction, there is a concrete sense that Schmitt is engaged in an attempt to create a language with which we are able to analyse contemporary world politics in all its increasing messiness. Understandably, the temptation persists to 'test' Schmitt's categorisation of the partisan against the contemporary political milieu.

Partisans and terrorists

In its exploration of the tension between the regular and the irregular, and its attempt to recast our basic understanding of political interaction at a time when the state has become a compromised locus of politics, *Theorie des Partisanen* is undoubtedly intended as a tool with which to examine and understand late modern politics. Schmitt is himself trying to use the category of partisan to understand and classify the broad spectrum of political-like activity taking place, and to elicit a deeper understanding of the interplay between the political decision and structures of political interaction. As early as 1969 Schmitt recognised that his four criteria of partisanship 'might become obsolete in a few years time'.[76] But prima facie, Schmitt appears here to be engaged in the same process of disentangling, categorising and understanding violence outside the state that has reached a new height of seriousness in our age of mass terror. In sharp distinction from the dated language of *Großraum*, it is the theory of the partisan that has prompted the widespread conclusion that Schmitt was 'a prescient analyst of political and legal trends, possessed with an uncanny

---

[75] *Ibid.*, p. 10.   [76] Schmitt, 'Gespräch über den Partisanen', pp. 635–6.

ability to identify dilemmas that would soon gain widespread attention'.[77]

It appears that Schmitt's *Theorie des Partisanen* might be a useful analytical tool. Firstly, in its finely drawn distinction between conventional, real and total enmity, it might allow us to generate a certain typology of state and non-state actors, and to distinguish between inherently conservative and inherently destabilising forms of political violence. That is to say, in Horn's account, we might be able to take forward Schmitt's own interest in distinguishing 'good' partisans from 'bad' partisans. Secondly, and somewhat more subtly, by raising the issue of the feedback relationship between regular and irregular, the ideas derived from *Theorie des Partisanen* might give us a language that allows us to consider the ongoing effect of partisanship on the way that states themselves operate in the international sphere. Irregular violence of the kind that concerned Schmitt poses a radically different set of normative questions from regular warfare. When confronted with irregular forces, existing regular actors, existing states, are required to create a new normative and legal language to situate and manage the experience. For Schmitt, it is fundamental that states get this process right, and find a way to neutralise the conceptual challenge that irregular violence poses to the existing regularity. He clearly envisaged that there would be a feedback relationship between the regular and the irregular. Finally, therefore, it might be fruitful to consider how Schmitt's categories can shed light on the changing nature of regular politics, and how the particular manifestations of irregularity may have much to say about the state of regular politics.

Terrorists and freedom fighters

The defensive partisan and the ideologically charged global revolutionary clearly represent two wholly distinct types of actors in Schmitt's scheme. Yet, if we cling to a primary distinction between regular and irregular violence, it is a distinction that might be easily and conveniently overlooked. The types certainly have features in common. They fall outside the conventions of international law and their methods are typically asymmetrical. The suspicion arises that the legitimacy or otherwise of violent irregular movements is primarily determined by whether or not such irregular violence is of value to the 'interested third party' – that is to say, according to the external context – rather than deriving internally from something distinctive about that particular group and its objectives. It is a cynicism commonly conveyed in the well-worn phrase, 'one man's

---

[77] Scheuerman, 'Carl Schmitt and the Road to Abu Ghraib', *Constellations* 13:1 (2006), 108–24 (p. 108).

terrorist is another man's freedom fighter'. Schmitt's categorisation of the four features of an authentic partisan, and his distinction of such partisans from aggressive revolutionaries, perhaps offer an analytical framework critically to assess the difference between authentic resistance and aggressive terrorism. Certainly, it is a framework that distinguishes 'terrorist acts' as a tactical device from terrorism as an existential characteristic.

Numerous other methods are available to assist in drawing this distinction, of course. There are extensive materials drawn from public international law that provide legal tools for identifying and labelling secessionist movements and resistance organisations, and for distinguishing legitimate and illegitimate actors. Where Schmitt's approach differs is in rejecting the language of legality and legitimacy, and instead placing the distinction in a wholly political sphere. Both types of actors are likely to stand outside the law. Neither will conduct themselves in accordance with the conventions of international law, and their violation of the law will always be a source both of strength and identity. The key distinction lies in the political *potentiality* of their relationship with the law. In other circumstances, the partisan could subscribe to a system of order in which he is, in essence, left alone. The global revolutionary cannot.

The point is as simple as it is profound. Irregular sources of violence will always stand in some sort of relationship to the existing regular (which, for the time being, we shall assume is sustainable and worth maintaining). In some instances, irregular fighters will resemble the Spanish partisans of 1808 in so far as they are trying to impose a distinction that coheres with the regular status quo (or status quo *ante*). However incoherently, they are making a claim for future regularity. One can imagine such a case being made on behalf of Shia militias in Iraq, or on behalf of Sinn Fein.[78] In other instances, the irregular fighter is irreconcilable with the existing order. Either his conception of political organisation is too radically distinct (in which case, he is attempting the tough feat of imposing a new regularity through force of arms),[79] or else he represents Schmitt's worst fear – the nihilistic rejection of regularity and order. One could endlessly debate which of these two outcomes is represented by al-Qaeda's mixture of tactics and objectives.[80]

---

[78] Müller suggests that Nicaraguan *Contras* and the Afghan *Mujahideen* as possible examples from the 1980s (although the latter might also serve as strong evidence of the slide into universal claims that Schmitt predicts for the partisan). Müller, *A Dangerous Mind*, p. 154.

[79] See p. 179 above.

[80] Michael Ignatieff famously characterised al-Qaeda as representing 'apocalyptic nihilism' in which there is no expectation 'of attaining a political objective'. M. Ignatieff, 'It's War – but It Doesn't Have to Be Dirty', *Guardian* (1 October 2001). For a critique of this characterisation of al-Qaeda as anti-political, see my discussion of Andreas Behnke below.

Grounding Schmitt's clean distinctions in reality may be immensely challenging. He argues that traditional, reactionary, 'communitarian' partisans are necessarily less dangerous because their violence knows the limits of territory and particularism. The global ideologue will engender limitless violence. Yet as Herfried Münkler argues in his study of Schmitt's *Theory of the Partisan*, such expectations may not hold true in the current climate. The reactionary partisan cannot reconcile himself to the norms and traditions of his enemy. He must cast the enemy in absolute terms. By contrast, the ideologue has a vested interest in persuading others of the justice of his cause, and so may very well be tempted to place limits on the extent of his violence. Schmitt's assumption that the former is preferable in terms of the level and duration of violence he engenders may thus be called into question.[81] It is necessary to look beyond the types of violence engendered, and return to the question of their political orientation.[82]

Schmitt is concerned that the failure to distinguish adequately between these two distinct figures will always be to the benefit of the latter – the more dangerous, expansive and ideological. In large part, this is because the latter is instinctively drawn towards the international sphere as part of his mode of being and, as such, acquires ideological allies as an adjunct to his partisan struggle. Additionally, his ideological 'dangerousness' prompts a careful and serious response even from those basically opposed to his universal ambitions. Schmitt illustrates the point by reference to Yugoslavia during the Second World War, attributing Tito's triumph over Mihailović to the energetic and 'aggressive nature of the international communist world-revolution'.[83] The Soviets supported Tito because they shared his ideological commitment. The British switched their

---

[81] See H. Münkler, *Gewalt und Ordnung: Das Bild des Krieges im politischen Denken*, Frankfurt am Main: Fischer Verlag (1992) pp. 127–41. I disagree, however, with Münkler's wider conclusion that this represents a failure on Schmitt's part to distinguish adequately between the two types of fighter. Münkler focusses primarily on the kinds of warfare that the two engender. Whilst such distinctions were important to Schmitt, his more pressing concern was with the potential relationship of the fighter to regularity. This is the primary distinction, and not the tactical manifestations of their form of violence. Indeed, given Schmitt's loathing of indirect violence and political hypocrisy, the idea that global revolutionaries might use limited and seductive methods of force would make them all the more fearful and contemptible.

[82] To an extent, Raymond Aron prefigured Münkler's critique, suggesting that Schmitt 'does not grasp the essential, for lack of rigorous discrimination between the levels of policy, tactics and law'. R. Aron, *Clausewitz: Philosopher of War* (trans. C. Booker and N. Stone), London: Routledge and Kegan Paul (1983), pp. 364–5. Both are certainly correct to point out that Schmitt is far too vague on the precise question of tactics, circuitously reducing the methods of irregular fighters to the fact of their irregularity.

[83] Schmitt, *Theorie des Partisanen*, p. 59.

support to Tito because they risked too much by frustrating him. Both would live to regret their choice. For Schmitt the conclusion is clear – only the authentic, reactionary partisan will restore order and equilibrium.

In his own analysis, this led Schmitt to a certain sympathy for Maoist partisans, whom he regarded as less destabilising in their external perspective than socialist revolutionaries infused with Lenin's reading of the function of partisanship. Indeed, Schmitt published an interview on the idea and theory of the partisan with the prominent German Maoist Joachim Schickel, in which he praises the prominence of the idea of *tao* – the element of land – in Mao's theory of partisan warfare.[84] The point for Schmitt is a dispositional one. Is a partisan concerned with his own land, and the imposition of meaning, ideas and policy in it? Does he seek to assert or regain authentic political control regardless of the international setting? Or does he reject the natural limits of terrain and ideas of home and difference, and instead apply his violence to abstract ends? As a distinction that transcends questions of legality and methodology, it perhaps continues to have some relevance to the sorts of distinctions we make today.

The response of states to the irregular

Horn is right to suggest that Schmitt's own concern was to identify authentic resistance movements from revolutionary activity. But if partisanship only makes sense in a relative context – in its relationship with the regular – it is always as significant for the questions it raises about the state of the regular as it is in its own right. As a conceptual challenge to the order of the status quo, the figure of the partisan creates a space in which other political actors must step outside the existing rules of the game. As long as he remains a partisan and does not fold back into being a light soldier controlled by a state, he does not allow his enemy the luxury of interacting with him within the context of existing rules and norms of warfare. Any attempt to distil impartial legal rules that govern the status of the irregular fighter is bound to fail. States must choose their response with care, since their immediate interests in the present confrontation may well conflict with their wider interest in maintaining the coherence of the existing international order. It is a dilemma that Schmitt recognised well.

In *Theory of the Partisan* Schmitt considers this feedback relationship between the irregular and the regular in the case of the French *Franktireurs*, or 'sharpshooters', who fought irregularly against the invading Prussian

---

[84] Schmitt, 'Gespräch über den Partisanen'.

army in 1870 (and, similarly, the Belgian 'sharpshooters' who resisted occupying forces in the First World War).[85] With its heightened sense of regularity, the Prussian army struggled to determine how it ought to respond politically and legally to the irregular resistance movement. Fuelled with indignation at such underhand tactics, and bolstered by juridical opinion that such activity was fundamentally illegal, the Prussians treated the sharpshooters mercilessly. Their response, Schmitt contends, was essentially legalistic. The sharpshooters acted illegally, beyond the line of conventional international and French domestic law, and so deserved to be despatched as spies (or terrorists). Schmitt holds this up as an example of how 'the more regular, uniformed opponent is respected as an enemy and never mistaken, even in bloodiest warfare, for a criminal, the more harshly the irregular fighter is treated as a criminal'.[86]

In a fully functioning system of states such a conclusion might be very valid, since the irregular fighter clearly does pose a challenge to the prevalent regular order. But for Schmitt, this question can never be reduced to law. It is always a political evaluation – the Prussians ought to have engaged in the question of the real enemy rather than relying on legal abstractions. Yes, the irregular French fighters fell outside the law. But this is of no relevance to their political status, and the question of the distinction between partisanship and terrorism. Rather, for Schmitt, it 'is conclusive for the problem of the partisan because it shows normative regulation to be judicially impossible'.[87] The partisan is a symptom of the limits of the normative order, and so, *eo ipso*, it is illogical to apply the existing legal categories to him.[88] He can only be conceived of politically through the concept of enmity.

Schmitt's historically depicted analysis of the challenges of irregular violence to all extant normative and juridical categories appears to pre-figure the debates surrounding the legitimacy and legality of responses to contemporary global terrorism with astonishing resonance. The problem remains of how to choose a language and modality with which to respond to terrorism. Is it a legal or a political problem? Were the attacks of 9/11 illegal acts of mass-murder, or acts of war? And, if the latter, can the

---

[85] Schmitt, *Theorie des Partisanen*, pp. 38–41.   [86] *Ibid.*, p. 39.   [87] *Ibid.*, p. 40.

[88] Schmitt offers a derisive account of attempts to create a juridical status for partisans in international law, most notably the inclusion of intermediate categories of combatants in the 1907 Hague Conventions and the 1949 Geneva Conventions. He concludes that attempts to extend the laws of war to 'militias, volunteer corps and spontaneous uprisings' only work in so far as such irregular fighters are 'organised', and, as such, do not really apply to the partisan at all. Despite recognition of the dilemma, international law has failed, according to Schmitt's account, to find a workable legal solution to the problem of irregular fighters. *Ibid.*, pp. 28–33.

parameters of that war with terrorists be conceived of within the existing parameters of international law, or is it an act of enmity that is inconsistent with that framework? Schmitt's language seems surprisingly relevant to the high-profile dilemmas that dominate much contemporary debate in international relations and public international law.

Scheuerman contends provocatively that 'the Bush Administration's legal arguments about the status of accused terrorists mirror crucial facets of Schmitt's logic [of] the impossibility of a successful codification of the laws of war for irregular fighters'.[89] The terrorist's lack of status within the boundaries of any existing set of legal norms is emphasised by his categorisation as an 'unlawful combatant'. With its stark imagery of indeterminacy, Guantanamo Bay is the symbol par excellence of this idea of a legal black hole. Scheuerman suggests that, in common with Schmitt, the US government interprets the inadequacy of existing legal provisions governing terrorism as 'evidence for the necessity of a fundamentally *norm-less* realm of decision making in which the executive possesses full discretionary authority'.[90] He argues that Schmitt's ideas dovetail with those of the Bush Administration's lawyers in their shared belief that a radically irregular enemy poses a purely political challenge, and that existing legal norms (specifically, in both instances, the Geneva Conventions) are simply inapplicable to such a scenario. In so far as such legal norms might attempt to address the problem, they fail.

Unsurprisingly, Scheuerman cannot provide any evidence that Alberto Gonzales or Jay Bybee have been directly influenced by Schmitt's ideas on the partisan, nor does he suggest such direct reception. To a certain extent, he is raising the spectre of Schmitt as a powerful (and somewhat mischievous) way to attack their legal conclusions. '[O]nce the cancer of *normlessness* is allowed into the legal system', he contends, 'it is only a matter of time before it infects healthy legal organs as well'.[91] Schmitt's theory of the partisan, according to this understanding, represents the theoretically complete account of legal indeterminacy, executive power and the limits of international law. He is holding up Schmitt as an example of where this sort of logic leads, and as a way to castigate the Bush Administration as fundamentally anti-liberal.

Despite his hostility to a 'Schmittian' conclusion, Scheuerman nevertheless agrees with Schmitt's diagnosis of the dilemma. Violence beyond the existing normative structure poses a challenge with divergent responses. Schmitt's categories remain prescient for the current debate, if only to be ultimately rejected. As an unapologetic liberal, Scheuerman

---

[89] Scheuerman, 'Carl Schmitt and the Road to Abu Ghraib', p. 118.
[90] *Ibid.* (Scheuerman's emphasis).   [91] *Ibid.*, p. 122 (Scheuerman's emphasis).

cannot accept Schmitt's conclusion that it is impossible to go on extending legal norms to new phenomena. Ultimately, Scheuerman implicitly accepts that productive conversation between the two sides of this debate might be impossible:

> But what if we refuse to endorse [Schmitt's] nostalgic preference of the traditional state system? Then a sympathetic reading of the argument would take the form of suggesting that the project for regulating irregular combatants by ordinary law must fail for another reason: it rests on a misguided quest to integrate incongruent models of interstate and international law. We cannot, in short, maintain core features of the (state-centered) Westphalian system while extending ambitious new protections to non-state actors.[92]

Scheuerman's conclusion, in other words, is that the present challenge of irregular violence requires a refiguring of the 'regular' away from an outmoded Westphalian model.

'Saving the concepts'

Scheuerman's conclusions embrace Schmitt's realisation that the partisan has the power to change the basis of the existing order.[93] Both Schmitt and Scheuerman subscribe to an interpretation of irregular violence, partisanship and terrorism as potent harbingers of change in the way that law and politics functions. In contrast to Schmitt, however, this realisation is positive for Scheuerman in so far as it might allow for the thorough privileging of the liberal individual, and the permeation of the solid structures of the Westphalian system. As with Schmitt's own study, therefore, the real object of concern is not simply the nature of the irregular fighter or the response of regular forces, but rather the historical dynamic that unfolds as a result of this confrontation of regular and irregular. Looking forwards, Schmitt can only begin to anticipate the wider ramification of this interaction, and hope for outcomes that reflect his own '[belief] that the traditional state system is normatively superior to recent attempts to modify it' by elevating the standing of the individual subject.[94]

Schmitt's focus on the contest for political meaning, and the maintenance of a solid regular political arena against external challenges, has provided a starting point for some scholars seeking to uncover a deeper

---

[92] *Ibid.*, p. 117.
[93] The phrase 'saving the concepts' is used repeatedly by Raymond Aron in the context of attempts by him and others to rescue a concrete conception of the distinction between war and peace and, as such, to save a Clausewitzian concept of war. See especially the conclusion to Aron, *Clausewitz*.
[94] Scheuerman, 'Carl Schmitt and the Road to Abu Ghraib', p. 116.

understanding of the political *meaning* of the current threat of terrorism at a conceptual level. Andreas Behnke, for instance, seeks to determine whether or not the terrorist attacks of 11 September 2001 should be considered as 'political acts'.[95] In his analysis of al-Qaeda from the perspective of Schmitt's criteria of partisanship, Behnke concludes that modern global terrorism confirms many of Schmitt's predictions of the vulnerable slide from particular political concerns to a universal urge to rid the world of evil. Al-Qaeda shows signs of tellurism in its avowed objective to defend the Arabian peninsula against American influence, and its conscious relationship to the political community of the *umma* constitutes a public and political commitment that distinguishes it from the radically private criminal.[96] And yet, in its extreme globalised violence, in its limitless imagination for the destiny of its own ideology, and in the absence of a credible basis for normalised future coexistence, these particular concerns are rapidly lost in a drive towards universalism.

Like Schmitt, Behnke focusses on the interaction of non-state groups with the international context. Schmitt explicitly attributed the increasing vulnerability of the local, defensive and particular partisan to a global international context that made its own liberal or socialist truth claims. Likewise, Behnke, following Hardt and Negri, concludes that the reframing of sovereign 'regularity' on moral, imperial and universal lines denies the space in which a particular partisan can exist, and instead ensures that 'in this area ... a Foe has emerged that mirrors the American universalist strategies in terms of its truth claims and the de-limitation of violence'.[97] In such a pervasive international context, locally stimulated forms of violent resistance are rapidly and effectively forced into a frame of absolutes, move away from their immediate political goals (such as the eviction of US forces from Saudi Arabia, or the establishment of a Palestinian state) and express universal motives.

Behnke's approach illustrates one possible way in which Schmitt's categories might be applied to the current situation. He picks up on Schmitt's concern that the phenomenon of partisanship will come to dominate all political discourse, and we will all literally become *Parteigänger* – adherents to ideas in a disorderly global environment. But in his determination to offer a critique of certain modes of American imperialism, and his focus on al-Qaeda at a macro level, Behnke misses the basic criticism that Schmitt's

---

[95] A. Behnke, 'Terrorising the Political: 9/11 within the Context of the Globalisation of Violence', *Millennium: Journal of International Studies* 33:2 (2004), 279–312.

[96] *Ibid.*, pp. 305–10.

[97] *Ibid.*, p. 300. M. Hardt and A Negri, *Empire*, Cambridge, MA: Harvard University Press (2000).

categories offer of the definitive *difference* between partisans and decontex-tualised terrorists or revolutionaries. He effectively argues that al-Qaeda should be read as problematic partisans, rather than recognising that Schmitt has already prefigured the fundamental distinction between autochthonous defenders of the homeland, and radically distinct actors on a global level. He thus enters Schmitt's critique at its end point – in a situation where all particular claims have been abandoned, and all that remains is a formless confrontation between imperial sovereignty on the one hand, and globalised irregular violence on the other.

It is clear that a group such as al-Qaeda has broken out of Schmitt's four-part ideal-typology of the partisan, and has become a decontext-ualised source of violence. The really interesting question that clearly concerned Schmitt was whether this feedback process was necessary, or whether there might be localised partisans who resisted this slide into a formless global context. Perhaps in this context al-Qaeda is the exception rather than the rule, and interesting (if less spectacular) contemporary illustrations of Schmitt's partisan phenomenon might be found among, say, Shia armed groups in Iraq or Hezbollah in Lebanon. Such groups display the sort of ambitious irregularity that always has the achievement of regularity in mind. They are conscious of their political aspirations, and conscious of the need to collapse back into the regular sphere in order ontologically to consolidate their gains. Behnke overstates his case for the effect of American hegemony. Schmitt had already accepted this as a political fact in the 1960s, yet was still concerned to search for localised, particular forms of resistance. Indeed, the question of the authentic partisan becomes all the more pertinent, on Schmitt's terms, if we accept Behnke's diagnosis of American universalist strategies.

The question that Behnke's critique asks – and the same question that troubled Schmitt in the 1960s – is whether this regularity of states and spaces actually constituted the regular at all. In the current climate, this relativist political dynamic lends itself to a post-structural solution. Drawing on Derrida, Alberto Moreiras poses the problem in these terms: 'The implication is of course that contemporary partisan or counterparti-san violence, no longer primarily statist, no longer happens in the name of sovereignty. If not sovereignty, then what? Messianisms, whether of the partisan or of the counterpartisan variety?'[98] Schmitt always recognised that political power rested on authority over the concepts of political life. Marking the fragility of the existing order, and offering an exit from the dominance of concepts such as state and order, the partisan is the natural

---

[98] A. Moreiras, 'A God without Sovereignty. Political *Jouissance*: The Passive Decision', *The New Centennial Review* 4:3 (2004), 71–108 (p. 72).

figure of hope for post-structural readers of Schmitt. It is a way out of the malaise that Schmitt fully anticipated, and intensely feared.

Partisans, the state, and order

Theory of the Partisan is Schmitt's most emphatic attempt to think through politics away from the detailed mechanics of the state. Without the structures drawn from Bodin and Hobbes, without the comprehensive organising principles of medieval religion, this is a dangerous and inchoate political world. It illustrates the innate potential for raw, authentic, political decisions that emerge from outside the existing normative order. And it reflects the mounting incapacity of that normative order – the *Nomos* of sovereign states and its tenuous shadow in post-war bipolarity – to contain and sustain politics. Schmitt cannot conclude whether the partisan is, in theory, a symbol of optimism for the perpetuation of politics or a devastating harbinger of ultimate dissolution. But more seriously than this, Schmitt cannot, in the final analysis, break the equation of state and the political that he always claims to have unravelled.[99] As with his theory of *Großraum*, Schmitt's attempt to innovate a radical new language of political action collapses back into his overriding concern for the historical fate of the state, and reproduces his wider critique from a new angle.

In the instant moment, the partisan is a political actor. This much is clear. He makes a decision on the real enemy, he embraces a (proto-) political community and, in the extreme instance, he resorts to violent confrontation justified by nothing more than the fact of difference. The four ideal-type criteria that Schmitt provides are narrowly drawn to emphasise the political nature of this disposition. There is a clear transposition of the raw ideas of *The Concept of the Political* into the ideal-type partisan. As an exercise in illustrating the independence of the categories of 'state' and 'political', *Theory of the Partisan* appears, at first glace, to work admirably. But, as we have seen, Schmitt's concern is to show that the decontextualised political decision is really of relevance only in so far as it creates a dynamic of regular with irregular. Its specific political potential is relational and not self-referential.

Without conventionality – without an order of the international as the ultimate reference point – Schmitt holds out little hope for the further

---

[99] As Schmitt put it in 1932, 'In one way or another "political" is generally juxtaposed to "state" or at least is brought into relation with it. The state thus appears as something political, the political as something pertaining to the state – obviously an unsatisfactory circle.' Schmitt, *The Concept of the Political*, p. 20.

containment of the political. It is not enough, therefore, that the partisan can make an authentically political choice outside the context of a state system. Without such a context, it seems, such a decision never gains traction – it never develops a meaning in a world-historical sense. In other words, the political decision is not a free, defining and autonomous act. Instead, it is already embedded in an international context that will determine its ultimate fate. In an international context that drives towards the restoration and maintenance of a conventional inter-state system, the autochthonous decision of the partisan will work itself out in favour of the state. The Spanish partisans were ultimately a part of the reassertion of Spanish sovereignty – a reassertion that became stabilised in the sovereign resurrection of the Spanish state in form. Likewise, the decisions of Generals York and Clausewitz *against* Napoleon became grounded politically in the assertion of Prussian *state* orientation. But in other world-political contexts, the very lack of form in the partisan's choice makes it an ideal companion for absolute enmity.

Schmitt is showing his hand here, and making it clear that he is normatively committed to a certain order of the political. Without conventionality, the actions of the partisan have no replicable meaning. And without meaning – without some form of historical permanence and without having a lasting impact on the consciousness of himself and his enemies – how can such acts be considered properly political? The authentic partisan is caught in a performative contradiction that he will usually resolve by attaining regularity – by folding himself back into a regular system of sovereignty. In other words, Schmitt can only envisage two eventual outcomes in every instance of partisan activity. The outbreak of 'real' enmity will fold back either into the recovery of conventional enmity, or the expansion of 'absolute' enmity.[100] No matter how authentic and 'Romantically' admirable, 'real' enmity lacks the stability to survive as a concept in time. In the very act of its emergence, it is already dead – exposed to the rival logics of order and disorder.

Far from offering a route out of the present malaise, *Theory of the Partisan* ends up profoundly pessimistic in tone. It represents a complementary narrative to Schmitt's grand narrative of the decline of the state and, with it, the decline in the possibility of order. For as long as the system of European states was based on a clear sense of enmity as politically legitimate, the partisan too had the opportunity to express a particularist position. His raw, 'real' enmity might have been regarded as a perversion of the more normatively sophisticated mechanics of inter-

---

[100] See the discussion of Slomp above.

state relations, but it was nevertheless a recognisable digression. Today though, the dual processes we examined in the first part of this work have narrowed the scope for a relationship between irregular partisans and the bedrock of regular states. The more homogeneous and static the international system becomes, the fewer in number the cracks and shadowlands in which the partisan can develop.

This pessimistic view of the stasis of the regular order is best summed up by Schmitt's discussion of the case of General Raoul Salan in Algeria.[101] Schmitt sees Salan as 'an instructive, symptomatic appearance of the last stage' of partisanship.[102] Whereas the partisans of Spain or the Tyrol fought an authentic and straightforward battle to define the providential enemy of the nation, Schmitt sees the colonial war in Algeria as evidence of the final, impossible narrowing of space to challenge and redefine real political orientation. For Schmitt, Salan is a tragic hero in the tradition of Generals York and Clausewitz – a true partisan who sought to act politically to remedy an absence of decision on the part of his president, a servant so loyal as to be driven to disloyalty. By juxtaposing Salan with York, Schmitt attempts to illustrate a structural change in the flexibility and political authenticity of the international system.[103] The Prussian generals could successfully disentangle the political fact of enmity from the norm of legal authority; Salan could not.

The irony of Salan's position is that the erosion of the state into a wholly normative and legal category has forced Salan, as an agent of regularity, into the role of a partisan, and has therefore made a paradox of his position.[104] The case of Salan shows the limits of a modern international setting in which all sense of existential legitimacy has been subsumed by normative categories. The fact that Salan ends up as a partisan between the Algerian partisan and the French republic shows the incompatibility of

---

[101] After a distinguished military career in Indochina, Salan achieved notoriety for the part he played leading a failed putsch in Algeria in 1961. He subsequently founded the terrorist group *Organisation armée secrète* (OAS) to oppose the conclusion of peace between France and the *Front de libération nationale* (FLN), and the consequent move towards Algerian independence. Limited resources exist on Salan in English. By far the best general overview of the surrounding events remains Alistair Horne's classic study *A Savage War of Peace: Algeria 1954–1962*, New York: New York Review of Books Press (2006).

[102] Schmitt, *Theorie des Partisanen*, p. 83.

[103] Schmitt suggests that 'the historian finds examples and parallels in history for all historical situations' (*ibid.*, p. 88). One might argue, however, that the attempt to draw a parallel between General York and General Salan is one analogy too far. If nothing else, Schmitt's intense sympathy for Salan exposes his political orientation in the context of decolonisation and the defence of European hegemony.

[104] 'The partisan can transform himself easily into a presentable uniformed officer; but to the good regular officer, that uniform is more than a costume.' *Ibid.*, p. 84.

modern political forms and any attempt at orientation through Schmittian enmity.

> The enemy is our own question as *Gestalt*. If we have determined our own *Gestalt* unambiguously, where does this double enemy come from? The enemy is not something to be eliminated out of a particular reason, something to be annihilated as worthless. The enemy stands on my own plane …
>
> Salan took the Algerian partisan for the absolute enemy. But all at once, a far worse enemy turned up on his own back: his own government, his own commander, his own brother.[105]

Through the figure of Salan, Schmitt delivers one last blast against the triumph of positivism in domestic and international law, the removal of concrete decisions, and the inversion of the relationship between authority and command.

> We have recalled that the partisan requires legitimation if he wants to remain in the sphere of the political instead of sinking into criminality. The question cannot be adjudicated by reference to the cheap antithesis, habitually mentioned today, of legality and legitimacy. For legality shows itself to be by far the stronger form of validity; indeed, it shows itself as that which it originally was for a republican, namely, the rational, progressive, one and only modern, in a word, highest form of legitimacy itself.

This triumph of legal form over political decision marks a tragic end for Schmitt. His commitment to the system of sovereign states derived always from his admiration for the capacity of that system to generate restraint. And restraint was only possible when a clear recognition of the validity of enmity gave rise to a conventional and predictable pattern of enmity: 'Every attempt at containing or fencing in war must involve the consideration that in relation to the concept of war enmity is the primary concept, and that the discrimination between various kinds of war is preceded by the discrimination between various kinds of enmity.'[106] The partisan can only realise forms of restraint if he is subsumed into the regular. But the case of Salan shows that the regular itself has lost any sense of the distinctions at play. It reserves the right to determine everything through the law, and to apply the categories of criminality to spheres that it must have the courage to treat as political. Schmitt sees no escape from 'the great misfortune' that has been wrought by the abdication of the state, and its pernicious infection by the 'destructive work of the professional revolutionary'.[107]

Today the question of the decision has been wholly subsumed by a legal category. There is no room for an appeal to 'legitimacy' and, as such, no

---

[105] *Ibid.*, pp. 87–8.   [106] *Ibid.*, p. 91.   [107] *Ibid.*, p. 92.

room to enforce a political decision against the prevailing legal order. The framework of law is now too omnipotent for a moment of rupture to take hold. For Schmitt, this is the ultimate expression of pessimism, since the triumph of positive law means the logical elimination of the political decision. Far from offering an alternative locus of politics, Schmitt's account of the partisan ends up confirming his pessimism of the age of the state. Rather than dying its painful but inevitable death, the state lives on as parody. The form has finally overtaken the substance, and a political structure that once achieved so much in the name of restraint has become a thin veil for absolute enmity:

This is a great misfortune, for with those containments of war, European man had succeeded in accomplishing a rare feat: the renunciation of criminalising opponents at war, in other words, relativising enmity, the negation of absolute enmity. *It really is something rare, indeed improbably human, to bring people to the point of renouncing the discrimination and defamation of their enemies.*[108]

This final statement could be regarded as a precise expression of Schmitt's resigned and foundationally uncertain passion for the achievements of European international law. It expresses the importance of a clear principle of enmity, and the contingency of a world intellectual-political context in which that clarity can be sustained. Through the figure of the partisan, as with every other attempt Schmitt makes to clarify the concepts of order and disorder, meaningful conclusions for the future remain painfully remote. The partisan takes over the state, and the statesman is forced into partisanship – this seems to be the pessimistic message of Schmitt's *Theory of the Partisan*. Within the horizon of modernity, even the most radical expressions of enmity serve to hasten the destruction of structures and divisions that might serve as barriers to universalism. Figures such as Salan are tragic for their untimeliness – for their noble but absurd attempts to construe patterns of enmity according to the old rules.

As a last word on the historical fate of the state system, Schmitt's study of the partisan raises the stakes still further in the search for a new principle of order. If the centralising logic of modern thought has managed to conflate the energy of the partisan and the hollow form of the state, how can we begin to conceive of new ordering principles that can securely contain a Schmittian vision of politics? There is something even Bakuninesque about the final pages of *Theory of the Partisan* – the corruption of the current form is absolute, and everything is to be treated with suspicion. The only remedy can be to embrace a total change, the outcome of which cannot be known. But for Schmitt the Christian, it is a

---

[108] *Ibid.* (my emphasis).

conclusion that does not invite us to go out and burn up the world in the hope of hastening the new dawn. As Meier argues, he understood his own efforts to play the role of a Christian Epimetheus to have led to his 'bad' and 'unworthy' accommodation with Nazism. Instead, Schmitt's final word on political order is that of the wistful yet hopeful believer in the Katechon – nothing.

8   Conclusion

World order occupied Schmitt for his entire life. He posited order as an ideal, but also as an eternal problem in political life. Schmitt was always seized of the fact that all order is fragile, and his comfort in the murky zone between stasis and chaos contains an important lesson for all theorists of world politics. Indeed, the name Carl Schmitt has virtually become a byword for the hard-headed acceptance of the uncomfortable 'facts' of human existence. But in spite of his many sophisticated attempts to focus his attention on order and disorder as discrete and autonomous subjects of study, Schmitt ultimately failed to separate his study of order from his study of the history of the state. Faced with what he regarded as the collapse of the existing order, Schmitt actually turned away from a *theoretical* approach to the problem of order, and increasingly focussed on the *historical* experience of the state in a painful effort to explain its decline.

His consideration of the problem of world order shows Schmitt in all his variety as a thinker. Schmitt draws extravagantly from politics and philosophy, law and theology, history and geopolitics. It reflects both his 'extreme talent' and his 'boundless vanity'.[1] And whilst such an approach creates great richness, it also leaves behind a confused and fractious intellectual legacy, in which little agreement can be reached on 'what Schmitt was really about'. Many students of international relations or political theory, for instance, will read Heinrich Meier's study of Schmitt as a religiously oriented thinker with great interest. The thesis that Meier advances is amply supported by the depth of religious metaphor, theory and conceptual development in Schmitt's own work. And whilst most readers will admit to there being great validity in a religious reading of Schmitt, there is a tendency to suggest that this reading remains to be studied on its own terms. For political readers, religion in Schmitt is

---

[1] Such was the assessment of Schmitt by the director of the Berlin Handelshochschule, Moritz Julius Bonn, who appointed Schmitt to a faculty position in 1928. See P. Caldwell, *Popular Sovereignty and the Crisis of German Constitutional Law: The Theory and Practice of Weimar Constitutionalism*, London: Duke University Press (1997), p. 218 n. 6.

an embarrassing sideshow somehow to be ignored, explained away, or ceded to obscure German-speaking theologians to debate.

The result is the typical multiplicity of snapshots that now characterise writing about Schmitt. There is Schmitt the theologian, beloved of German theological writers who regard his fundamental achievement as the development of Christological political concepts, and who see him as Karl Barth's fellow traveller in the development of a theory of secularisation under conditions of modernity. There is Schmitt the jurist, whose exemplary studies of constitutional theory and the constitutional basis of dictatorship are important contributions to twentieth-century public jurisprudence. There is, of course, Schmitt the magician of political concepts, who surpassed Weber in offering precise, comprehensive and comprehensible ideas in reaction to the crisis of German political order in the first third of the twentieth century. There is even, perhaps, Schmitt the geographer, with his bold vision of the importance of spatial concepts in shaping the possibility of political order.

This multiple Schmitt has offered a seemingly bottomless well for those seeking ideas and well-crafted concepts to illuminate a particular legal, political or theological position. And it is equally characteristic of the various Schmittisms that exist today that, of necessity, they must disavow various of Schmitt's other, less supportive interests or ideas. For instance, the spectre of the Antichrist and the restraining power of politics is, *eo ipso*, inconsistent with a serious, secular, radical-Left political theory, such as that espoused by Chantal Mouffe.[2] From the opposite perspective, theological readers of Schmitt are less compelled to ignore the fact that Schmitt was a serious legal and political theorist, and that he showed deep concern for the concrete issues of his day. Yet even they are inevitably drawn towards the conclusion that such concerns were of merely ephemeral concern. The temptation exists to downplay Schmitt's very real and destructive engagement in immediate political questions. And every compartmentalised reading encourages attempts to detach selected ideas from the controversy of Schmitt's engagement with Nazism, rather than reading his theories and his political choices as part of a continuum (albeit hardly a necessary or inevitable one).

Our objective here has been to offer one possible insight into the productive relationship between Schmitt's concern for the meaningfulness of history; his fear of and belief in apocalyptic endings; and his real, detailed and dedicated search for conceptual solutions to the precise problems of his age. Far from embodying distinct concerns that may be

---

[2] See C. Mouffe, 'Schmitt's Vision of a Multipolar World Order', *The South Atlantic Quarterly* 104:2 (Spring 2005), 245–51.

boxed separately, as if they represent two detached careers emanating from the same mind, Schmitt's conceptual political activism achieved its urgency and vitality from his unique sense of meaning. And, as one might expect, this concern for meaning grew over time, both as Schmitt matured intellectually, and as his concerns for the stability of the political order depicted in *The Concept of the Political* reached a climax after about 1941. A career that started out rooted in relatively modest concerns of constitutionality and a fairly instinctive sense of the importance of a political pluriverse blossomed (if one might allow the term) into a fuller and more reflective consideration of why these challenged political facts mattered so deeply.

We have taken *The Concept of the Political* as the high point of Schmitt's achievement for so long, especially in the English-speaking world, that we have often succumbed to the temptation to ignore Schmitt's own contemplation of the context and importance of those ideas. To a very great extent, the remainder of Schmitt's intellectual career offers answers to the question that *The Concept of the Political* leaves glaringly unanswered – why should we value the *seriousness* of a specifically political life, when the alternative is a peaceful world of fun and entertainment? *The one normative prescription in* The Concept of the Political *is that life should be serious.* Such an open normative concept clearly required clarification, and this is precisely what his religiously informed ideas on history and political space provide.

Schmitt's development of theological themes expresses a multivalent reading of 'theology'. On the one hand, he is concerned with disciplined theological themes. In his early study of the Catholic church as a quasi-political institution, and in his consideration of the elision of concepts of miracle and authority, Schmitt tries to apply the language of a theologian to political problems. But underlying such approaches is a concern for theology in its most basic sense – as the study of *theos*. That is, the study of meaning. In the absence of any real contemporary *political* effort to grasp the nettle, and to enforce a definition of meaning, Schmitt turned instead to a consideration of how interpretations of meaning had been enforced historically. The duties of Schmitt's state go beyond protecting the physical life of its citizens, and extend to providing the only credible mechanism for creating meaning in human life.[3] For Schmitt, the alternative to a

---

[3] Indeed, there is always something inherently problematic about the reading of *protego et obligo* as relating simply to the physical life of citizens, since the ultimate ratio of protection is compelling men to die for the sake of their own protection. Unlike Hobbes, Schmitt makes existential claims about the duty of obedience. For Schmitt, men die for the state not only because of the abstract logic of their own protection, but also more directly, from the fact that they die in the protection of a credible definition of themselves.

political pluriverse is a form of nihilism. It is open to interpretation whether this nihilism is a necessarily *Christological* form of apocalypse, or whether it is simply the absence of meaning per se.

Politics is always a matter of life and death for Schmitt. The political derives its concrete reality from the 'real potential for physical killing'.[4] But one might say that his ideas of *international* politics are about the comprehensibility of the patterns of life and death. Killing in a vacuum would not be politics as Schmitt understood it. Schmitt's politics requires rules of grammar.[5] The historical picture Schmitt presents in *The Nomos of the Earth* and elsewhere is a picture of both the functioning and fragility of various grammatical arrangements of the political. It is a great pity that he ended up doing so little to develop a fuller picture of the functioning of politics in pre-modern eras. Schmitt celebrates the supposed unity of order and orientation of Roman and medieval orders, yet the actual content of politics in these orders remains fatally underdeveloped. In the end, it is only the system of states, in all its fallibility, that remains. Given that his primary concern is to understand the decline of that system, it is all the more surprising that Schmitt spends comparatively little time trying to understand previous shifts from one nomic arrangement of the political to another. He posits the change from medieval to modern as a fundamental change in the concrete orientation of political life, yet offers little analysis of how this change takes place, and why this change should be regarded as more significant or consequential than others.

Perhaps Schmitt's endist pessimism would have been more persuasive if he had had a better point of comparison with which to illustrate the *unique* dangers of the present age. Indeed, it is the ambiguities of Schmitt's critique of modernity per se that perhaps present the greatest problems in attempting to apply his critical categories to real or perceived political problems. Schmitt's great intellectual heroes, de Maistre and Donoso Cortes, are both fundamentally anti-modern in so far as the advent of liberalism and the spirit of the American and French revolutions are taken as symptomatic of modernity. Schmitt, by contrast, takes a more structural and longer-term perspective, in which the advent of liberalism is

---

[4] C. Schmitt, *The Concept of the Political* (trans. G. Schwab), Chicago: University of Chicago Press (1996), p. 33.

[5] Schmitt outlines this basic understanding of the importance of a possibility of 'normal' discourse as early as 1922, in *Political Theology*. There he writes that '[t]here exists no norm that is applicable to chaos. For a legal order to make sense, a normal situation must exist, and he is sovereign who definitively decides whether this normal situation actually exists.' C. Schmitt, *Political Theology* (trans. G. Schwab), Cambridge, MA: MIT Press (2005), p. 13. Of course, the 'normal situation' of international politics is an infinitely more complicated beast than the normal domestic situation, but the insistence on the incommensurability of chaos and normality nevertheless pertains.

itself a side effect of the changing structure of the international system in the seventeenth century. As Schmitt's study of Hobbes seeks to illustrate, an essentially *positive* and authentically political attempt to locate politics firmly and absolutely within the state is inverted (by Spinoza and others) to a situation in which the state is the servant of the people. In such circumstances, Schmitt fears that the state (and with it all authority and all difference) can be dispensed with.

The international is even more important in Schmitt's critique of the present than first appears. For him, the processes of liberal dissolution and the elimination of difference cannot be understood without the context of the state system, and the arcane structure of political life that developed out of the seventeenth century. With its simple stratification of the relationship between the state and the citizen (and its vulnerability to a reductive polarity of the citizen versus the state), the state is uniquely vulnerable as a political institution. Yet at the same time, Schmitt applauds the simplicity of a system of states for its potential to display the stark reality of politics as antagonism. Whereas the *complexio oppositorum* of medieval Europe contained inherent complexities that would frame and occasionally obscure the reality of the political, Schmitt sees that the Hobbesian state is the first political structure that embraces enmity as its *ultima ratio*. The problem, as Schmitt sees it, is that such a clear-headed realisation has provoked such discomfort that, ever since, man has been engaged in futile attempts to build new complexities that will disguise and temper these cold political realities.

The canvas on which Schmitt paints the story of modernity stretches, therefore, from the Thirty Years' War rather than the French Revolutionary Wars. And, pre-eminently, this story is the problematic tale of the decline of the state and, with it, the decline of European hegemony. Caught in a moment of transition of great importance but ambiguous duration, Schmitt was to take faltering steps in his assessment of this process. It is clear that he could not lightly abandon his emotional and intellectual commitment to the European state as the locus of politics. Recognising the difficulties of political design and the ever-present danger of chaos, the state of Hobbes and Westphalia remained an astonishingly successful point of certainty for an unprecedented period of time. And its key attribute, above any other, was that it could still show the occasional capacity to inspire belief, and compel obedience.

One might credibly say that Schmitt's intense focus on the Leviathan made him a prescient forerunner of the recent shift in international political theory towards issues of epistemology. He clearly recognised the state to be a contingent entity, the success of which was wrapped up with its capacity to define a public truth, and to orient both the physical and emotive faith of its people. He understood the dangers that result from radically discordant truth claims, and the potential for such divergent claims to result in extreme violence. In so far as he had one, Schmitt's 'project' was to allow for diverse truth claims in a context that could ultimately tolerate that diversity.

It was always going to be a challenge for Schmitt to look beyond the state in pursuit of this project, all the more so because the state was so integral to Schmitt's concept of the political. Even as late as 1948, he could still force himself to believe in the continuity of the age of the state and the continuing historical achievement of the seventeenth century. The Leviathan, he would write, 'is and remains the clear Catechism for the foundational concept of state (*staatlichen*) and international (*zwischen-staatlichen*) law of modernity, which has not yet been subsumed by a new civil war'.[6] Such occasional and continuing professions of his own faith in the system of states expose a weakness in Schmitt's embrace of the present problems. How, one wonders, could he credibly have viewed even his own idiosyncratic reading of the *Leviathan* as a solution to the political fragmentation of 1948? The challenge Schmitt appears to set for himself is to provide theoretical innovations to avoid or foreshorten this 'new civil war'. It is a challenge he surely fails to meet.

On the one hand, Schmitt developed a theory of a new politics of large spaces that was essentially a fudge. Certainly, it embraces all of the geopolitical aspects of Schmitt's critique of the modern state. It recognises that technology and modern weaponry are inconsistent with the small territorial boundaries of the modern state. It draws lessons from the model of the United States, and its continental projection of power across the American continent. And, as such, it is very much a theory of its time, in its appeal to some kind of pan-European politics as the only credible antidote to the bipolarity of Russia and America. But when we relate the theory of *Großraum* to Schmitt's more fundamental concerns, it is evidently little more than a flourishing delay tactic. If the *Großraum* is intended to contain politics, then it clearly faces an astonishing task in creating (or enforcing) the bonds under which the logic of *protego et obligo* gains traction. On the other hand, if the *Großraum* is seen as a simple arbitrary imposition, then surely it will generate new horizons of antagonism both *within* and *between* the various *Großräume*. In short, there is no reason to believe in the *Großraum* as a response to all the problems of dissolution and the erosion of authority that Schmitt diagnoses.

---

[6] C. Schmitt, unpublished review of Norberto Bobbio's *Elementi filosofici sul cittadino di Thomas Hobbes*, Torino (1948), HStAD RW265 19000.

Even in the radically discontinuous figure of the partisan, Schmitt is still essentially rehearsing his attachment to the state, and his regret at its passing. At first it seems that the partisan will mark a radical new turn in his thought. There is a glamorous romance about Schmitt's depiction of the partisan, and from the Spanish partisans of 1808 to Mao's Long March, he appears to identify with the ambitions of those who take up arms and fight an irregular war. They like me, Schmitt seems to say, believe in the necessity of having something to believe in, are willing to decide on the real enemy, and accept the fact that the political is a matter of life and death. Ultimately, though, Schmitt concedes that there is too little difference between the Romantic partisan who seeks to define new political divisions, and the Romanticism of the radical individual who turns every event into something aesthetic.[7] Ultimately, the partisan steps into the regular sphere for his actions and orientation to have any historical meaning and, as such, he relies upon a pre-existing definition of the regular. Without the dynamic of his relationship with the regular, the partisan is nothing but a violent criminal. As with his other supposed attempts to chart a new course of global politics, Schmitt's study of the partisan ends up as yet another mournful reflection on the state we're in. Each reflection adds more layers of complexity to Schmitt's position, but ultimately diminishes any confidence that there can be a Schmittian solution to Schmittian problems.

One must not attempt to distinguish between 'legitimate' and 'illegitimate' uses of Schmitt in thinking about contemporary international problems. As this study has shown, Schmitt opens up so many underdeveloped avenues of enquiry that might fruitfully be adapted and exploited in situating current problems. It is hardly surprising that he has attracted such a curious range of readers, and that advocacy of a Schmitt revival has come from diverse angles. What is less clear is whether there is any credible prospect of a productively discrete 'Schmittian' approach to problems in international political theory. Each invocation of Schmitt comes with caveats or attempts to explain away less appealing, supportive or savoury aspects of his intellectual output. At the most extreme, such attempts treat Schmitt's accommodation with Nazism as nothing more than an act of opportunism, as if his virulent anti-liberalism and Christological antipathy to the historical effects of Judaism in Europe didn't at least somewhat predispose Schmitt to Nazism vis-à-vis the other credible options at the time. Treating Schmitt as a character severable at our own convenience might be handy for the contemporary theorist, but it

---

[7] The very Romanticism, that is, that Schmitt had gone to such lengths to criticise in his 1919 work *Political Romanticism* (trans. G. Oakes), Cambridge, MA: MIT Press (1986).

also ignores much that is so rich and so tragic about his career as a chronicler of the end of the *jus publicum Europaeum*.

Schmitt diagnosed the need for radical innovation in the concepts of the political as the only corrective to an age of global civil war. Yet the very seriousness of the issues at stake appeared to hamper his efforts in contributing to that search. The only ideal to which Schmitt could subscribe was that human life should be serious. And he could never formulate an understanding of seriousness that did not, in the extreme instance, compel killing and dying in the name of a belief.

Appendix. Carl Schmitt in international relations: a bibliographic essay

Fully twenty-six papers were presented to the Standing Group on International Relations panel on 'The International Political Thought of Carl Schmitt' at the 2004 conference in the Hague.[1] It gave the impression of a dam bursting in international relations (IR), and of a widespread, pent-up interest in the possible applications of Schmitt in IR theory flooding out. Participants were drawn from fields as diverse as international law, political theory, theology, literary theory, intellectual history and IR itself. Inevitably such a diverse gathering generated much debate at cross-purposes. But this reception was quite exceptional for the vast range of theoretical applications to which Schmitt's work was put.

With apologies for the necessity of creating simplistic typologies, it is suggested that the emergence of Schmitt into international political theory can be traced broadly within traditions of thought associated variously with the Left and Right of the political spectrum. Such a distinction is inevitably open to challenge, and rightly so. What it emphasises, however, is that most of the interest shown in Schmitt over the past twenty or so years has come from thinkers who self-consciously inhabit the outer fringes of political discourse, and whose work is not especially concerned with its own poltical respectability. What these approaches share is their adoption of Schmitt as a theorist of the necessity of a political pluriverse, to be cited against the apparent advance of global liberal hegemony. Schmitt was, of course, implacably opposed to those who regarded the political and moral unity of the world as the pinnacle of human achievement and the gateway to utopian paradise. World unity was dangerous and nihilistic. At best, such unity was a futile chimera, the pursuit of which would lead mankind into dangerous and bloody escalation of conflict. At worst, the pursuit could be successful, resulting in a facile and depoliticised world. Furthermore, and especially in his pre-war writings,

---

[1] Several of these papers were collected and published in L. Odysseos and F. Petito (eds.), *The International Political Thought of Carl Schmitt: Terror, Liberal War and the Crisis of Global Order*, London: Routledge (2007).

Schmitt condemns the use of liberal universalism as a cloak that hides the particular political interest of those who espouse it. These two strands of Schmitt's critique of liberal universalism have been taken up respectively by the Right and the Left.

Schmitt and poltical realism

The emphasis in Schmitt's work on the primacy of the political decision and the immutability of war as a human possibility resonates naturally with a 'realist' interpretation of international relations. For instance, as Scheuerman has amply illustrated, Schmitt had a profound influence on forming the 'harder' edges of Hans Morgenthau's political realism, and the latter's concern for the role of the nation state as bearer of authentic human meaning.[2] Schmitt himself has been characterised as a realist of sorts, to be read alongside other theorists of political power and *raison d'état*.[3] In his pre-war writings in particular, Schmitt showed an intimate concern for the requirements of pragmatic and power-oriented foreign policy that read like classic expressions of realist IR theory.[4] He also produced a highly sympathetic study of Meinecke's theory of *Staatsräson*.[5]

This implacable opposition to the creation of a global state, and concern to impose limits to the intrusion of international law inside the boundaries of the state, have made Schmitt an apparently valuable resource to realists, broadly conceived. Gary Ulmen – described by one of his closest collaborators as a 'pro-New Deal American nationalist'[6] – is one of the most prominent protagonists in the attempt to deploy Schmitt against the replacement of the international order with 'free-floating concepts [that]

---

[2] W. Scheuerman, 'Another Hidden Dialogue: Carl Schmitt and Hans Morgenthau', in *Carl Schmitt: The End of Law*, Lanham, MD: Rowman and Littlefield (1999), pp. 225–52. See also W. Scheuerman, 'Carl Schmitt and Hans Morgenthau: Realism and Beyond', in M. C. Williams (ed.), *Realism Reconsidered: The Legacy of Hans Morgenthau in International Relations*, Oxford: Oxford University Press (2007). For consideration of Morgenthau's links to Schmitt in the context of the American Right, see A. Söllner, 'German Conservatism in America: Morgenthau's Political Realism', *Telos* 72 (Summer 1987), 161–72. For a thoughtful contrast of Schmitt and Morgenthau see C. Brown, 'The Twilight of International Morality: Hans J. Morgenthau and Carl Schmitt on the End of the *Jus Publicum Europaeum*', in Williams, *Realism Reconsidered*, pp. 42–61.

[3] See, for instance, E. Bolsinger, *The Autonomy of the Political: Carl Schmitt's and Lenin's Political Realism*, London: Greenwood Press (2001); E. Vad, *Strategie und Sicherheitspolitik: Perspektiven im Werk Carl Schmitt*, Opladen: Westdeutscher Verlag (1996).

[4] See C. Schmitt, 'Die Rheinlande als Objekt internationaler Politk', in *Positionen und Begriffe im Kampf mit Weimar–Genf–Versailles, 1923–1939*, Berlin: Duncker and Humblot (1970), pp. 29–37.

[5] C. Schmitt, 'Zu Friedrich Meineckes Idee der Staatsräson', in *Positionen und Begriffe*, pp. 51–9.

[6] P. Gottfried, 'Forgotten but Not Gone', *American Outlook Magazine* (Autumn 2001).

do not constitute institutional standards but have only the value of ideo-logical slogans'.[7] Ulmen takes up Schmitt's critique of the just-war tradi-tion, and shares the view that denial of war as a tool of rational politics is both dangerous and hypocritical, and will result in the use of war as a form of religious or ideological domination rather than a part of acceptable *raison d'état*.[8]

In addition to his basic hostility to a normatively based global politics, Schmitt also appeals to certain contemporary realists for his apparent ability to avoid the stasis that might result from an unrealistic continued attachment to notions of Westphalian politics. In his distinction of politics from the state form, Schmitt appears to hold out the possibility of restruc-turing political realism time after time, adapting the basic premise of power politics to new structures of global power. In characterising the contemporary value of Schmitt's *Nomos of the Earth*, Ulmen argues that '[g]lobalization and new, larger political entities require a new political realism and a new political theory dealing with a new type of law regulating "international" relations. This global order will fail if it does not take into account the accomplishments of the only truly global order of the earth developed so far: the *jus publicum Europaeum*.'[9]

In other words, Schmitt appears to offer hopes of a new conceptual depth to political realism, allowing a constructive engagement in debates on globalisation and the changing political competence of the state. The necessity of 'the political' as part and parcel of the human condition can be defended, whilst the future competence of the state can be debated. In particular, Schmitt's interest in the possibility of a new spatial basis for politics proves an attractive line of enquiry to those realists aware of the potential need to move beyond the rigid old assumptions of specifically *state* power as the basic component of world politics.

The use of Schmitt in this vein does not prevent the simultaneous, ongoing defence of the state. Paul Gottfried calls on Schmitt in support of his argument against what he regards as the dominant, passive liberal-ism of the contemporary 'managerial state'. Gottfried understands power to be the primary political category, and castigates the modern Western tendency to obfuscate power and render it an exercise of bare manage-ment. This managerial tendency is made all the worse by a tendency towards the incorporation of a false and hypocritical moralism into the

---

[7] G. Ulmen, 'Toward a New World Order: Introduction to Schmitt's *The Land Appropriation of a New World*', *Telos* 109 (Autumn 1996), 3–27 (p. 26).

[8] G. Ulmen, 'Just Wars or Just Enemies?', *Telos* 109 (Autumn 1996), 99–113 (p. 112).

[9] G. Ulmen, 'Introduction' to C. Schmitt, *The Nomos of the Earth*, New York: Telos Press (2005), pp. 9–34 (p. 34).

function of government. Whilst the domestic effects of this obfuscation of power are Weberian in character, Gottfried draws heavily on Schmitt in arguing that the managerial state must be abandoned in favour of clear, hard-headed, realist political dynamics in foreign policy too.[10]

This association of Schmitt with calls for a renewed realism in world politics has inevitably raised the question of an underground influence on contemporary US policy-making. The suggestion that Schmitt is 'Dick Cheney's Eminence Grise' is based in part on the exercise of a form of executive power domestically that, it is argued, corresponds to Schmitt's theory of dictatorial power.[11] But there is a clear international dimension to the attempt to draw this linkage. Levinson, for instance, draws on the idea of 'lines of amity' in describing the policy of torture in Iraq as essentially 'Schmittian'.[12] And besides all else, those seeking to trace a line of heritage from Carl Schmitt to the neo-con hate figures need do little more than stress the productive relationship that Leo Strauss had with Schmitt, and then stress the influence of the former.

For the most part, the characterisation of Bush foreign policy as 'Schmittian' is polemical and unrealistic, and does further damage to attempts to study Schmitt's political theory dispassionately and effectively. A brief survey of the literature in this area reveals a large volume of impressionistic attempts to draw some correlation, and surprisingly little interest in the only realistic avenues of influence. In other words, there is much interest in the idea that the 'label Schmittian [seems] a good fit', and little grafting to discover the nature of any influence.[13] The notion that the neo-cons were 'born under a Schmittian star' does little to enhance our understanding of what a 'Schmittian' foreign policy might actually be.[14]

This approach of using 'Schmittian' as a term of intellectual abuse has also played a part in describing Huntingdon's 'Clash of Civilisations' thesis as somehow infused with Carl Schmitt's concern for the political world as a pluriverse in which violence remains an ever present possibility. Whilst Huntingdon's contention that conflict is an immutable part of the societal condition might draw on *The Concept of the Political*, there is no

---

[10] P. Gottfried, *After Liberalism: Mass Democracy in the Managerial State*, Princeton: Princeton University Press (1999).

[11] B. Boyd, 'Carl Schmitt: Dick Cheney's Eminence Grise', *Executive Intelligence Review* (6 January 2006), 35–7.

[12] S. V. Levinson, 'Torture in Iraq', *Daedalus* 133:3 (Summer 2004), 5–9.

[13] M. Specter, 'Perpetual War or Perpetual Peace? Schmitt, Habermas and Theories of American Empire'. Unpublished lecture given to the Internationales Forschungszentrum Kulkturwissenschaften, Vienna, 26 April 2004.

[14] *Ibid.*

necessity that it should do so. One hardly needs Schmitt to make the point that perpetual peace might be the least likely outcome. And, as Ulmen points out, Huntingdon has a fundamentally different notion of the mechanics of political agency from Schmitt.[15] For Huntingdon, conflict emerges from culture, whereas for Schmitt the ultimate political *ratio* must be the act of command and inscription. Huntingdon is seeking sociological foundations that are too rigid to correspond to Schmitt's basic understanding of the political.

Furthermore, it might be added that Huntingdon's emphasis on the inscription of cultural hatred and the concomitant notion that the future *Nomos* he describes will witness radical instability is at odds with the dispassionate description of enmity that Schmitt puts forward. There is no need for Schmitt's enemies to hate one another, and their enmity is more perfect for its lack of hatred. By contrast, hate, infused with heavily layered cultural, religious, linguistic and racial difference, is the very basis of the divisions that characterise Huntingdon's schema. In many respects, Huntingdon seems to believe that the temperate enmity that Schmitt clings to has been subsumed by the very cultural aspects that Schmitt always insisted were subordinate to the basic fact of division. For Huntingdon, culture defines the political, whereas in Schmitt's concept the political is the form-giving principle (in its ideal-type at least).

Schmitt and the European Right

As a man unequivocally of the hard Right, Schmitt is quite naturally a sympathetic figure for the hard Right of the present. In truth, Schmitt has been omnipresent, giving intellectual succour to the German-speaking Right throughout his years of internal exile. Jan-Werner Müller's superb study of Schmitt's influence in European thought cast light on Schmitt's shadowy but astonishingly effective influence throughout German, French and Spanish intellectual circles.[16] Schmitt's continuing influence on the Right is no less real as a result of its shadowy secrecy. Public figures on the Right always had more to lose from an acknowledged engagement with the *Kronjurist* of the Third Reich than those on the Left, and especially so in Germany, where the process of intellectual rehabilitation was such an arduous and delicate process for so many. It is instructive, for instance, that German legal theorists of the 1950s such as Ernst Forsthoff,

---

[15] See Ulmen, 'Toward a New World Order'.

[16] J.-W. Müller, *A Dangerous Mind: Carl Schmitt in Post-War European Thought*, New Haven: Yale University Press (2003).

Rüdiger Altmann and Hermann Lübbe were necessarily low-key in their appropriation of Schmitt's constitutional concepts.[17]

As a result of the reputational sensitivities at stake in Germany, Schmitt's influence on the right was more implicit than explicit. Hanno Kesting and Reinhard Koselleck were both informal pupils of Schmitt.[18] Meanwhile, Roman Schnur drew on *The Nomos of the Earth* in his study of the effect of utopianism on international law, and in expressing his hope for a renewed national ethic that could contain an element of liberalism within the nation.[19] Although this process of reception and advocacy was largely clandestine, Müller's study suggests that the impact of Schmitt in the development of ideas of world order on the Right was ongoing and potent, both in Germany and beyond.

Partly as a result of the bars to the invocation of Schmitt in Germany, open reference to his work has been most prominent among the New Right in France, Italy and Spain. In large part these theorists have latched on to Schmitt's innate Eurocentrism, and his suggestion of a new ordering of world politics in which the political uniqueness of Europe is emphasised in the creation of its own *Großraum*. Led by Alain de Benoist, the political-legal primacy of Europe depicted in *The Nomos of the Earth* has been overlaid with a theory of European cultural superiority in support of a radical right-wing vision of world order. Schmitt thus provides several isolated intellectual tools that the *Nouvelle Droit* have carefully utilised. The superiority of Europe in *The Nomos of the Earth* is coupled to the possibility of *Großraum* politics, and these two appropriations are both read in the light of the friend–enemy distinction as a call to radical political action. Whilst the way in which these concepts have been recoupled might seem logically dubious, it is worth remembering that the likes of Julien Freund and Gianfranco Miglio were pupils and associates of Schmitt, and so perhaps lay the best claim to representing a 'Schmittian' concept of international order.[20]

It should come as little surprise that Schmitt can be utilised in support of an essentially fascist view of the function of foreign policy. There is, after all, a pretty self-evident precedent for this. Whether or not this amounts to the adoption of Schmitt in IR, and whether there can even be a fascist theory of international relations, are for others to judge. The point rather is to stress that, for all the creative and dynamic uses of

---

[17] *Ibid.*, pp. 76–86.   [18] *Ibid.*, pp. 104–15.

[19] R. Schnur, 'Weltfriedensidee und Weltbürgerkrieg 1791/92', *Der Staat* 2 (1963), 297–317.

[20] Schmitt's thought has been appropriated widely within the New Right, including a considerable focus on his *Verfassungslehre*. Recent works of a more explicitly international flavour include J. Freund, 'Schmitt's Political Thought', *Telos* 102 (Winter 1995), 11–42; and A. de Benoist, 'Qu'est-ce que la souveraineté?', *Elements* 96 (November 1999), 24–35.

Schmitt's thought in attempting to theorise contemporary international relations, it is important to remember that Schmitt is subject to pretty unambiguous application in the interests of the contemporary hard Right. Again, whether or not this observation should be taken as a 'warning' is for others to decide.

Marxisti Schmittiani and afterwards

Schmitt's critique of a Wilsonian world order resonates equally on the Left among those who seek to challenge the Washington consensus, the abusive nature of supposedly 'benign' US hegemony and the erosion of local political difference. This approach is both the highest-profile and most surprisingly counterintuitive use of Schmitt in thinking about contemporary world politics. The strange relationship between Schmitt and the New Left began in earnest in 1968, when their shared hostility to the 'banality' of liberal parliamentarism was thrown into sharp relief.

Initially, this effect was especially strong in Italy, where those on the Left who attempted to apply Schmitt's concept of enmity in an absolute hostility to liberalism were derided as the *Marxisti Schmittiani*.[21] According to Mario Tronti and his associates, placing enmity at the heart of a vision of politics not only negated the very logic of liberalism, but was also a spur to increased radicalism. Schmitt could be used to bring together an almost syndicalist notion of political unity with the sheer aggression of the enmity distinction. Furthermore, the identification of political unity as a concept prior to and distinct from the state was deployed as a further theoretical prop in support of revolutionary action to tear down the stale, outmoded and hypocritical edifice of the bourgeois state.

In recent years, some of the *Marxisti Schmittiani* have radically adjusted the balance away from discredited Marxism and towards a more thoroughgoing adoption of Schmitt as a talisman of the Left. Much work in this area has centred on the ideas of radical democracy and agonal pluralism in opposition to the allegedly apolitical and dominating stasis of the liberal state. As with the critique from the Right, this approach draws intimately on Schmitt's sustained assault on supposedly universal values of liberalism as a cloak for political interests and as a means of eroding identity.

Such a critique is international in its manifestation since the whole objective is to assert the validity and necessity of difference, yet tends to

---

[21] Müller, *A Dangerous Mind*, p. 178.

focus more narrowly on the alleged hypocrisy of Western universalism.[22] The universalism that Schmitt feared on its own terms as the negation of politics is recast by the Left as a particular, identifiable phenomenon – namely the triumph of Western liberal capitalism. Assertion of 'the political' thus becomes a defence against a form of universalism to be feared and despised, rather than the necessary, *de facto* assertion of 'the political' on its own terms against an idea of universalism that remains abstract. Slavoj Žižek summarises the appeal of Schmitt to those on the Left concerned with this defence against liberal hegemony:

> ... the way to counteract the re-emerging ultra-politics is not more tolerance, more compassion and multicultural understanding, but the *return of the political proper*, that is, the reassertion of the dimension of antagonism which, far from denying universality, is cosubstantial with it. That is the key component of the proper *leftist* stance as opposed to the rightist assertion of one's particular identity ... true universalists are those ... who engage in a passionate struggle for the assertion of a Truth that compels them.[23]

In other words, Schmitt's emphasis on the particular nature of politics is useful at this time, and in this context, because the universalism on offer to us is unacceptable. Liberal universalism cannot represent true freedom and as such must be resisted by the reassertion of particular identities, and the exposition of Western claims to benign leadership as fraud and hypocrisy. Schmitt thus provides a theoretical underpinning to a form of bunker mentality that continues to hope for the ultimate achievement of the 'Truth that compels them'. It need hardly be stressed that this sense for the role of 'the political' is radically at odds with the hostility that Schmitt felt per se towards universalism. Schmitt's fear was of universalism qua universalism. Just as his analysis of the state is underpinned by a foundational sense of the meaning of politics, his critique of liberalism is underpinned by a foundational fear of world unity. His concerns are clearly not co-extensive with those Left Schmittians whose primary fear is liberalism itself.

This use of Schmitt is motivated by a desire to find an active and political response to the current situation. The objective is to theorise a response to the triumph of liberalism that is more satisfactory than

---

[22] As William Rasch puts it, 'Not only is conflict within the system outlawed, but also that among the systems, for universal morality always results in "reconciliation", whether one wants it or not. Such "outlawry" never operates neutrally; such "reconciliation" always camouflages a differend and masquerades as peace.' W. Rasch, 'Conflict as a Vocation: Carl Schmitt and the Possibility of Politics', *Theory, Culture and Society* 17:6 (2000), 1–32 (p. 26).

[23] S. Žižek, 'Carl Schmitt in the Age of Post-Politics', in C. Mouffe (ed.), *The Challenge of Carl Schmitt*, London: Verso (1999), pp. 18–37 (p. 35).

Adorno's fatalistic advocacy of 'near asceticism as a response to a modernity in which even culture becomes an industry'.[24] For William Rasch *et al.*, recourse to Schmitt is all about 'establishing the *logical possibility of legitimate political opposition*'.[25] As Chantal Mouffe argues, 'the central problem that our current unipolar world is facing is that it is impossible for antagonisms to find legitimate forms of expression'.[26] Schmitt provides a point of departure for creating an assertive and linguistically novel arena to attack the current political consensus. He is seen as providing 'vocabularies that do not just emphatically repeat philosophically more sophisticated versions of the liberal ideology of painless, effortless, universal equality'.[27]

Those who seek to apply Schmitt in this direction adopt varying degrees of theoretical sophistication, but are collectively driven by their ability to identify with his basic contention that modern liberalism and its international manifestations are intellectually and morally bankrupt. A strange substitute for a discredited Marxism of old, Schmitt has emerged as an ally of convenience in the raging debates against globalisation and the triumph of American power. His appeal in this context lies, most basically, in the way that he 'lifted [the] veil' between law and political fact, and in so doing helped to answer the 'question that never ceases to reverberate in the history of Western politics: what does it mean to act politically?'[28] Schmitt continues to be a spur to leftist radicalism in the extremity of the political position he presents.[29]

Leftist Schmittians have been given a second wind by the work of the Italian professor of aesthetics Giorgio Agamben, and his theory of 'bare life'. Agamben argues that the contemporary world order has eradicated the sense of interior and exterior that characterised the *jus publicum*

---

[24] W. Rasch, *Sovereignty and Its Discontents: On the Primacy of Conflict and the Structure of the Political*, London: Birkbeck Law Press (2004), p. 1.

[25] *Ibid.*, p. 13.

[26] C. Mouffe, 'Carl Schmitt's Warning on the Dangers of a Unipolar World', in Odysseos and Petito, *Carl Schmitt*, pp. 147–53 (p. 152).

[27] W. Rasch, 'Lines in the Sand: Enmity as a Structuring Principle', *The South Atlantic Quarterly* 104:2 (Spring 2005), 253–62 (p. 261).

[28] G. Agamben, *State of Exception* (trans. K. Attell), Chicago: University of Chicago Press, 2005) p. 2.

[29] Most recently, Schmitt's critique of liberalism is deployed as an explanation for the current phenomenon of global terrorism. As Mouffe argues:

> There is certainly a correlation between the now unchallenged power of the United States and the proliferation of terrorist groups. Of course, in no way do I want to pretend that this is the only explanation. Terrorism has always existed, and it is due to a multiplicity of factors. *But it undeniably tends to flourish in circumstances where there are no legitimate political channels for the expression of grievances.* (Mouffe, 'Schmitt's Vision of a Multipolar World Order', p. 250 (my emphasis))

Europaeum described by Schmitt. This has exposed the 'bare life' of individuals who assert an exterior unto themselves, and stand in contra-distinction to the homogeneous Empire of liberal civil society. Agamben subscribes to Schmitt's fear that denial of the basic, legal distinctions of the state leads inexorably to a violent and uncontrollable hyperpo-liticisation, and takes a critical interest in Schmitt's development of a *Partisanentheorie* as a way of thinking about the political effects of resist-ance to hegemony.[30] Jan-Werner Müller argues, not implausibly, that this 'Schmittian' pessimism about a world without meaningful political divi-sions can be traced from Schmitt, via Agamben, to the influential work of Hardt and Negri.[31] We will return later, in this context, to the viability of using Schmitt's thoughts on the partisan in this sort of application.

What remains here, however, is a certain perplexity at Schmitt's sticking power on the European Left. It is certainly understandable that Schmitt formed an object of interest and a useful shock factor to Mario Tronti and his associates in the 1960s. Understandable, too, would be the strategic and occasional deployment of Schmittian concepts and phrases in support of a broader, and conceptually distinct emancipatory project. Yet in the circles where his thought is celebrated, Schmitt looks like a godfather above the intellectual landscape. The epithet 'Schmittian' is adopted with a certain intellectual and moral pride, perhaps as a badge of intellec-tual bravery. Uncovering the reasons for this inverse dogmatism would require a thesis unto itself, and would probably prove a futile exercise in deductive psychology anyway. The one factor that emerges again, how-ever, is Schmitt's seductive and self-contained style. Once one climbs on board with his conceptual language, it becomes increasingly difficult to disembark and draw alternative, dispassionate linkages. Such, again, are the strengths and weaknesses of such a compelling *Begriffsmagie*.

It is impossible to improve upon Müller's withering assessment of the use of Schmitt by the contemporary Left:

Schmitt's apocalyptic vision that almost *anything* was preferable to liberalism had apparently invaded the Marxist imagination – and often been made into a form of messianism … But as long as the Left continued to lack an alternative social reality, it would be all the more likely that it would have to resort to rusty and double-edged Schmittian swords in its battle against global capitalism.[32]

---

[30] See G. Agamben, *'Homo sacer': Sovereign Power and Bare Life* (trans. D. Heller-Roazen), Stanford: Stanford University Press (1998). Following the advent of the 'War on Terror', Agamben takes up the theme of the state of exception and the exercise of executive power in *State of Exception* (2005).

[31] M. Hardt and A. Negri, *Empire*, Cambridge, MA: Harvard University Press (2000). See Müller, *A Dangerous Mind*, p. 229.

[32] Müller, *A Dangerous Mind*, pp. 231–2.

Nowhere was the contemporary use of Schmitt in the theory and polemic of contemporary international relations made clearer than in debates over the use of force in Kosovo. For 'Schmittians' Kosovo represented the hypocrisy and danger of liberal foreign policy in microcosm. The West claims to speak in the name of an abstract 'humanity' whilst all the time pursuing its own political goals. According to the critics, the inconsistency of the two objectives becomes clear in the failure to obtain a UN mandate. The critique mounted by Danilo Zolo and others directly echoes Schmitt's critique of the claims of the Allied powers to act in the universal interest, in the 1923 Ruhr crisis, in 1939, or again in the great confrontations of the Cold War.[33]

Schmitt was also utilised in the critique of the methods of warfare deployed in Kosovo, emphasising as they did the indirect and responsibility-free use of force that characterises modern Western warfare (or, as Schmitt might have had it, *potestas indirecta*). Thus the use of sanctions regimes, bombing from high altitude and the techniques of psychological warfare all fall within the banner of indirect and hypocritical power.

Pure economic imperialism will also apply a stronger, but still economic, and therefore (according to this terminology) nonpolitical, essentially peaceful means of force. A 1921 League of Nations resolution enumerates as examples: economic sanctions and severance of the food supply from the civilian population ...

War is condemned but executions, sanctions, punitive expeditions, pacifications, protection of treaties, international police, and measures to assure peace remain. The adversary is thus no longer called an enemy but a disturber of the peace and is thereby designated to be an outlaw of humanity.[34]

For these readers of Schmitt, such criticisms penned in 1932 are equally true of the foreign policy goals and methods of NATO.[35]

Challenges to Schmitt

Given the appeal of Schmitt to radicals of seemingly every persuasion, it was only a matter of time before Schmitt appeared in post-modern debates on the viability of the state concept. We needn't linger too long

---

[33] See D. Zolo, *Invoking Humanity: War, Law and Global Order* (trans. F. Poole and G. Poole), London: Continuum (2002).

[34] C. Schmitt, *The Concept of the Poltical* (trans. G. Schwab), Chicago: University of Chicago Press (1996), pp. 78–9.

[35] For the Schmittians of the Right, by contrast, Kosovo seemed dangerous precisely because it appeared to shepherd in a new paradigm in international law that, once in place, might prove hard to shift. See for instance C. Schreuer, 'The Waning of the Nation State: Towards a New Paradigm for International Law ', *European Journal of International Law* 4:1 (1993), 447–71.

here, other than to note that the value of Schmitt to post-modernism centres on the impossible question of whether or not his concept of the political is foundational or not. Even Jacques Derrida, whose *Politics of Friendship* is in part an extended engagement with Schmitt's thought, declined to reach any conclusions on the matter. He held out the possibility that Schmitt is essentially a diagnostic thinker, whose basic concern for the contingency of foundational concepts on the concrete reality of confrontation could be proto-post-structuralist to some degree.[36] This question cannot be answered, of course, without thorough consideration of the degree to which Schmitt was irreversibly attached to the state-form, despite the potential freedom created by his independent concept of the political.

One could dwell indefinitely here on points of intersection and divergence between Schmitt and post-structural ideas. In certain respects, this work as a whole addresses the question of his approach to foundations and the temporality of concepts, and so places him in a context where such points of intersection might hopefully become evident. It is worth noting that this concern for political design, and Schmitt's continued quest to define the deep institutions of political life, do and will continue to make him an interesting point of reference in post-structural thinking on global order. There is doubtless a case for arguing that Schmitt himself is a sort of a post-structural thinker, since the focus of his theory is on the problematic aspects of this process of definition and maintenance of concepts.

The point, for the time being, is to highlight the fact that Schmitt's work has been, and is likely to be, invoked in mainstream IR through the work of those whose primary concern is with philosophies of knowledge. Schmitt will be of manifest value as both a resource and a challenge to those who question the logical possibility of ordering concepts and the political presuppositions that drive the agenda of political theorists of all shades. It remains to be seen how this process will take shape, and whether the gap in language between Schmitt's ideas of truth and the scepticism of those who deal with him will be bridged.

Taking Schmitt as the challenge

Schmitt's rehabilitation as a thinker to be read and taken seriously, if not to be admired, is by now sufficiently advanced as to have engaged the attention of those beyond the radical Left and Right, and their

---

[36] See J. Derrida, *The Politics of Friendship* (trans. G. Collins), London: Verso (1997), p. 104.

post-structuralist critics. Whilst many in the 'mainstream' would doubtless prefer to continue the 'ostrich' approach of the past sixty years, and consign Schmitt to history, this appears to be an increasingly unviable and unnecessary attitude. Whilst perhaps the most tepid approach to using Schmitt in international political theory, there is nothing intrinsically flawed in reading Schmitt as a conceptual challenge requiring of a response. This, after all, was the dominant attitude with which Schmitt was initially received into Anglo-American political theory in the 1980s – a process that produced much good analytical research.

On the one hand, this approach can focus on the 'lessons' that Schmitt can teach us. He can be read as exemplifying the dangers of losing sight of a sense of academic moral responsibility and of uncoupling the power of thought from its political uses. Mark Lilla makes much of this point in his consideration of Schmitt as one of a number of 'reckless minds' who, in their various ways, aggravated the dangerous potential of their thought with foolhardy forays into politics.[37] Lilla addresses the question of the responsibility that intellectuals bear for the policy application of their ideas, and takes parallel snapshots of Heidegger's complicity in Nazism, and Foucault's strange applause for the Ayatollahs. In itself, the argument in favour of responsible scholarship is sound, but there is something of the schoolmistress to start a liberal 'engagement' with Schmitt on such terms.

More productive examples of responding to the 'challenge' of Schmitt on the international level have tended to follow the lead of David Dyzenhaus in accepting and seeking to address Schmitt's challenge to a liberal concept of neutrality. Schmitt can be used in this way as a stalking horse within liberalism (including debates on a liberal foreign policy) in order to attack excessive formalism and the hiding of politics behind formless legalism. Dyzenhaus himself, although ultimately rejecting Schmitt, nevertheless deploys Schmitt's critique of liberal neutrality against the legalist concept of political power advocated by Dworkin and, to a lesser extent, Rawls.[38] Ironically, given the legendary antipathy between the two men, this approach is suggestive of the use of Schmitt as a weapon of attack in support of a more Habermasian, deliberative democracy against the formal legalism of Anglo-American liberalism.[39]

---

[37] M. Lilla, *The Reckless Mind: Intellectuals in Politics*, New York: New York Times Books (2001).

[38] D. Dyzenhaus, *Legality and Legitimacy: Carl Schmitt, Hans Kelsen and Herman Heller in Weimar*, Oxford: Oxford University Press (1999).

[39] Such a consequence would doubtless be equally distasteful for both Schmitt and Habermas. Whilst acknowledging Schmitt's intellectual capability, Habermas condemns his 'crude anti-Semitism and toadying to the Nazi authorities', characterising him as

One of the more original liberal arguments in support of Schmitt is that deployed by Renato Cristi regarding his theory of 'authoritarian liberalism'.[40] Cristi argues that the fundamental character of the stable modern state, according to Schmitt, is the unquestioned sovereign authority of its government both internally and externally. Provided sovereignty as the locus of decision is not undermined, the nature of governance itself can be inherently liberal (in the sense that it is participatory and guarantees civic freedoms). Indeed, in *The Nomos of the Earth* and *The Crisis of Parliamentary Democracy*, Schmitt does hold up the national liberalism of nineteenth-century liberalism as combining certain 'freedoms' with a stable political framework. However, Cristi's exemplary cases of Singapore and various Latin American democracies more or less make the point that the privilege Schmitt grants to the exercise of sovereignty is necessarily at odds with the logic of liberalism. Whilst the phrase 'authoritarian liberalism' might adequately *describe* a historical situation, the concept is ultimately oxymoronic if one subscribes to Schmitt's notion of authority.

His use as a challenge, and as a tool occasionally to critique the political nature of Western liberalism, has its merits, but, as with the leftist use of Schmitt, one wonders how far the use of Schmitt in particular is necessary. There is a hollowness to the assertion of some need to be watchful for the pitfalls of which Schmitt serves as warning. For those who yearn for the arrival of cosmopolitan internationalism (or, for the more optimistic among them, celebrate its arrival), Schmitt necessarily represents the past. And this is necessarily so, since the achievement of such a condition in reality was the political nadir that Schmitt so feared, and worked so tirelessly in seeking to avert.

On the other hand, if there is a timelessness to Schmitt's insights, then the fundamental insight that should be of concern to international political theory is the assertion, to borrow Robert Frost's phrase, that good fences make good neighbours. If 'the political' really is immutable, and conflict is an omnipresent possibility in man's social condition, then Schmitt's concern for the stability of the *Nomos* becomes paramount. The challenge then would be to re-create the successful 'bracketing' of

fascinated 'above all [by] the aesthetics of violence'. J. Habermas, *The New Conservatism* (trans. S. W. Nicholson), Cambridge MA: MIT Press (1989). Ellen Kennedy provoked fury by arguing for a logical connection between Schmitt and Habermas. Pointing out connections between Habermas' *Stuctural Transformation* and Reinhard Koselleck's *Critique and Crisis*, Kennedy argues that the latter's self-professed debt to Schmitt silently extends to the Frankfurt School. E. Kennedy, 'Carl Schmitt and the Frankfurt School', *Telos* 71 (Spring 1987), 37–66.

40 R. Cristi, *Carl Schmitt and Authoritarian Liberalism: Strong State, Free Economy*, Cardiff: Cardiff University Press (1998).

war and to emulate the 'one singular accomplishment of continental European jurists and governments in the seventeenth and eighteenth centuries, an accomplishment that was perpetuated in the nineteenth century: the rationalization and humanization of war'.[41]

Whether or not Schmitt's views on international order present a challenge depends on the degree to which one shares his fear of nihilism. For those who welcomed Fukuyama's prognosis of an end to history, Schmitt's fundamental concern will be incomprehensible. By contrast, for those who would prefer an anarchy in which one knows where one stands, to a universalism in which one is nowhere and everywhere at once, he will offer some source of inspiration:

[In the Middle Ages] there had been tumultuous conditions of a terrible sort, also on European soil – conditions of 'anarchy', but not of 'nihilism' in the sense of the ninteenth and twentieth centuries. If 'nihilism' is not to become an empty phrase, one must comprehend the specific negativity whereby it obtains its historical place: its *topos*. Only in this way can the nihilism of the nineteenth and twentieth centuries be distinguished from the anarchistic conditions of the Christian Middle Ages. In the connection between *utopia* and *nihilism*, it becomes apparent that only a conclusive and fundamental separation of order and orientation can be called 'nihilism' in an historically specific sense.[42]

---

[41] C. Schmitt, *The Nomos of the Earth in the International Law of the* Jus Publicum Europaeum (trans. G. Ulmen), New York: Telos Press (2004), p. 149.

[42] *Ibid.*, p. 66.

Bibliography

Works by Carl Schmitt

'The Age of Neutralizations and Depoliticizations' [1929] (trans. M. Konzett and J. P. McCormick), *Telos* 96 (Summer 1993), 130–42

Antworten in Nürnberg (ed. H. Quaritsch). Berlin: Duncker and Humblot (2000)

'Appropriation/Distribution/Production: Towards a Proper Formulation of the Basic Questions of any Social or Economic Order' [1953] (trans. G. Ulmen), *Telos* 95 (Spring 1993), 52–64

'Beschleuniger wider Willen, oder: Die Problematik der westlichen Hemisphäre' [1942], in *Staat, Großraum, Nomos*, pp. 431–40

'Clausewitz als politischer Denker: Bemerkungen und Hinweise', *Der Staat* 6:4 (1967), 479–502

The Concept of the Political [1927] (trans. G. Schwab). Chicago: University of Chicago Press (1996) [1932 edition]

The Crisis of Parliamentary Democracy [1923] (trans. E. Kennedy). Cambridge, MA: MIT Press (1985) [1926 edn]

Die Diktatur. Berlin: Duncker and Humblot (1921)

Donoso Cortes in gesamteuropäischer Interpretation. Cologne: Greven Verlag (1950)

'Drei Möglichkeiten eines christlichen Geschichtsbildes', *Universitas* 5:8 (August 1950), 927–31

'Die Einheit der Welt' [1952], in *Staat, Großraum, Nomos*, pp. 496–512

Ex captivitate salus. Cologne: Greven Verlag (1950)

Frieden oder Pazifismus? Arbeiten zum Völkerrecht und zur internationalen Politik 1924–1978 (Berlin: Duncker and Humblot, 2005)

'Der Führer schützt das Recht', *Deutschen Juristenzeitung* 39:15 (1934), 945–50

'Gespräch über den Partisanen: Carl Schmitt und Joachim Schickel' [1969], in *Staat, Großraum, Nomos*, pp. 619–42

Glossarium: Aufzeichnungen der Jahre 1947–1951. Berlin: Duncker and Humblot (1991)

Das internationalrechtliche Verbrechen des Angriffskrieges und der Grundsatz Nullum crimen, nulla poena sine lege. Berlin: Duncker and Humblot (1994)

Land und Meer. Stuttgart: Klett–Cotta (1954)

Legality and Legitimacy [1932] (trans. J. Seitzer). Durham NC: Duke University Press (2004)

The Leviathan in the State Theory of Thomas Hobbes: Meaning and Failure of a Political Symbol [1938] (trans. G. Schwab). Westport, CT: Greenwood Press (1996)

'Nationalsozialismus und Völkerrecht' [1938], in *Frieden oder Pazifismus?: Arbeiten zum Völkerrecht und zur internationalen Politik 1924–1978* (ed. G. Maschke), Berlin: Duncker and Humblot (2005), pp. 391–421

The Nomos of the Earth in the International Law of the Jus Publicum Europaeum (trans. G. Ulmen). New York: Telos Press (2004)

'Die Ordnung der Welt nach dem zweiten Weltkrieg' [1962], in *Staat, Großraum, Nomos*, pp. 592–618

Political Romanticism [1919] (trans. G. Oakes). Cambridge, MA: MIT Press (1986) [1925 edn]

Political Theology [1922] (trans. G. Schwab). Cambridge, MA: MIT Press (2005) [1934 edn]

Politische Theologie II: Die Legende der Erledigung jeder politischen Theologie. Berlin: Duncker and Humblot (1970)

Positionen und Begriffe im Kampf mit Weimar–Genf–Versailles, 1923–1939. Berlin: Duncker and Humblot (1994)

'Die Rheinlande als Objekt internationaler Politik' [1925], in *Positionen und Begriffe*, pp. 29–37

Römischer Katholizismus und politische Form [1923] (2nd edn). Cologne: Klett–Cotta (1925)

'Der Staat als Mechanismus bei Hobbes und Descartes' [1937], in *Staat, Großraum, Nomos*, pp. 139–51

Staat, Bewegung, Volk: Dreigliederung der politischen Einheit. Hamburg: HAVA (1933)

Staat, Großraum, Nomos: Arbeiten aus den Jahren 1916–1969 (ed. G. Maschke). Berlin: Duncker and Humblot (1995)

'The State as Mechanism in Hobbes und Descartes', in *The Leviathan*, pp. 91–104 (pp. 99–100)

'Strong State and Sound Economy' [1932] (trans. R. Cristi), in R. Cristi, *Carl Schmitt and Authoritarian Liberalism*. Cardiff: University of Wales Press (1998), pp. 212–32

Theorie des Partisanen: Zwischenbemerkung zum Begriff des Politischen. Berlin: Duncker and Humblot (1963)

'The Theory of the Partisan: A Commentary/Remark on the Concept of the Political' [1963] (trans. A. C. Goodson), *The New Centennial Review* 4:3 (2004), 1–78

'Theory of the Partisan' [1963] (trans. G. Ulmen), *Telos* 127 (Spring 2004), 11–78

Theory of the Partisan [1963] (trans. G. Ulmen). New York: Telos Press (2007)

Über die drei Arten des rechtswissenschaftlichen Denkens. Hamburg: HAVA (1934)

Unpublished review of Norberto Bobbio's *Elementi filosofici sul cittadino di Thomas Hobbes*. Torino (1948). HStAD RW265 19000

'Völkerrechtliche Formen des Modernen Imperialismus' [1932], in *Positionen und Begriffe*, pp. 184–203

'Völkerrechtliche Großraumordnung mit Interventionsverbot für raumfremde Mächte' [1941], in *Staat, Großraum, Nomos*, pp. 269–371

'Völkerrechtliche Probleme im Rheingebiet' [1928], in *Positionen und Begriffe*, pp. 111–23

Die Wendung zum diskriminierenden Kriegsbegriff. Berlin: Duncker and Humblot (1938)

'Die Wendung zum totalen Staat' [1931], in *Positionen und Begriffe*, pp. 166–78

Der Wert des Staates und die Bedeutung des Einzelnen. Tübingen: Paul Siebeck (1914)
'Zu Friedrich Meineckes Idee der Staatsräson' [1926], in *Positionen und Begriffe*, pp. 51–9

Other works

Agamben, G. *'Homo sacer': Sovereign Power and Bare Life* (trans. D. Heller-Roazen). Stanford: Stanford University Press (1998)
  State of Exception (trans. K. Attell). Chicago: University of Chicago Press (2005)
Aron, R. *Clausewitz: Philosopher of War* (trans. C. Booker and N. Stone). London: Routledge and Kegan Paul (1983)
Balakrishnan, G. *The Enemy: An Intellectual Portrait of Carl Schmitt.* London: Verso (2000)
Baumann, Z. *Modernity and the Holocaust.* Cambridge: Polity Press (1991)
Behnke, A. 'Terrorising the Political: 9/11 within the Context of the Globalisation of Violence', *Millennium: Journal of International Studies* 33:2 (2004), 279–312
Bendersky, J. *Carl Schmitt: Theorist for the Reich.* Princeton: Princeton University Press (1983)
  'Carl Schmitt at Nuremberg', *Telos* 72 (Summer 1987), 91–6
  'Carl Schmitt's Path to Nuremberg: A Sixty Year Reassessment', *Telos* 139 (Summer 2007), 6–34
  'The Expendable Kronjurist: Carl Schmitt and National Socialism, 1933–1936', *Journal of Contemporary History* 14:2 (1979), 309–28
  (transcr.). 'Interrogation of Carl Schmitt by Robert Kempner', *Telos* 72 (Summer 1987), 97–107
  (transcr.). 'The "Fourth" (Second) Interrogation of Carl Schmitt at Nuremberg', *Telos* 139 (Summer 2007), 35–43
Bodin, J. *On Sovereignty* (trans. J. H. Franklin). Cambridge: Cambridge University Press (1992)
Bolsinger, E. *The Autonomy of the Political: Carl Schmitt's and Lenin's Political Realism.* London: Greenwood Press (2001)
Boyd, B. 'Carl Schmitt: Dick Cheney's Eminence Grise', *Executive Intelligence Review* (6 January 2006), 35–7
Brown, C. *Sovereignty, Rights and Justice.* Cambridge: Polity (2002)
  'The Twilight of International Morality: Hans J. Morgenthau and Carl Schmitt on the End of the *Jus Publicum Europaeum*', in M. C. Williams (ed.), *Realism Reconsidered*, pp. 42–61
  Understanding International Relations. London: Palgrave (2001)
Caldwell, P. C. 'Controversies over Carl Schmitt: A Review of Recent Literature', *The Journal of Modern History* 77 (June, 2005), 357–87
  Popular Sovereignty and the Crisis of German Constitutional Law: The Theory and Practice of Weimar Constitutionalism. London: Duke University Press (1997)
Carty, A. 'Carl Schmitt's Critique of Liberal International Legal Order between 1933 and 1945', *Leiden Journal of International Law* 14 (2001), 25–76

Colombo, A. 'Challenging the State: Carl Schmitt and "Realist Institutionalism"'. Paper presented to the 5th Pan-European International Relations Conference, The Hague, September 2004

'L'Europa e la società internazionale: gli aspetti culturali e istituzionale della convivenza internazionale in Raymond Aron, Martin Wight e Carl Schmitt', *Quaderni di scienza politica* 2 (1999), 251–302

Cristi, R. *Carl Schmitt and Authoritarian Liberalism: Strong State, Free Economy.* Cardiff: Cardiff University Press (1998)

de Benoist, A. 'Qu'est-ce que la souveraineté?', *Elements* 96 (November 1999), 24–35

Derrida, J. *The Politics of Friendship* (trans. G. Collins). London: Verso (1997)

Dostoyevsky, F. *The Brothers Karamazov* (trans. D. McDuff). London: Penguin (2003)

Dyzenhaus, D. *Legality and Legitimacy: Carl Schmitt, Hans Kelsen and Herman Heller in Weimar.* Oxford: Oxford University Press (1999)

Ellul, J. *The Technological Society.* London: Jonathan Cape (1965)

Fasching, D. J. *The Thought of Jacques Ellul: A Systematic Exposition.* New York: Edward Mellen Press (1981)

Frei, C. *Hans J. Morgenthau: An Intellectual Biography.* Baton Rouge: Louisiana State University Press (2001)

Freund, J. 'Schmitt's Political Thought', *Telos* 102 (Winter 1995), 11–42

Gasché, R. 'The Partisan and the Philosopher', *The New Centennial Review* 4:3 (2004), 9–34

Goodson, A. C. 'About Schmitt: Partisans and Theory', *The New Centennial Review* 4:3 (2004), 1–7

'*Pro aris et focis*: Schmitt's Partisans in Münkler's Theory of War', *The New Centennial Review* 4:3 (2004), 145–59

Gottfried, P. *After Liberalism: Mass Democracy in the Managerial State.* Princeton: Princeton University Press (1999)

Carl Schmitt. London: The Claridge Press (1990)

'Forgotten but Not Gone', *American Outlook Magazine* (Autumn 2001)

Habermas, J. *The New Conservatism* (trans. S. W. Nicholson). Cambridge, MA: MIT Press (1990)

'Verrufener Fortschritt – verkanntes Jahrhundert: zur Kritik der Geschichtsphilosophie', *Merkur* 14 (1960), 112–21

Hardt, M. and Negri, A. *Empire.* Cambridge, MA: Harvard University Press (2000)

Harste, G. 'Jean Bodin on Sovereignty, State and Central Administration: Unity or Complexity?', *Distinktion: Scandinavian Journal of Social Theory* 2 (2001), 35–52

Herf, J. *Reactionary Modernism: Technology, Culture, and Politics in Weimar and the Third Reich.* Cambridge: Cambridge University Press (1986)

Herwig, H. H. 'The Influence of A. T. Mahan upon German Sea Power', in J. B. Hattendorf (ed.). *The Influence of History upon Mahan: The Proceedings of a Conference Marking the Centenary of Alfred Thayer Mahan's* The Influence of Sea Power upon History. Newport, RI: Diane Publishing (1991), pp. 67–80

Heuser, B. *Reading Clausewitz*. London: Pimlico (2002)

Hobbes, T. *A Dialogue between a Philosopher and a Student of the Common Laws of England* (ed. J. Cropsey). Chicago: University of Chicago Press (1997)
  Leviathan. Oxford: Oxford World's Classics (1998)
  Man and Citizen: De homine *and* De cive (ed. B. Gert). Indianapolis: Hackett (1991)

Holmes, S. *The Anatomy of Antiliberalism*. Cambridge, MA: Harvard University Press (1994)

Horn, E. '*Waldgänger*, Traitor, Partisan: Figures of Political Irregularity in West German Postwar Thought', *The New Centennial Review* 4:3 (2004), 125–43

Horne, A. *A Savage War of Peace: Algeria 1954–1962*. New York: New York Review of Books Press (2006)

Howse, R. 'Europe and the New World Order: Lessons from Alexandre Kojève's Engagement with Schmitt's *Nomos of the Earth*', *Leiden Journal of International Law* 19:1 (2006), 93–103

Ignatieff, M. 'It's War – but It Doesn't Have to Be Dirty', *Guardian* (1 October 2001)

Joerges, C. and Ghaleigh, N. S. (eds.). *Darker Legacies of Law in Europe: The Shadow of National Socialism and Fascism over Europe and Its Legal Traditions*. Oxford: Hart (2003)

Jünger, E 'Der Waldgang', in *Werke*, 22 vols., Vol. V: *Essays I*. Stuttgart: Klett–Cotta (1960), pp. 291–388

Kant, I. *The Philosophy of Law: An Exposition of the Fundamental Principles of Jurisprudence as the Science of Right* (trans. W. Hastie). Edinburgh: T. & T. Clark (1887)

Kateb, G. 'Aestheticism and Morality: Their Cooperation and Hostility', *Political Theory* 28:1 (2000), 5–37

Kelly, D. *The State of the Political: Conceptions of Politics and the State in the Thought of Max Weber, Carl Schmitt and Franz Neumann*. Oxford: Oxford University Press (2003)

Kennedy, E. 'Carl Schmitt and the Frankfurt School', *Telos* 71 (Spring 1987), 37–66
  Constitutional Failure: Carl Schmitt in Weimar. Princeton: Princeton University Press (2005)

Kershaw, I. *The Hitler Myth: Image and Reality in The Third Reich*. Oxford: Oxford Paperbacks (2001)

Kervégan, J.-F. 'Carl Schmitt and "World Unity"', in C. Mouffe (ed.), *The Challenge of Carl Schmitt*. London: Verso (1999), pp. 54–74

Kiesel, H. (ed.). *Ernst Jünger–Carl Schmitt Briefe, 1930–1983*. Stuttgart: Klett–Cotta (1999)

Kissinger, H. *Diplomacy*. New York: Simon and Schuster (1994)

Klein, J. 'Adolf Grabowsky: ein vergessener Politikwissenschaftler', in B. Hafeneger and W. Schäfer (eds.), *Aufbruch zwischen Mangel und Verweigerung*. Marburg: Marburg Rathaus Verlag (2000), pp. 393–410

Koenen, A. *Der Fall Carl Schmitt: Sein Aufstieg zum 'Kronjuristen des Dritten Reiches'*. Darmstadt: Wissenschaftliche Buchgesellschaft (1995)

Köllreuter, O. *Das politische Geschicht Japans*. Berlin: Heymann (1940)

Kojève, A. 'L'Empire latin', *La regle du jeu* 1:1 (1990), 89–123

Koselleck, R. *Critique and Crisis: Enlightenment and the Pathogenesis of Modern Society* Oxford: Berg (1988)

> *Futures Past: On the Semantics of Historical Time* (trans. K. Tribe). New York: Columbia University Press (2004)

Langhans-Ratzeburg, M. *Begriff und Aufgaben der Geographischen Rechtswissenschaft (Geojurisprudenz)*. Berlin: Vowinckel (1928)

Laughland, J. *The Tainted Source: The Undemocratic Origins of the European Idea.* London: Little and Brown (1997)

Levinson, S. V. 'Torture in Iraq', *Daedalus* 133:3 (Summer 2004), 5–9

Lewis, M. W. and Wigen, K. E. *The Myth of Continents: A Critique of Metageography.* Berkeley: University of California Press (1997)

Lilla, M. *The Reckless Mind: Intellectuals in Politics*. New York: New York Times Books (2001)

Locke, J. *Two Treatises of Government* (ed. P. Laslett). Cambridge: Cambridge University Press (1988)

Löwith, K. *Meaning in History*. Chicago: University of Chicago Press (1949)

> 'Der okkasionelle Dezisionismus von Carl Schmitt', in *Saemtliche Schriften*, 9 vols., Vol. VIII (ed. K. Stichweh and M. B. de Launay). Stuttgart: Metzler Verlag (1984), pp. 93–127

McCormick, J. E. 'Dilemmas of Dictatorship: Carl Schmitt and Constitutional Emergency Powers', *The Canadian Journal of Law and Jurisprudence* 10:1 (1997), 163–87

> 'Introduction to Carl Schmitt's "The Age of Neutralizations and Depoliticizations"', *Telos* 96 (1993), 19–30

Mahan, A. T. *The Influence of Sea Power upon History 1660–1783*. Boston, MA: Little, Brown and Co. (1890)

Majer, D. *Nationalsozialismus im Lichte der juristischen Zeitgeschichte*. Baden-Baden: Nomos Verlagsgesellschaft (2002)

Malcolm, N. *Aspects of Hobbes*. Oxford: Clarendon Press (2002)

Marcuse, H. *Negations*. Boston, MA: Beacon (1968)

Martinich, A. P. *The Two Gods of Leviathan: Thomas Hobbes on Religion and Politics.* Cambridge: Cambridge University Press (2003)

Marx, K. and Engels, F. *The Communist Manifesto* (trans. S. Moore). London: Penguin Classics (2002)

März, J. *Landmächte und Seemächte*. Berlin: Zentral Verlag (1928)

Maschke, G. *Der Tod Carl Schmitts*. Vienna: Karolinger (1987)

Meier, H. *Carl Schmitt and Leo Strauss: The Hidden Dialogue* (trans. J. H. Lomax). Chicago: University of Chicago Press (1995)

> *The Lesson of Carl Schmitt: Four Chapters on the Distinction between Political Theology and Political Philosophy* (trans. M. Brainard). Chicago: University of Chicago Press (1998)

Mommsen, W. J. *Max Weber and German Politics, 1890–1920* (trans. M. S. Steinberg). Chicago: University of Chicago Press (1990)

Moreiras, A. 'A God without Sovereignty. Political *Jouissance*: The Passive Decision', *The New Centennial Review* 4:3 (2004), 71–108

Morgenthau, H. *Politics among Nations* (5th edn). New York: Knopf (1978)

Mouffe, C. (ed.). *The Challenge of Carl Schmitt*. London: Verso (1999)
  'Carl Schmitt's Warning on the Dangers of a Unipolar World', in L. Odysseos
    and F. Petito (eds.), *The International Political Thought of Carl Schmitt*,
    pp. 147–53
  'Schmitt's Vision of a Multipolar World Order', *The South Atlantic Quarterly*
    104:2 (Spring 2005), 245–51
Müller, J.-W. 'Carl Schmitt's Method: Between Ideology, Demonology and
    Myth', *Journal of Political Ideologies* 4:1 (1999), 61–85
  A Dangerous Mind: Carl Schmitt in Post-War European Thought. New Haven:
    Yale University Press (2003)
Münkler, H. *Gewalt und Ordnung: Das Bild des Krieges im politischen Denken*.
    Frankfurt am Main: Fischer Verlag (1992)
Murphy, D. T. *The Heroic Earth: Geopolitical Thought in Weimar Germany
    1918–1933*. London: Kent State University Press (1997)
Norris, A. 'A Mine that Explodes Silently: Carl Schmitt in Weimar and After',
    Political Theory 33:6 (December 2005), 887–98
  'Sovereignty, Exception, and Norm', *Journal of Law and Society* 34:1 (March
    2007), 31–45
Odysseos, L. and Petito, F. *The International Political Thought of Carl Schmitt:
    Terror, Liberal War and the Crisis of Global Order*. London: Routledge (2007)
Ojakangas, M. *A Philosophy of Concrete Life: Carl Schmitt and the Political Thought of
    Late Modernity*. Bern: Peter Lang (2006)
Ortino, S. 'Space Revolution and Legal Order'. Paper presented to the 5th Pan-
    European International Relations Conference, The Hague, September 2004
Osiander, A. *The States System of Europe, 1640–1990*. Oxford: Oxford University
    Press (1994)
Pan, D. 'Political Aesthetics: Carl Schmitt on Hamlet', *Telos* 72 (Summer 1987),
    153–9
Pourciau, S. 'Bodily Negation: Carl Schmitt on the Meaning of Meaning', *Modern
    Language Notes* 120:5 (December 2005), 1066–90
Rasch, W. 'Conflict as a Vocation: Carl Schmitt and the Possibility of Politics',
    Theory, Culture and Society 17:6 (2000), 1–32
  'Lines in the Sand: Enmity as a Structuring Principle', *The South Atlantic
    Quarterly* 104:2 (Spring 2005), 253–62
  *Sovereignty and Its Discontents: On the Primacy of Conflict and the Structure of the
    Political*. London: Birkbeck Law Press (2004)
Scheuerman, W. 'Carl Schmitt and Hans Morgenthau: Realism and Beyond', in
    M. C. Williams (ed.). *Realism Reconsidered*, pp. 62–92
  'Carl Schmitt and the Road to Abu Ghraib', *Constellations* 13:1 (2006), 108–24
  Carl Schmitt: The End of Law. Lanham, MD: Rowman and Littlefield (1999)
  'International Law as Historical Myth', *Constellations* 11:4 (2004), 537–50
  Liberal Democracy and the Social Acceleration of Time. Baltimore, MD: Johns
    Hopkins University Press (2004)
Schnur, R. 'Weltfriedensidee und Weltbürgerkrieg 1791/92', *Der Staat* 2 (1963),
    297–317
Schreuer, C. 'The Waning of the Nation State: Towards a New Paradigm for
    International Law', *European Journal of International Law* 4:1 (1993), 447–71

Schroers, R. *Der Partisan: Ein Beitrag zur politischen Anthropologie* Berlin: Kiepenhauer and Witsch (1961)

Schwab, G. *The Challenge of the Exception: An Introduction to the Political Ideas of Carl Schmitt between 1921 and 1936* (2nd edn). Westport, CT: Greenwood Press (1989)

Shklar, J. *After Utopia: The Decline of Political Faith.* Princeton: Princeton University Press (1969)

Slomp, G. 'Carl Schmitt's Five Arguments against Just War', *Cambridge Review of International Affairs* 19:3 (2006), 435–47

'The Theory of the Partisan: Carl Schmitt's Neglected Legacy', *History of Political Thought* 26:3 (2005), 502–19

Söllner, A. 'German Conservatism in America: Morgenthau's Political Realism', *Telos* 72 (Summer 1987), 161–72

Sombart, N. *Jugend in Berlin.* Munich: Carl Hanser (1984)

Specter, M. 'Perpetual War or Perpetual Peace? Schmitt, Habermas and Theories of American Empire'. Unpublished lecture given to the Internationales Forschungszentrum Kulkturwissenschaften, Vienna, 26 April 2004

Stirk, P. 'Schmitt's "Völkerrechtliche Großraumordnung"', *History of Political Thought* 20:2 (1999), 357–74

Strauss, L. 'Notes on Carl Schmitt: *The Concept of the Political*', in H. Meier (ed.), *Carl Schmitt and Leo Strauss: The Hidden Dialogue* (trans. J. H. Lomax). Chicago: University of Chicago Press (1995), pp. 83–4

Strong, T. B. 'Foreword' to C. Schmitt, *The Concept of the Political* (trans. G. Schwab). Chicago: University of Chicago Press (1996), pp. ix–xxviii

Taubes, J. *The Political Theology of Paul* (trans. D. Hollander). Stanford: Stanford University Press (2004)

Toulmin, S. *Cosmopolis: The Hidden Agenda of Modernity.* Chicago: University of Chicago Press (1990)

Ulmen, G. 'Introduction' to C. Schmitt, *The Nomos of the Earth.* New York: Telos Press (2005), pp. 9–34

'Just Wars or Just Enemies?', *Telos* 109 (Autumn 1996), 99–113

'Toward a New World Order: Introduction to Schmitt's *The Land Appropriation of a New World*', *Telos* 109 (Autumn 1996), 3–27

Vad, E. *Strategie und Sicherheitspolitik: Perspektiven im Werk Carl Schmitt.* Opladen: Westdeutscher Verlag (1996)

Vagts, D. 'International Law in the Third Reich', *The American Journal of International Law* 84:3 (1990), 661–704

van Laak, D. and Villinger, I. *Nachlaß Carl Schmitt: Verzeichnis des Bestandes im Nordrhein-Westfälischen Hauptstaatsarchiv.* Siegburg: Republica-Verlag (1993)

Vogel, W. *Das neue Europa, und seine historisch-geographischen Grundlagen.* Bonn: Schroeder (1925)

'Rhein und Donau als Staatenbilder', *Zeitschrift für Geopolitik* 1 (1924), 63–78

Wight, M. *International Theory: The Three Traditions.* London: Leicester University Press (1991)

'Western Values in International Relations', in H. Butterfield and M. Wight (eds.), *Diplomatic Investigations: Essays in the Theory of International Relations.* London: George Allen and Unwin (1966), pp. 89–131

Williams, M. C. (ed.). *The Realist Tradition and the Limits of International Relations.*
    Cambridge: Cambridge University Press (2005)
    'Why Ideas Matter in International Relations: Hans Morgenthau, Classical
    Realism and the Moral Construction of Power Politics', *International
    Organization* 58 (2004), 633–65
Wolin, R. 'Carl Schmitt: The Conservative Revolutionary Habitus and the
    Aesthetics of Horror', *Political Theory* 20:3 (1992), 424–47
Zarmanian, T. 'Carl Schmitt and the Problem of Legal Order: From Domestic to
    International', *Leiden Journal of International Law* 19 (2006), 41–67
Žižek, S. 'Carl Schmitt in the Age of Post-Politics', in C. Mouffe (ed.), *The
    Challenge of Carl Schmitt*, pp. 18–37
    The Ticklish Subject: The Absent Centre of Political Ontology. London: Verso (1999)
Zolo, D. *Invoking Humanity: War, Law and Global Order* (trans. F. Poole and
    G. Poole). London: Continuum (2002)

Index

Abravanel, Isaac, 88
Adorno, Theodor, 210–211
Agamben, Giorgio, 212
'Age of Neutralisations and
　　Depoliticisations, The', 110–118
al-Qaeda, 181, 187
　and partisanship, 188
Altmann, Rüdiger, 208
anarchy
　and law, 22
Antichrist, 4
　and experience of time, 110
　and peace, 49–52
　and the sovereign state, 49–54
anti-Semitism
　and Liberalism, 57
　and the *Großraum* concept,
　　138–139
　and the Katechon, 56–57
　of Schmitt, 54–59, 131
apocalypse, 4, 10
Aron, Raymond, 182
Atlanticism, 8–9

Barth, Karl, 196
Behnke, Andreas
　and partisans, 188
belief (public and private), 45–46,
　　47–48
Bendersky, Joseph, 6, 131
Benoist, Alain de, 63, 208
'Beschleuniger wider Willen', 119–122
Bodin, Jean, 18, 35–36,
　　41, 189
Bonald, Louis Vicomte de, 39
Bosch, Hieronymous, 43
British Empire, 135
Brown, Chris, 11, 79
Bruegel, the Elder, 43
Brueghel, Pieter the Younger, 43
Bull, Hedley, 22
Burckhardt, Jacob, 7

Calvinism, 89, 92–93
Clausewitz, Carl von, 59, 61, 167,
　　172–174, 190
　and Raoul Salan, 191
Colombo, Alessandro, 24
Columbus, Christopher, 90
complexio oppositorum, 8, 35, 44, 60, 76–78,
　　106, 199
Concept of the Political, The, 5–6, 11, 14–18,
　　52, 54, 60, 71, 108, 111, 147, 164,
　　179, 197
　and *The Theory of the Partisan*, 165–170
Congress of Vienna (1815), 37, 159,
　　168, 174
Crisis of Parliamentary Democracy, The, 48
Cristi, Renato, 216
Cromwell, Oliver, 55

Darwin, Charles, 86
de Maistre, Joseph, 17
Derrida, Jacques, 188, 214
Descartes, René, 114
Diktatur Die, 85
Disraeli, Benjamin, 141
Donoso Cortes, Juan, 39, 98, 158, 198
Dostoevsky, Fyodor, 61
Dworkin, Ronald, 215
Dyzenhaus, David, 215

England, 8, 38, 90–91
enmity, 14–17
　'absolute', 169–170
　and order, 13
　of General Salan, 191–193
　public nature, 16
　'real', 167–169, 190
Erastus, Thomas, 41
Ex captivitate salus, 156–158

Federal Republic of Germany
　constitution of, 156
Fichte, Johann Gottlieb, 172

227

Forsthoff, Ernst, 207
Foucault, Michel, 215
France, 91–92
Franz Joseph I, Emperor of Austria, 52
Frederick the Great, 46
Freemasonry, 46
French Revolution, 21
Freund, Julien, 208
friend–enemy distinction, 14–17
Fukuyama, Francis, 217

geopolitics, 95–101
Germany
  as a Reich, 136
  Federal Republic of, *see* Federal Republic
    of Germany
Glossarium, 55–56, 58
Gneisenau, August von, 172
Goodson, A. C., 156
Gottfried, Paul, 55, 205–206
Grabowsky, Adolf, 96
Großraum, 4–5, 126–155, 200
  and anti-Semitism, 138–139
  and the Monroe Doctrine,
    134–136
  and Nazi aggression, 139
  and territory, 141–147
  and the Cold War, 148–150
  as a *Leistungsraum*, 145
  internal relations of, 137
  political idea of, 137–141
Grotius, Hugo, 114

Hahlweg, Werner, 172
Haushofer, Karl, 97, 98, 99
Hegel, G. F. W., 12
  and philosophies of history, 37
  and the German state, 2
Heidegger, Martin, 56, 215
Herder, Johann Gottfried, 12, 31
Hezbollah, 188
history,
  philosophies of, 7–8
Hobbes, Thomas, 8–9, 18, 101,
    114, 189
  and IR theory, 63–68
  De cive, 65
  distinction between public and private,
    46–47
  Leviathan, 39–48, 59–61
  theory and practice, 37–38
Horn, Eva, 164, 175
horror vacui, 93–95
Hughes, Charles Evans, 135
Huntingdon, Samuel, 128, 206–207

interessierte Dritte, 178–179
international law
  and anarchy, 22, 105–106
  and irregular fighters, 169
  and *Nomos*, 24
  and sovereignty, 20–22
  and the *jus publicum Europaeum*, 17–22
  and third-party recognition, 178–179
  and treaty positivism, 147
  in medieval Europe, 75–78
  Schmitt's academic interest in, 128–132
IR theory,
  and Thomas Hobbes, 63–68
  Schmitt's relevance to, 3, 11, 13–14,
    203–217

Jünger, Ernst, 26, 45, 56
jus publicum Europaeum, 7, 13, 17–22, 36,
    45, 95, 106, 116, 124, 129, 159, 160,
    164, 169
  and *Nomos*, 24
justus hostis, 21, 74, 174

Kant, Immanuel, 46, 83
Kapp, Ernst, 74
Katechon, 49–54, 63, 78, 110, 194
  and anti-Semitism, 56–57
  and modern politics, 121–125
  and Nazism, 56
Kelly, Duncan, 113
Kelsen, Hans, 58
Kennedy, Ellen, 132
Kesting, Hanno, 208
Kjellen, Rudolf, 96, 97
Köllreuter, Otto, 96
Koselleck, Reinhard, 123–124, 208
Kosovo, 213

Land and Sea, 9
land appropriation, 84–85
  of the New World, 93–95
Land und Meer, 110, 164, 177
Langhans-Ratzeburg, Manfred, 96, 97
League of Nations, 130
Lebensraum, 97
Lenin, V. I., 54, 170
  reading of Clausewitz, 174
Leviathan
  and epistemology, 199, 200
  as mechanism, 44–45
  as myth, 42–44
  tripartite structure, 59–61
  unravelling of, 46–47
*Leviathan in the State Theory of Thomas
    Hobbes, The*, 37–38, 40–47, 110

liberalism,
  and anti-Semitism, 57
  Schmitt's critique of, 6–7, 126–127
Lilla, Mark, 215
Locke, John, 83–84
Löwith, Karl, 50, 54
Lübbe, Hermann, 208
Lukács, György, 54
Lutheranism, 92

Mackinder, Halford, 97
Mahan, Alfred Thayer, 97, 99
Maistre, Joseph de, 39, 98, 158, 198
Majer, Diemut, 138
Malcolm, Noel, 65
Marcuse, Herbert, 15
Martinich, A. P., 68
Marx, Karl, 54
März, Joseph, 99
Masaryk, Tomáš, 52
Maschke, Günter, 131
Meier, Heinrich, 2, 40, 49, 50, 51, 52, 53,
  109, 175, 195
Meinecke, Friedrich, 7, 204
Mendelssohn, Moses, 46, 55
Miglio, Gianfranco, 208
Mihailović, Draža, 182–183
miracle, 45–46, 47–48, 114
Monroe Doctrine (1823), 37, 134–136
More, Thomas, 94
Morgenthau, Hans, 64, 204
  personal relationship with Schmitt, 38
Moreiras, Alberto, 105, 188
Mouffe, Chantal, 196, 211
Müller, Jan-Werner, 27, 62, 63
Münkler, Herfried, 182
Murphy, David, 97
Muscovy Company, 90

Napoleon
  and forms of enmity, 170
  and Spanish partisans, 162
  resistance movements against, 159
'Nationalsozialismus und Völkerrecht', 130
Nazism
  legal foundations, 130–131
  Schmitt's relationship with, 31–32,
    37, 148
neutralisation, 110–118
  and technology, 113–118
New World (discovery), 93–95
9/11, see September 11, 2001 (attacks)
Nomos, 22–26
  and territory, 72–73
  and the jus publicum Europaeum, 24

and universality, 73
as a constitutive act, 23
as a fence-word, 23
as international law, 24
pre-global examples of, 73–78
shadow of permanence, 106–108
Nomos of the Earth, The, 3, 12, 13, 22–26, 48,
  52, 160, 164, 198
Nuremberg Trials, 157
  interrogation of Schmitt, 1, 156

Ojakangas, Mika, 52, 109
Ortino, Sergio, 25, 73

Pan, David, 138
partisan, 159–194, 201
  and irregularity, 162
  and technology, 175–178
  and terrorism, 179–189
  and the state, 189–194
  as philosophical abstraction, 170–175
  mobility, 163
  political stance, 162
  telluric nature, 163
Paul, St
  2 Thessalonians, 49
Pearl Harbor, attack on (1941), 119
Peloponnesian Wars, 80
Piłsudski, Józef, 52
Plato
  Schmitt's interpretation of, 16
Plettenberg, 2, 27
Political Romanticism, 31
Political Theology, 11, 52, 108
Positionen und Begriffe, 11
Prussia, 157, 167
  army of, 183–165
  Landsturm Edict (1813), 172
Pufendorf, Samuel von, 38, 46

Rasch, William, 211
Ratzel, Friedrich, 96, 97
Rawls, John, 215
Rheinlande als Objekt internationaler Politik,
  Die, 129
Röhm, Ernst, 37
Roman Catholicism and Political Form, 76–78
Roosevelt, Franklin Delano, 121
Russia, 113–114

Salan, Raoul, 191–193
Scharnhorst, Gerhard von, 172
Schelsky, Helmut, 42
Scheuerman, William, 27, 64, 103, 204
  and modern terrorism, 185–186

Schickel, Joachim, 183
Schnur, Roman, 208
Schroers, Rolf, 178
Schwab, George, 11, 54, 55
sea (as element), 85–87
  and emptiness, 93–95
  elemental decision in favour, 87–93
Second World War (1939–1945), 119–121
September 11, 2001 (attacks), 184
Serbia, 57
Sinn Fein, 181
Slomp, Gabriella, 5, 165–168
Sombart, Nicolaus, 148
sovereign state
  and the Antichrist, 49–54
  and the partisan, 189–194
  origins, 35–36
sovereignty
  and international law, 20–22
  fragility of, 46–47
  the sovereign decision, 25–26
Spanish Civil War (1936–9), 119
spatial revolution, 78–82
Spengler, Oswald, 100
Spinoza, Benedict, 46, 48, 55, 57, 58,
    114, 199
Staat, Grossraum, Nomos, 11
Stahl, F. J., 54
Staufenberg plot (1944), 157
Stirk, Peter, 137, 139
Strauss, Leo, 6, 16, 39, 42, 49, 64, 206

Taubes, Jacob, 10, 47, 78
tellurism, 163
  and technology, 175–178
territory, 8–9
  and foundationalism, 101
  and Großraum, 141–147
  and Nomos, 72–73
  and spatial revolution, 78–82
  and technology, 116
  as the foundation of the modern state, 20
  man's orientation to, 82–85
  private ownership, 83
terrorism
  and the partisan, 179–189
Thales of Miletus, 82

Theory of the Partisan, 5, 159–194
  and The Concept of the Political, 165–170
Thirty Years' War, 18, 21, 40, 79, 81, 199
Thomasius, Christian, 46
Tito, Josip, 182–183
Tönnies, Ferdinand, 41
Tordesillas, Treaty of (1494), 92
Toulmin, Stephen, 124
Treaty of Westphalia (1658), 18
Tronti, Mario, 209, 212
Tyrol
  resistance to Napoleon, 161

Über die drei Arten des rechtswissenschaftlichen
    Denkens, 54
Ulmen, Gary, 11, 204–205
United States of America, 119–121
  and the Monroe Doctrine, 134–136

Vagts, Detlev, 133
Venetian republic, 75
Verfassungslehre, 129
Versailles, Treaty of (1919), 96, 97,
    130, 157
Vitoria, Francisco de, 75–76
Vogel, Arthur, 96, 99, 100–101, 136
'Völkerrechtliche Probleme des
    Rheingebiets', 129

war
  bracketing of, 21, 79, 80
warfare
  and technology, 115–117
Weber, Max, 39, 196
Weimar Constitution
  Article 9
Weiß, Konrad, 51
Wendung zum diskriminierenden Kriegsbegriff,
    Die, 149, 170
Williams, Michael, 65

York, Graf von Wartenburg, 167, 190
  and Raoul Salan, 191

Zarmanian, Thalin, 24, 25
Žižek, Slavoj, 122, 210
Zolo, Danilo, 213